£9.99

ICON CRITICAL GUIDES

Elizabeth Gaskell

Mary Barton
North and South

EDITED BY ALISON CHAPMAN

Series editor: Richard Beynon

ICON B

Published in 1999 by Icon Books Ltd.,
Grange Road, Duxford, Cambridge CB2 4QF
e-mail: icon@mistral.co.uk
www.iconbooks.co.uk

Distributed in the UK, Europe, Canada, South Africa and Asia by the
Penguin Group: Penguin Books Ltd., 27 Wrights Lane, London W8 5TZ

Published in Australia in 1999 by Allen & Unwin Pty. Ltd.,
PO Box 8500, 9 Atchison Street, St. Leonards, NSW 2065

Series editor: Richard Beynon
Series devised by: Christopher Cox
Cover design: Christos Kondeatis
Typesetting: Wayzgoose

ISBN 1 84046 037 7

Printed and bound in Great Britain by
Cox & Wyman Ltd., Reading

Contents

'This Unhappy State of Things': Marxist Literary Criticism and the 'Social-Problem' Novel

The rise in literary criticism inspired by the Marxist critique of class structures revolutionises approaches to Gaskell's social-problem novels, with the result that Gaskell is reclaimed as a major Victorian novelist. The interest in biographical criticism is on the wane, although it continues to shadow some analyses. Extracts start with Raymond Williams, perhaps the most significant Gaskell critic of this period, continuing through all the major responses to the two novels until the rise of feminist studies inflects the interest in class with gender. The major extracts are taken from Kathleen Tillotson's *Novels of the Eighteen-Forties* and John Lucas's crucial essay, 'Gaskell and Brotherhood'.

Feminist Neglect and Feminist Celebration: the 1980s

As critics respond in this decade to the new Gaskell that Marxists uncovered, class and gender become interconnected issues. Feminist readings challenge the Marxist disapproval of Gaskell's investment in romance and melodrama and, crucially, thus destabilise the valorised binary public/private that leftist critique had, sometimes inadvertently, maintained. Some feminists, however, remain ambivalent about Gaskell's celebration of motherhood and domesticity. The major extract is taken from Catherine Gallagher's magisterial study, *The Industrial Reformation of English Fiction: 1832–1867*, which finally establishes and restores Gaskell as an important Victorian intellectual and brilliantly demonstrates *Mary Barton*'s generic hybridity.

Recovering Contexts: New Historicism in the 1990s

The most recent Gaskell criticism aims to situate her work within its various contexts and to explore contradictions and complexities as proof of her engagement with the most vital cultural, social and political issues of her day, rather than artistic failings. Following Foucault's interest in history as a series of 'local and unstable centres of power', Gaskell criticism looks to the dispossessed as illustration of the fiction's multiple power relationships; in particular, the streetwalker, the working class, the mother. Major extracts are by Hilary Schor, Catherine Barnes Stevenson, and Linda Hughes and Peter Lund.

A NOTE ON REFERENCES

Cross-references to the extracts printed in this Guide, and page references to the Penguin 1985 edition of *Mary Barton*, edited and with an
introduction by Macdonald Davy and to the Oxford University Press
1973 edition of *North and South*, edited and with an introduction by
Angus Easson, are given in brackets in the text of the Guide. Other page
references are given in the endnotes. The quotations from *Mary Barton*
and from *North and South* cited in the extracts retain the variants of the
critics' editions.

INTRODUCTION

Reading (as) Conflict: Approaching Gaskell's Fiction

■ I suppose we all *do* strengthen each other by clashing together, and earnestly talking our thoughts, and ideas. The very disturbance we thus are to each other rouses us up, and makes us more healthy. □
Elizabeth Gaskell to Lady Kay-Shuttleworth, 14 May 1850[1]

Most of Elizabeth Gaskell's critics note the remarkable sequence of clashing in her novels: clashing between rich and poor, employer and worker, north and south, men and women, realism and romance. But critics, too, often inadvertently, are engaged in another type of clash, the clash between critic and text, for they offer varied and contradictory readings of Gaskell's work. Indeed, Elizabeth Gaskell has been, more than most of her contemporary novelists, at the mercy of the fashions of literary criticism. As a result, we are presented with a variety of Gaskells, partly epitomised by the transition her authorial signature undergoes at the hands of the critics from 'Mrs Gaskell' to 'Elizabeth Gaskell'.

Gaskell's contemporary critics, responding to *Mary Barton* and *North and South*, vigorously debated whether or not the author was a radical and dangerous sympathiser with the poor. The industrial novels were by no means, however, the most contentious for her contemporaries. The daring and courageous portrayal of a fallen woman in *Ruth* (1853) provokes outrage and hostility among her contemporary critics and friends (the book was burnt in some circles).[2] In a letter to Anne Robson, Gaskell expects people to declare it 'an unfit subject for fiction' (January 1853).[3] But Gaskell also wrote a quite different fiction. As chapter two discusses, at her death she was remembered and praised as the author of the pastoral *Cranford* (1851–53), set in Knutsford, Cheshire, where Gaskell spent part of her childhood with her aunt, Mrs Lumb. Gaskell is also the author of supernatural fiction, which sits uneasily with critics' portrayals of her as a realist writer.[4] The next phase of critical opinion mostly represented her as a 'proper authoress', a feminine writer with conservative middle-class views. Then, with the advent of Marxist literary criticism, Gaskell becomes a radical again, but a radical whose sympathies with the poor are tempered, and the fiction blemished, by her middle-class background. In the 1980s, Gaskell and her fiction are again dramatically refashioned. We are presented with an intellectual Gaskell, whose ideological contradictions are complex but fruitful, bearing witness to the interactions of class and gender in the 1840s. Gaskell's fiction continues to be read in its socio-political, religious and cultural contexts in the 1990s by new historicist critics interested in approaching the fiction's intersection with history. Gaskell continues to be reclaimed as radical, with one critic pronouncing that '*Mary Barton* is one of the most *militant* pieces of fiction to come out of the nineteenth century'.[5]

All these diverse and contradictory critiques of Gaskell's industrial fiction are rather dizzying, if not disheartening, for today's reader. This Guide to *Mary Barton* and *North and South* steers the reader around and through the different phases of the last 150 years of Gaskell criticism, presents the most fruitful of approaches, and suggests why a critic's opinions are shaped within his or her context. Finally, the Guide offers a genealogy or intertextuality of literary criticism, for Gaskell's readers are often hypersensitive to, or hypercritical of, competing interpretations. In other words, the reader is offered a guide not only to secondary criticism, but also to the *politics* of that criticism.

Politics, in fact, is something no reader of Gaskell can ignore, despite the fact that many of her earlier critics attempt to suppress or elide the political side of her work. She wrote in revolutionary times. Raymond Williams, a Marxist critic, makes clear why socio-political contexts to the late 1840s are inextricably linked to the English novel:

■ I keep thinking about those twenty months, in 1847 and 1848, in which these novels were published: *Dombey and Son, Wuthering Heights, Vanity Fair, Jane Eyre, Mary Barton, Tancred, Town and Country, The Tenant of Wildfell Hall.*

What was it just then that emerged in England? It was of course no sudden process of just a few months. But we can see, looking back, those months as decisive. The English novel before then had its major achievements; it had Defoe and Fielding, Richardson and Jane Austen and Walter Scott. But now in the 1840s it had a new and major *generation*. For the next eighty years the novel was to be the major form in English literature. And this was unprecedented. What these months seem to mark above all is a new kind of consciousness, and we have to learn to see what this is, and some ways of relating it to the new and unprecedented civilisation in which it took shape.

The changes in society had been long in the making: the Industrial

Revolution, the struggle for democracy, the growth of cities and towns. But these also, in the 1840s, reached a point of consciousness which was in its turn decisive. The twelve years from Dickens's first novel to his radically innovating *Dombey and Son* were also the years of the crisis of Chartism. The first industrial civilisation in the history of the world had come to a critical and defining stage. By the end of the 1840s the English were the first predominantly urban people in the long history of human societies. The institutions of an urban culture, from music-halls and popular Sunday newspapers to public parks, museums and libraries, were all decisively established in those years. There was critical legislation on public health and on working-hours in factories. A major economic decision, on free trade and the repeal of the corn laws, had begun a long realignment of politics. In the struggle and disturbance of those years the future, of course, was not known. But the sense of crisis, of major and radical issues and decisions, was both acute and general. It is then not surprising that in just this decade a particular kind of literature – already known and widely read, but still not very highly regarded – should come to take on a new life, a newly significant and relevant life. Here, in these hands, a generation of writers, in very different ways, found the common forms that mattered, in response to a new and varied but still common experience.

There were of course immediate and related reasons for the new importance of the novel. Reading of all kinds was increasing. Between the 1820s and 1860 the annual number of new books rose from 580 to over 2,600, and much of the increase was in novels. New methods of binding and printing had brought book-prices down. In the period in which these novels were published there were new cheap libraries: the Parlour and the Railway: not led, of course, by the new generation, but by others: Lytton, Marryat, G.P.R. James. The reading of newspapers and magazines was increasing rapidly, though the major period of expansion was still twenty years ahead. In every way the reading-public was still a minority, and the book-reading public especially so. But serial publication of fiction, in the new family magazines, was significantly expanding the number of readers of novels. Direct market factors were important to writers in more pressing and evident ways.

But this is no simple case, in the end, of demand and supply. Several of the best new writers were involved in the market, and with their eyes wide open to it: Dickens above all. But what was written and what had to be written had many other sources. The crisis of the society and the expansion of reading were themselves related. More and more people felt the need for this kind of knowledge and experience, as customary ways broke down or receded. But beyond even this, as we can see most clearly from the novels themselves, the new pressures and disturbances were not simple moulds out of which new forms came. The men and women who were writing – some at the centre of opinion-forming and the market, some distant and isolated – took from the disturbance of these years another impetus: a crisis of experience, often quite personally felt and endured, which when it emerged in novels was much more than a reaction to existing and acknowledged public features. It was a creative working, a discovery, often alone at the table; a transformation and innovation which composed a generation out of what seemed separate work and experience. It brought in new feelings, people, relationships; rhythms newly known, discovered, articulated; defining the society, rather than merely reflecting it; defining it in novels, which had each its own significant and particular life. It was not the society or its crisis which produced the novels. The society and the novels – our general names for those myriad and related primary experiences – came from a pressing and varied experience which was not yet history; which had no new forms, no significant moments, until these were made and given by direct human actions.[6] □

One of the most profound and pervasive influences on Gaskell, Thomas Carlyle, voices this sense of crisis and helped to shape new forms that embody what Raymond Williams terms the 'new consciousness'. In *Chartism* (1839), he anxiously calls for an enquiry into what he terms the 'Condition-of-England Question':[7]

■ A feeling very generally exists that the condition and disposition of the Working Classes is a rather ominous matter at present; that something ought to be said, something ought to be done, in regard to it. And surely, at an epoch of history when the 'National Petition' carts itself in waggons along the streets, and is presented 'bound with iron hoops, four men bearing it', to a Reformed House of Commons; and Chartism numbered by the million and half, taking nothing by its iron-hooped Petition, breaks out into brickbats, cheap pikes, and even into sputterings of conflagration, such very general feeling cannot be considered unnatural! To us individually this matter appears, and has for many years appeared, to be the most ominous of all practical matters whatever; a matter in regard to which if something be not done, something will *do* itself one day, and in a fashion that will please nobody. The time is verily come for acting in it; how much more for consultation about acting in it, for speech and articulate inquiry about it![8] □

By the time Carlyle published *Past and Present* in 1843, there is an increasing note of desperation at the prevailing illusion among the middle and upper classes that all is well:

■ The condition of England, on which many pamphlets are now in the course of publication, and many thoughts unpublished are going on in every reflective head, is justly regarded as one of the most ominous, and withal one of the strangest, ever seen in this world. England is full of wealth, of multifarious produce, supply for human want in every kind; yet England is dying of inanition. With unabated bounty the land of England blooms and grows; waving with yellow harvests; thick-studded with workshops, industrial implements, with fifteen millions of workers, understood to be the strongest, the cunningest and the willingest our Earth ever had; these men are here; the work they have done, the fruit they have realised is here, abundant, exuberant on every hand of us: and behold, some baleful fiat as of Enchantment has gone forth, saying, 'Touch it not, ye workers, ye master-workers, ye master-idlers; none of you can touch it, no man of you shall be the better for it; this is enchanted fruit!' On the poor workers such fiat falls first, in its rudest shape; but on the rich master-workers too it falls; neither can the rich master-idlers, nor any richest or highest man escape, but all are like to be brought low with it, and made 'poor' enough, in the money sense or a far fataler one.[9] □

The most famous of responses to the plight of the working class is Fredrick Engels's *The Condition of the Working Class in England*, published in German in 1845. He concurs with Carlyle that the destitution of the poor is ignored by the middle and upper classes. Outlining the street plan of Manchester, Engels notes that the poor can be easily bypassed:

■ The town itself is peculiarly built, so that a person may live in it for years, and go in and out daily without coming into contact with a working-people's quarter or even with workers, that is, so long as he confines himself to his business or to pleasure walks. This arises chiefly from the fact, that by unconscious tacit agreement, as well as with out-spoken conscious determination, the working-people's quarters are sharply separated from the sections of the city reserved for the middle-class; or, if this does not succeed, they are concealed with the cloak of charity.[10] □

Someone who did, however, have contact with the working class was Gaskell, as her comment makes clear in the Preface to *Mary Barton*: '[the poor] elbowed me daily in the busy streets of the town where I resided'.[11] The description of the living conditions of the poor in Manchester that Engels gives, from his own experience in the city, discloses the full horror of what Gaskell, too, must have witnessed:[12]

■ Immediately under the railway [Ducie] bridge there stands a court, the filth and horrors of which surpass all the others by far, just because it was hitherto so shut off, so secluded that the way to it could not be found without a good deal of trouble, I should never have discovered it myself, without the breaks made by the railway, though I thought I knew this whole region thoroughly. Passing along a rough bank, among stakes and washing-lines, one penetrates into this chaos of small one-storied, one-roomed huts, in most of which there is no artificial floor; kitchen, living and sleeping-room all in one. In such a hole, scarcely five feet long by six broad, I found two beds – and such bedsteads and beds! – which, with a staircase and chimney-place, exactly fitted the room. In several others I found absolutely nothing, while the door stood open, and the inhabitants leaned against it. Everywhere before the doors refuse and offal; that any sort of pavement lay underneath could not be seen but only felt, here and there, with the feet. This whole collection of cattle-sheds for human beings was surrounded on two sides by houses and a factory, and on the third by the river, and besides the narrow stair up the bank, a narrow doorway alone led out into another almost equally ill-built, ill-kept labyrinth of dwellings.[13]

[. . .]

Such is the Old Town of Manchester, and on re-reading my description, I am forced to admit that instead of being exaggerated, it is far from black enough to convey a true impression of the filth, ruin, and uninhabitableness, the defiance of all considerations of cleanliness, ventilation, and health which characterise the construction of this single district, containing at least twenty to thirty thousand inhabitants. And such a district exists in the heart of the second city of England, the first manufacturing city of the world. If any one wishes to see in how little space a human being can move, how little air – and *such* air! – he can breathe, how little of civilisation he may share and yet live, it is only necessary to travel hither. True, this is the *Old* Town, and the people of Manchester emphasise the fact whenever any one mentions to them the frightful condition of this Hell upon Earth; but what does that prove? Everything which here arouses horror and indignation is of recent origin, belongs to the *industrial epoch*.[14] □

Perhaps, given all the controversy surrounding the 'proper' reading of Gaskell and the revolutionary years in which her industrial fiction was written, it comes as no surprise that *Mary Barton* and *North and South* were both conceived, written and published at great personal cost to the author. Writing was, in the case of *Mary Barton*, literally and symbolically born out of pain at the death of her infant son; executed in physical discomfort in the case of *North and South*; and, once her fiction was in the hand of reviewers and friends, it invariably continued to give her emotional distress.[15] Chapter one gives the background to Gaskell's writing and extracts from her correspondence that make her psychical and physical suffering clear. Luckily, for Gaskell, the financial rewards partly compensated, although legally the profits belonged to her husband who, notoriously, 'buttoned up' her £20 profits for the short story 'Lizzie Leigh'.[16] Gaskell, in fact, commanded an increasing price for her novels. The initial copyright for *Mary Barton* was £100; for *Ruth*, £500; for the *Life of Charlotte Brontë*, £800; for *Sylvia's Lovers* (1863), £1,000; for *Wives and Daughters* (1864–66), £2,000.[17]

Before these details seduce us with the 'charming' historical personage of Gaskell (a term frequently used to describe her and, as Hilary Schor comments, to dismiss her),[18] however, it is important to remember that for a long time Gaskell criticism was under the shadow of a particular biographical representation of the author, as elucidated in chapter two. Virginia Woolf's review of Mrs Ellis Chadwick's *Mrs Gaskell: Haunts, Homes and Stories* perceptively argues that, despite the charm of Elizabeth Gaskell, it is difficult to recover her character: 'it is delightful to see how cleverly she vanishes'.[19] Hilary M. Schor notes, 'some notes sounded early in the criticism resound still: Gaskell is a lovely lady; she is a deeply moral woman; she is, whatever else is said, a "minor writer"'.[20] This, she continues, has had a serious and detrimental impact on criticism of Gaskell:

■ No Victorian novelist has suffered more than Gaskell from an unwillingness to look for the *un*conventional ending, or what D. A. Miller has called the 'discontents' of narrative. It would, one supposes on reading these critics, have seemed bad manners to probe too deeply into the stylistic or sexual politics of 'Mrs Gaskell' – at least as that figure has been imagined (smiling, gentle, tolerant) on the borders of the (major) Victorian novelists.[21] □

While these biographical readings clearly misrepresent Gaskell and her fiction, they are valuable to today's reader for the way in which they reveal competing ideological tensions as the critics try to come to terms with the fact that a Victorian middle-class woman, indeed the wife of a minister, wrote about social and political issues. Rather than dismiss the biographical approach to *Mary Barton* and *North and South*, we should consider what sort of questions they ask and prompt about her work and how these questions have mutated and evolved through subsequent criticism. Implicitly, and sometimes explicitly, the reader of this Guide will find that certain issues are elided. For example, the early critics tried to ignore the prostitute in *Mary Barton* and the fact that the narrative shows a complex and sophisticated understanding of political economy, despite the Preface's denial. But throughout the history of Gaskell criticism, readers return to the same two questions, although formulated in different ways or obliquely addressed: What are the limits of realist fiction? Are the industrial novels conservative or subversive? Criticism from the 1950s onwards, as chapters three, four and five demonstrate, has usefully argued that the terms of these questions need to be rethought, to avoid pointless and tiresome value judgements about what material, style or structures ought to be excluded from realism. Instead of expecting to find a coherent unified narrative, and holding on to that as the standard of the Victorian realist novel, such criticism listens out for the ideological clashes that, as Gaskell advises, produce robust and vigorous fiction, fiction that is exciting to read, and fiction that restores Gaskell to her position as a major Victorian novelist. I hope that the reader will follow this book both forwards and backwards, being attentive both to the history of Gaskell criticism but also attuned to his or her own position as a reader of the 1990s, taking into account what is most to be gained from contemporary literary criticism.

Hilary M. Schor's meta-critical article on Gaskell summarises and celebrates the new vibrancy in Gaskell studies:

■ There is a kind of excitement in Gaskell scholarship these days, an energy and pleasure rare even in the already heady circles of Victorian studies, as if individual critics who thought they had secretly discovered the real thing suddenly realized everyone else had discovered it too. Much of the impetus for this revival has come from the feminist project of transforming the canon, of – echoing the charge of Virginia Woolf – 'if we were women', thinking 'back through our mothers', but Gaskell has benefited as well from recent work in social history and the social problem novel, from work that stresses the ideological contradictions and social tensions behind the literary text. In the movement of fiction studies away from more purely aesthetic judgements, and in the decline of often equally ahistorical structuralist criticism, the socially dense, narratorially complicated, historically motivated work of a novelist like Gaskell has proven particularly fruitful; to study the transformation in Gaskell scholarship can offer a similarly fruitful understanding of our own critical approaches, of 'the way we live now,' in Victorian studies.[22] □

A cautionary note is, however, struck in the following extract. While many responses to Gaskell have a meta-critical element, Deanna L. Davis's article shows how feminist critics' ambivalent attitude to motherhood has radically coloured and confused readings of Gaskell.[23]

■ Unlike her contemporaries Charlotte Brontë and George Eliot, Elizabeth Gaskell has occupied a shadowy position in feminist criticism: neglected by some critics because of her conservative values, uneasily respected by others for achieving literary and financial success. When seeming to warrant study at all, she has often bewildered feminist critics who do not find in her work the kind of protest that makes Brontë and George Eliot seem such modern women. Yet it is too easy to dismiss Gaskell as simply a less powerful and talented writer than her more acclaimed cohorts. The manner in which she has been dismissed suggests that Gaskell's treatment by feminist critics has more to do with the psychology and politics of feminist criticism than with any real lack in Gaskell's fiction. The feminine nurturance on which she grounded her life and work has appeared to many feminist critics as unappealing at best and traitorous at worst. In the eyes of a few recent critics, however, that emphasis on nurturance has become not only the most attractive part of Gaskell's work but also the most potentially subversive. For such reappraisals come at a time when feminists are reevaluating their perceptions of the same 'feminine' values that Gaskell endorsed and reconsidering the figure who most completely embodies them: the mother. Thus the root of both the feminist neglect and the feminist celebration of Elizabeth Gaskell is the equivocal status of the mother within feminism and feminist criticism themselves. Both responses unconsciously gesture toward the most troubling issues surrounding mothering, issues that touch the individual psyches of feminist women as much as they affect feminist political and social agendas. For her feminist critics, Gaskell becomes the focus of the daughter's anxieties and dreams: her treatment of mothering provokes both the daughter's longing for maternal nurturance and her fears of becoming a mothering woman herself.[24] □

This extract should prompt readers of all inclinations – biographical, Marxist, feminist, new historicist, and those who exceed such categorisation – to reflect on the politics of their own critical praxis. But, as Gaskell admits, controversy is healthy, not least in the clashing of the hugely divergent readings of her industrial fiction. I hope the clashes within this Guide inspire and rouse the reader.

CHAPTER ONE

Telling Tales: Contemporary Reviews

■ Some say the masters are very sore, but I'm sure I *believe* I wrote truth. □

Elizabeth Gaskell[1]

The anonymous publication of *Mary Barton: A Tale of Manchester Life* in 1848 caused a sensation. This was a year of revolution in Europe and the novel's socio-political subject matter marked a major new turn in British fiction, especially fiction by women, to which many reviewers responded with either excitement or unease. Ironically, Gaskell wrote *Mary Barton* before the Paris uprising in 1848, a context that led her publisher to insist upon an explanatory preface in a vain attempt to assuage the conservative middle-class fears of her readership.[2] By the time Gaskell published her fourth novel *North and South* in 1854–55, she was an established author, although, crucially, the suitability of her political and economic subject matter for fiction by women was still in dispute. While Gaskell was anxious in her letters to assert both veracity and good faith as the motives of her writing, she was stung by comments that her fiction was dangerously subversive. Both author and reviewers, however, agreed that both novels were engaged in a radical new departure. In fact, Gaskell was very nervous about the reception of her novels – perhaps partly for this reason – and always made sure she was out of the way, if it was at all possible, upon their publication.[3] To Mary Ewart, who had accurately guessed the authorship of *Mary Barton*, Gaskell confides: 'I am almost frightened at my own action in writing it'.[4] After the anonymous publication of *Mary Barton*, she found the strain of the attempts to identify the novelist extremely stressful. To her publisher Edward Chapman she complains: 'hitherto the whole affair of publication has been one of extreme annoyance to me'.[5] As a serial publication, *North and South's* episodic entry into the public domain did not enable Gaskell to take complete sanctuary from the response (indeed, critical responses to the instalments affected the outcome of future parts), although she wrote in the comfortable retreat of Florence Nightingale's family house.[6] To Anna Jameson she divulges her plans after the two volume publication of the novel: 'I am going to follow your plan and run away from reviewers'.[7]

Mary Barton

Gaskell's first novel was born out of grief at the loss of her nine-month-old son William in August 1845 and written to assuage the pain at the suggestion of her husband.[8] In Gaskell's correspondence she divulges that the circumstances surrounding her act of writing *Mary Barton* are crucial to the shape and texture of the novel. She asserts, in a letter to Catherine Winkworth, that these circumstances are imbedded in the grain of the narrative:

■ It is a painful subject and *must* be painful, and I felt it all so deeply myself I could hardly be light-hearted any part of the time I was writing it.[9] □

To Mrs Greg, in a letter probably dated in early 1849, she confides that 'I took refuge in the invention to exclude the memory of painful scenes':

■ It is no wonder then that the whole book seems to be written in the minor key; indeed, the very design seems to me to require this treatment. I acknowledge the fault of there being too heavy a shadow over the book; but I doubt if the story could have been deeply realised without these shadows.[10] □

In the Preface to *Mary Barton*, Gaskell alludes briefly to the reason for her writing the novel and also makes clear how other aspects of her experience have fed into the narrative, principally her contact with the working class in her home city of Manchester. The Preface asserts the veracity of the subject matter, based on the author's direct experience of and sympathy with the life of the poor. Indeed, such experience is described as direct physical contact, for the working class 'elbow' her every day on the city's streets. But the author's direct encounters with the poor lead her to consider the 'romance' of their lives: a word that sits uneasily alongside realism. She significantly, and more rhetorically than truthfully, denies any knowledge of the economic principles behind the issues of her plot.[11] The Preface fuelled the novel's controversial reception and is worth quoting in full:

■ Three years ago I became anxious (from circumstances that need not be more fully alluded to)[12] to employ myself in writing a work of fiction. Living in Manchester, but with a deep relish and fond

17

admiration for the country, my first thought was to find a frame-work for my story in some rural scene; and I had already made a little progress in a tale,[13] the period of which was more than a century ago, and the place on the borders of Yorkshire, when I bethought me how deep might be the romance in the lives of some of those who elbowed me daily in the busy streets of the town in which I resided. I had always felt a deep sympathy for the care-worn men, who looked as if doomed to struggle through their lives in strange alternations between work and want; tossed to and fro by circumstances, apparently in even a greater degree than other men. A little manifestation of this sympathy, and a little attention to the expression of feelings on the part of some of the work-people with whom I was acquainted, had laid open to me the hearts of one or two of the more thoughtful among them; I saw that they were sore and irritable against the rich, the even tenor of whose seemingly happy lives appeared to increase the anguish caused by the lottery-like nature of their own. Whether the bitter complaints made by them of the neglect which they experienced from the prosperous – especially from the masters whose fortunes they had helped to build up – were well founded or no, it is not for me to judge. It is enough to say, that this belief of the injustice and unkindness which they endure from their fellow-creatures taints what might be resignation to God's will, and turns it to revenge in many of the poor uneducated factory-workers of Manchester.

The more I reflected on this unhappy state of things between those so bound to each other by common interests, as the employers and the employed must ever be, the more anxious I became to give some utterance to the agony which, from time to time, convulses this dumb people; the agony of suffering without the sympathy of the happy, or of erroneously believing that such is the case. If it be an error that the woes, which come with ever returning tide-like flood to overwhelm the workmen in our manufacturing towns, pass unregarded by all but the sufferers, it is at any rate an error so bitter in its consequences to all parties, that whatever public effort can do in the way of merciful deeds, or helpless love in the way of 'widow's mites'[14] could do, should be done, and that speedily, to disabuse the work-people of so miserable a misapprehension. At present they seem to me to be left in a state, wherein lamentations and tears are thrown aside as useless, but in which the lips are compressed for curses, and the hands clenched and ready to smite.

I know nothing of Political Economy,[15] or the theories of trade. I have tried to write truthfully; and if my accounts agree or clash with any system, the agreement or disagreement is unintentional.

To myself the idea which I have formed of the state of feeling among too many of the factory-people in Manchester, and which I endeavoured to represent in this tale (completed above a year ago), has received some confirmation from the events which have so recently occurred among a similar class on the Continent.[16]

October 1848[17] □

The novel's truthfulness was the most controversial aspect for the contemporary reviewers. Not only the author's Preface but also its generic associations with realism stake *Mary Barton*'s claim to veracity. As a literary construct, realism does not mean that fiction *is* life but that it *represents* life and is convincing psychologically, socially and rhetorically.[18] The issue is complicated, however, by two interrelated factors. Firstly, the Victorian gender ideology of female literary creativity shaped women's writing according to their experience and then, in a double bind, constrained that experience within the private domestic sphere of the home. Family life, maternal feelings, and emotions were the supposed subject matter of both middle-class women's lives and middle-class women's writing.[19] Gaskell, of course, took refuge in anonymity, but her Preface clearly marks the novel as not necessarily by a woman, but certainly a *feminine* narrative, encoded with the expectations of women's writing.[20] In a familiar gesture of the nineteenth century, many readers and reviewers took the novel's feminine attributes to be indicative of female authorship. John Forster, for example, comments:

■ Unquestionably the book is a woman's. If one of its casual remarks had not betrayed this (it would seem unintentionally), we might have known it from the delicate points of the portraiture where women and children are in question, from the minuteness of the domestic details, from certain gentle intimations of piety and pity perceptible throughout, and from the mixed diffidence and daring with which the question of employers and employed is treated in the course of it.[21] □

Carlyle, who had greatly influenced the conception of the novel, knows to address his letter of admiration to 'Dear *Madam* (for I catch the *treble* of that fine melodious voice very well)'.[22] Maria Edgeworth also guesses correctly, but for rather different reasons: 'I opine that [the author] is a *she* – From the great abilities, and from the power of drawing *from* the life and *to* the life so as to give the impression and strong interest of reality'.[23]

A second factor is the novel's uneasy mixture of the generic conventions of realism and romance, something that contemporary reviewers gesture to and more recent criticism tries to unravel. While the majority of reviewers accept and praise *Mary Barton*'s veracity, its realism is hotly contested in the most negative commentaries. That which studies published in the last decade take to be proof of the novel's ideological complexity is, for reviewers in the late 1840s, grounds to debate the value of the novel. An unsigned review in the *Literary Gazette* of 28 October 1848 states categorically that 'there is no invention in these volumes',[24] while John Forster in the *Examiner* asserts that 'she [the author] seems to write according to her knowledge'.[25] This terminology is reiterated throughout the copious positive reviews of *Mary Barton*: the narrative is absolutely true to life, self-evidently realistic, drawn from experience. Samuel Bamford concords, in a letter to Gaskell, 'you have drawn a fearfully true picture'.[26] Some reviewers, writing within the gender ideology of female creativity, assume that the novel's truthfulness is a direct reflex of the author's high moral fibre. In the *Christian Examiner* for March 1849, J. E. Bradford notes that:

■ The reader is made to feel that true religion, the spirit of Christianity, is the all-pervading principle in the mind of the writer, whose own beautiful character breathes through every page of the book. There is no effort, no straining after effect. So simply and naturally is the fearful story told, that we feel as if we were listening to a true tale from the lips of a friend; we forget that what we have been told is only a fiction; heart seems to speak to heart, and leaves its impress there.[27] □

Gaskell, no doubt reading the debate about the novel's truthfulness in the reviews, states in a letter to Mary Ewart:

■ I can only say I wanted to represent the subject in the light in which some of the workmen certainly consider to be *true*, not that I dare to say it is the abstract absolute truth.

That some of the men do view the subject in the way I have tried to represent, I have personal evidence; and I think somewhere in the first volume you may find a sentence stating that my intention was simply to represent the view many of the work-people take. But independently of any explicit statement of my intention, I do think that we must all acknowledge that there are duties connected with the manufacturing system not fully understood as yet, and evils existing in relation to it which may be remedied in some degree, although we as yet do not see how; but surely there is no harm in directing the attention to the existence of such evils. No one can feel more deeply than I how *wicked* it is to do anything to excite class against class; and the sin has been most unconscious if I have done so.[28] □

To Eliza Fox she confides that: 'nobody and nothing was real [. . .] in M. Barton, but the character of John Barton; the circumstances are different, but the character and some of the speeches are exactly a poor man I know'.[29]

The negative reviews are all hostile to the novel's claim of realism and complain about both the representation of the employers and the author's understanding of political economy. The unsigned review in the *British Quarterly Review* dislikes the novel's 'one-sided picture'.[30] It complains that the depiction of the employers is grossly inaccurate:

■ [Quotes, with omissions, the novel's Preface, 'I saw that they were . . . and ready to smite'.]

This, it must be confessed, is a sufficiently doleful and alarming picture. We did not believe it to be a true one, and we have taken some pains to arrive at a just view of the case. We have talked both with operatives and with employers, and do not hesitate to say that the tone of feeling which the tale before us represents as general among the working population of Manchester, is one, which, if it exists at all now, is confined within comparatively narrow limits. We have observed nothing of it, nor have we, in the course of our inquiries, met with any one who had, – that is, as a feeling participated in by any considerable number. No doubt there are discontented men, filled with vague ideas of a levelling and communistic character; for socialism and chartism have not been idle in these parts. And there are unjust and grasping employers – men who inflict heavy deductions of wages in the shape of fines and abatements, if they do not lower the ostensible rate of remuneration for labour, who are ready, when the occasion presents itself, to throw their factory-hands out of employ, or who keep up some of the evil features of the truck system, such as compelling every spinner in their employ (if they possess cottage property for the residence of the work people) to pay the rent of a cottage, whether he chooses or has occasion to occupy one, or not. It may readily be understood, that when such employers and such workpeople come in contact, the result will be a feeling of bitter dislike, and angry jealousy on the part of the latter towards the former. Happily, however, such masters have never been average specimens of their class, and their number is becoming smaller and smaller continually. In fact, the system does not pay. Attention to the well-being, physical and mental, of the operatives in their employ, is found by the masters to be, in the long run, much the more economical plan of the two. An organised system of skilled labour, such as is seen in operation in a factory, cannot be replaced so readily as it can be broken up. So that unless the emergency be of the most pressing kind, a millowner has the strongest motives for keeping his workpeople together. And then again, it is of the utmost advantage, in every point of view, to secure skilful and orderly workmen, especially for the superior departments of the work; and these of course soon find out the kind of masters whom it is most for their interest to serve. There have from the first been employers connected with the manufacturers of Lancashire, who have set a most commendable and noble example of attention to the interests of those in their service; and both philanthropy and self-interest have led to the extensive imitation of that example; and without forgetting that there are exceptions, it may safely be affirmed that the millowners, as a body, may challenge comparison with any class of employers in the country. On the other hand, we have met with one accordant testimony as to the improved state of feeling that exists on the part of the working classes, taken as a whole, toward the masters. The relations between the two, and the essential connection of their mutual interests, have come to be much better understood; a result which, again, has been in part brought about by the searching investigations to which the struggle for commercial freedom gave rise. We have no hesitation, therefore, in pronouncing much of that state of things which the tale before us exhibits to be in part greatly exaggerated, as compared with what has at any time existed, and in part quite out of date.[31] □

The *Manchester Guardian*'s unsigned review similarly empathises with the employers. Written on the occasion of the novel's third edition, it accuses the author of dangerous errors and states that 'the authoress has sinned gravely against truth, in matters of fact either above her comprehension, or beyond her sphere of knowledge'.[32] W.R. Greg, in *The Edinburgh Review*, also rehearses ideological objections to the novel's apparent message and suggests that, although the benevolence of the author cannot be doubted, the working class must be wholly responsible for improving their condition:

■ The plain truth cannot be too boldy spoken, nor too frequently repeated: the working classes, and they only, can raise their own condition; to themselves alone must they look for their elevation in the social scale; their own intellect and their own virtues must work out their salvation; their fate and their future are in their own hands, – and in theirs alone.[33] □

While either approval or condemnation of the novel is based wholly on ideological premises in contemporary reviews, the judgements revolve implicitly and explicitly around a generic issue: the appropriate subject matter for fiction, and for fiction written by women. Henry Fothergill Chorley, in an unsigned review in the *Athenaeum*, states:

■ How far it may be kind, wise, or right to make Fiction the vehicle for a plain and matter-of-fact exposition of social evils, is a question of limitations which will not be unanimously settled in our time. The theory and practice of 'Agitation' are, as all the world knows, adjusted by a sliding scale, on which 'Choleric word' and 'Flat Blasphemy' indicate every conceivable degree of heat and excitement, according to conscience, convenience, or chances of success – as it may be. But we have met with few pictures of life among the working classes at once so forceful and fair as 'Mary Barton.' The truth of it is terrible. The writer is superior to melodramatic seductions, and has described misery, temptation, distress and shame as they really exist. Only twice has he (?) had recourse to the worn-out machinery of the novelist, – and then he has used it with a master's hand. But he is excellent in the anatomy of feelings and motives, in the display of character, in the life-like and simple use of dialogue: – and the result is, a painful interest very rare in our experience.[34] □

An unsigned review of *Mary Barton* in the *Critic* gives a similar judgement, but significantly juxtaposes the harsh realism of the novel with the traditional romance genre found in novels:

■ Manchester Life will strike many as a very unfit subject for a novel; the romance of spinning-jennies, devil's dust, and power-looms; the poetry of steam-chimneys, manufactories, trades-unions, and anti-corn-law leagues! Yet is the author true to nature in his topic and its treatment. He has found ample food for his fancy, even here; he has woven a tale of profound interest, although it is but a common story of every-day life; he has discovered that the smoky atmosphere of the metropolis of manufactories covers the same passions, good and bad, as did the azure sky that hung over the castles of the Norman barons.[35] □

There were, however, more negative remarks about the choice of subject matter. The poet Elizabeth Barrett Browning, writing from Florence to Mary Russell Mitford, expresses her dissatisfaction with the novel's interest in class issues. This is perhaps surprising, given Barrett Browning's *Aurora Leigh* (1856), which seeks, in its novel-poem format, to expand and question the boundaries of genre and explicitly address taboo subjects such as the fallen woman.[36]

■ For 'Mary Barton' I am a little disappointed, do you know. I have just done reading it. There is power and truth – she can shake and she can pierce – but I wish half the book away, it is so tedious every now and then; and besides I want more beauty, more air from the universal world – these class-books must always be defective as works of art.[37] □

Gaskell, in fact, was aware that her novel would present a new genre: narrative as a 'tragic poem'.[38] As the following extract makes clear, from a letter to Miss Lamont on 5 January 1849, she is articulate in expressing her aesthetic:

■ 'John Barton' was the original name [of the novel], as being the central figure to my mind; indeed I had so long felt that the bewildered life of an ignorant thoughtful man of strong power of sympathy, dwelling in a town so full of striking contrasts as this is, was a tragic poem, that in writing he was [?] my 'hero'; and it was a London thought coming through the London publisher that it must be called *Mary* B. So many people overlook John B. or see him merely to misunderstand him, that if you were a stranger and had only said that one thing (that the book shd have been called *John* B) I should have had pleasure in feeling that my own idea was recognised; how much more am I pleased then when the whole letter comes from one whom I so much liked and admired in our few & far between glimpses as I did you. Some people here are very angry and say the book will do harm; and for a time I have been shaken and sorry; but I have such firm faith that the earnest expression of any one's feeling can only do good in the long run, – that God will cause the errors to be temporary[,] the truth to be eternal, that I try not to mind too much what people say either in blame or praise.[39] □

To Mrs Greg she writes:

■ 'John Barton' was the original title of the book. Round the character of John Barton all the others formed themselves; he was my hero, *the* person with whom all my sympathies went, with whom I tried to identify myself at the time, because I believed from personal observation that such men were not uncommon, and would well reward such sympathy and love as should throw light down upon their groping search after the causes of suffering, and the reason why suffering is sent, and what they can do to lighten it.[40] □

While many critics recognised the importance of sympathy in the novel, few appreciated quite how radical Gaskell's intentions had been, as she herself notes in a letter to her publisher Edward Chapman: 'no one seems to see my idea of a tragic poem'.[41] J.J. Taylor perceptively terms the novel a 'Poem in prose' and notes what he terms Gaskell's '*concetto* style', or her juxtaposition of a series of unresolved opposites through the narrative (which would also become an organising principle behind *North and South*).[42] Indeed, it is important for contemporary reviewers that, in fiction, these opposites – rich and poor, employer and employed – are not resolved. Rather, they applaud Gaskell's suggestion that mutual sympathy of one class for the other, rather than a political solution, would greatly improve the lives of the poor.[43]

Maria Edgeworth writes to Mary Holland that the book resembles a Greek tragedy for *Mary* Barton.[44] Her comments astutely cover not just the ideological premise of the novel but also some of its formal narrative features which would become the focus of later criticism. Early in 1849, she writes to Honora Beaufort:

■ – Hopelessness remains in the readers worn out mind – No remedy proposed – But emigration which is only an evasion, an escape not a remedy.[45]

The benefit of *character* even is not justly allowed to the good hero – as it surely would have been by his associates in real life – .

There are about a dozen too many deaths – and death is unavoidable and deathbed scenes in my opinion very objectionable in a moral & social point of view. Death bed spies are hateful Moralists – But after boring you with all this I advise you to read the book & you will do it more justice than I have done.[46] □

To Mary Holland on 27 December 1848, Edgeworth comments on the ideological basis of the narrative:

■ In truth there is no bodily or mental evil to which flesh is heir which this author cannot describe most feelingly. The evils consequent upon over-manufacturing or over-population or both conjoined and acting as cause and effect; the misery and the hateful passions engendered by the love of gain & the accumulation of riches; and the selfishness and want of thought and want of feeling in Master Manufacturers are most admirably described and the consequences produced on the inferior class of employed or unemployed workmen are most ably shown in action. [. . .]

The fault of this book is that it leaves but a melancholy, I almost feel hopeless, impression. When the box of evils was opened Hope should have been left sticking to the lid.

It is all too true

But what can we do

What can be done –

It is in fact very difficult to say – for we cannot. Make a new division & equal distribution without *revolution* & even if we could do this without revolution & injustice to the present possessors, of what *permanent* avail could it be? Wealth must immediately & incessantly tend to reaccumulate unless the efforts of *Industry* & in wages are stopped & this stoppage could not increase human happiness. There must then be rich & poor – *Laborers & Masters*.

All that can be done is to prevent the laborers from being made slaves and to deter the masters from becoming tyrants. Such a powerful writer as the author of *Mary Barton could* tend to this beneficial purpose by his pathetic representations and appeals to the feelings of pity and remorse.[47] □

North and South

After the controversy and vigorous debate that greeted the publication of *Mary Barton*, Gaskell turned away from industrial concerns to address and celebrate the pastoral idyll of Knutsford in her next novel, *Cranford* (1851–53). This has the effect of establishing Gaskell among her critics as a writer with two personae: as Hilary Schor notes, 'one is the Gaskell of the social novel, the other, the Gaskell of *Cranford* – a division of Hebraic and Hellenic proportions'.[48] But, after the publication of *Ruth*, in her fourth novel she returns to the problematic and inequitable relationship between employers and workmen. Arthur Pollard, among others, suggests that this is an attempt to respond to the controversial reception of her first novel: 'there is much in *North and South* to suggest that she was trying to redress the balance of the scales which some had felt she had so wrongly weighted in one direction in *Mary Barton*'.[49] Julia Swindells concurs:

■ Gaskell's vulnerability in relation to attacks on the class and gender interests of *Mary Barton* is later manifest in the writing of *North and South*. Although she had resisted one direct attempt to persuade her to 're-write' *Mary Barton*, giving the narrative perspective as that of the employer rather than the worker, the manufacturer, Thornton, in the later novel is clearly a concession to that kind of persuasion. Perhaps this signifies too her further entry into literary professionalism by the time of the later novel.[50] □

That relationship between employers and workmen, however, was also the subject of Dickens's *Hard Times*, which immediately preceded *North and South* (1854–55) in his periodical *Household Words*. Dickens was by turns Gaskell's editor, rival, influence and flatterer. After reading *Ruth*, and as the final instalments of *Cranford* were sent to his printer, Dickens wrote to Gaskell with his praise: 'as to future work . . . you cannot write too much for Household Words . . . I receive you, ever, (if Mr Gaskell will allow me to say so) with open arms'.[51] Gaskell replied with her plans for what was to become *North and South*, and Dickens responded positively: 'I have no doubt that you may do a great deal of good by pursuing it in Household Words'.[52] Once Gaskell began writing the first instalments in February 1854, she was alarmed by the similarity of Dickens's *Hard Times*, and wrote to him for assurance that he was not, unlike her, planning a strike.[53] Although, in this instance, Gaskell was pacified, Dickens's authorship of *Hard Times* and the publication of its instalments overlapped with Gaskell's work on *North and South*, which she sent to him in parts for his comments. The influence of each book on the other is mapped by a recent critic, Jerome Meckier (see chapter four). In addition to the strain of responding to and anticipating a rival's similar material, Gaskell found the pressures of writing for serial publication distressing and over-taxing. To Eliza Fox she declares that 'it has all been a terrible weight on me and has made me have some of the most felling headaches I ever had in my life'.[54] The deadlines and space constraints were a particular strain, as she tells Anna Jameson on 30 January 1855: 'if the story had been poured just warm out of the mind, it would have taken a much larger mould. It was the cruel necessity of compressing it that hampered me'.[55]

To Dickens, sending an instalment that is too long, she writes the only letter that has survived from her side of the correspondence about the novel: 'I never wish to see it's [*sic*] face again; but, *if you will keep the MS for me, & shorten it as you think best for HW*, I shall be very glad. Shortened I see it must be'.[56] In an earlier letter to Jameson, Gaskell out-lines the effect serial publication had on her novel:

■ I made a half-promise (as perhaps I told you,) to Mr Dickens, which he understood as a whole one [to publish in *Household Words*]; and though I had the plot and characters in my head long ago, I have often been in despair about the working of them out; because of course, in this way of publishing it, I had to write pretty hard without waiting for the happy leisure hours. And then 20 numbers was, I found[,] my allowance; instead of the too scant 22, which I had fancied were included in 'five months'; and at last the story is huddled & hurried up; especially in the rapidity with which the sudden death of Mr Bell, succeeds to the sudden death of Mr Hale. But what could I do? Every page was grudged me, just at last, when I did certainly infringe all the bounds & limits they set me as to quantity. Just at the very last I was compelled to desperate compression. But now I am not sure if, when the barrier gives way between 2 such characters as Mr Thornton and Margaret it would not go all smash in a moment, – and I don't feel quite certain that I dislike the end as it now stands. But, it is being republished as a whole, in two vols.; – and the question is shall I alter & enlarge what is already written, bad & hurried-up though it be? I can not insert small pieces here & there – I feel as if I must throw myself back a certain distance in the story, & re-write it from there; retaining the present incidents, but filling up intervals of time &c &c. Would you give me your *very* valuable opinion as to this?[57] □

When the two-volume edition appeared Gaskell had revised her text and includes a preface explaining the changes: 'various short passages have been inserted, and several new chapters added'.[58]

The literary partnership had not been happy on Dickens's part, either. On 14 October 1854, after six weeks of publishing instalments of *North and South*, sales figures for *Household Words* had dropped significantly. Dickens wrote to his assistant editor: 'I am sorry to hear of the Sale dropping, but I am not surprised. Mrs Gaskell's story, so divided, is wearisome in the last degree'.[59] Again, to Wills, comes this infamous outburst against what he saw as Gaskell's intractability: 'If I were Mr. G. Oh Heaven how I would beat her!'[60]

Most of the heat generated by *North and South* occurred in the private correspondence, and no doubt drawing rooms, of Gaskell and Dickens. Although not reviewed as widely as *Mary Barton*, responses to the novel raise similar issues. Some of the comments on the suitability of the working-class struggles in Manchester as a subject for fiction are combined with political opposition to Gaskell's sympathy with the poor and with a misogynistic patronism. The *Leader*'s unsigned review scathingly declares that 'so much of the book as relates to Lancashire is full of errors which it is inconceivable for a resident in Manchester to have made, and which none but a lady could have so made'.[61] After listing the perceived inaccuracies, the reviewer continues:

■ If our objections seem too technical, we have to allege in excuse that we take so deep in [*sic*] interest in the questions that agitate Lancashire and its trade arrangements; are so convinced that nothing but sound, strong, masculine, practical insight can aid their solution; are so sure that in this, above all other social complications, sentimental yearnings and feverish idealisations only complicate matters; are so certain that if there are two classes that should give trade and masters-and-men questions a wide berth, those classes are clergymen and women; that we have taken especial pains to show, and it could only be shown by such technicalities, that our authoress knows too little of the Cotton Trade to be entitled to increase the confusion by writing about it.[62] □

Other readers also doubt whether the subject matter is suitable for fiction. Henry Fothergill Chorley, in an unsigned review in the *Athenaeum*, states:

■ She [Gaskell] deals with the difficulties of morals needlessly, and too fearlessly, because, as we have again and again said, the riddle propounded cannot be solved in fiction; and because by all one-sided handling of such matters, – when passions become engaged and generous feelings are persuaded, and when the temptation must be dwelt upon as cruel, in apology for the offence, – there is always a danger of unmooring the eager and the inexperienced from their anchorage.[63] □

Charlotte Brontë, herself no stranger to controversial subject matter, writes to Gaskell, inaccurately anticipating the contents of the remaining instalments:

■ What has appeared I like well, and better, each fresh number; best of all the last (to-day's). The Subject seems to me difficult: at first, I had groaned over it: if you had any narrowness of views or bitterness of feeling toward the Church or her Clergy, I should groan over it still; but I think I see the ground you are about to take as far as the Church is concerned; not that of attack on her, but of a defence of those who conscientiously differ from her, and feel it a duty to leave her fold. Well – it is good ground, but still rugged for the steps of Fiction; stony – thorny it will prove at times – I fear. It seems to me that you under-stand well the Genius of the North.[64] □

Reviewers continued to see similarities between the fiction of Gaskell and that of Dickens. Margaret Oliphant perceptively comments on the tension in both novels between the public and the private:

■ There is one feature of resemblance in Mrs Gaskell's last work [*North and South*] and Mr Dickens' *Hard Times*. We are prepared in both for the discussion of an important social question; and in both, the story gradually slides off the public topic to pursue a course of its own.[65] □

Richard Holt in the *National Review*, however, complains that characters are secondary to ideas:

■ [*North and South*] has much of the great power of its author, but its plot is sadly disjointed, and the interstices are 'viewy'. The characters do not move gradually through the narrative, but, so to say, get through it, in kangaroo fashion, by a series of little successive springs, and the characters are rather subordinated to the 'views', than the 'views' to the characters. The story is clearly rather incoherent, and the incident invented, as emergency dictated, to get up periodic interest when the book became too discussional.[66] □

This is one of the rare attentions to the formal features of Gaskell's fiction, rather than the type of subject matter she chooses to focus upon, and the reviewer astutely detects the thorny issue of periodic publication that caused Gaskell much angst. Other reviewers note the continued interest in narrative that evolves around a series of oppositions. To the binaries rich/poor and employer/workman from *Mary Barton*, *North and South* adds geography and gender. The latter is not picked up explicitly by readers until the feminist criticism of recent years, but the issue of location is hotly debated.[67] Some contemporary reviewers, such as the unsigned review in the *Leader*, deny that the portrayal of either is representative: 'as [it] relates to anything special to either the North or the South, or to those two Districts in contrast, it is not so successful: it is, not to mince matters, a failure'.[68] Other reviewers, rather than worrying whether the depiction of North and/versus South is accurate, admire the dynamic behind the opposition, such as in the last extract from the *Manchester Weekly Advertiser*:

■ 'North and South' seems to us, both in conception and execution, the best of Mrs Gaskell's fictions. It aims, nobly and generously, at reconciling two long-opposed sections of English society, by exhibiting to each the true worth of the other. The rugged industrial energy of the 'north' is brought face to face with the culture and refinement of the 'south', and after a little mutual misapprehension and hostility, there is established between them a firm friendship, based on the appreciation that arises out of better knowledge.[69] □

CHAPTER TWO

A Proper Authoress: Biographical Criticism

■ I do not see why the public have any more to do with me than to buy or reject the wares I supply to them. □

Elizabeth Gaskell[1]

Although Elizabeth Gaskell flinches from her readers' and potential biographers' exploration and exploitation of her personal life, the responses to her fiction in the critically barren period between their publication and the evolution of sociological criticism are fascinated by her character. This is not a mode of critical practice unique to Gaskell; on the contrary, it was the fate of all major women writers of the nineteenth century, in particular Emily and Charlotte Brontë, Christina Rossetti and Elizabeth Barrett.[2] The particular disadvantage that such an approach has to Gaskell studies, leaving aside the critical ideology underpinning this methodology, is to produce a rather blinkered attempt to match her fiction according to the norms of a woman writer's appropriate subject matter. Thus, the radical aspect of Gaskell's fictions has been elided. Furthermore, the approach relegated Gaskell as a minor Victorian novelist. In this period of eighty-five years, critical attention to Gaskell, and in particular to her industrial novels *Mary Barton* and *North and South*, is both lukewarm and minimal in comparison to the huge interest generated by *Mary Barton*'s publication and by Marxist literary criticism from the 1950s.

Charles de Moüy's appreciative article in the *Revue Européene* on 1 September 1861 sees Gaskell as an objective writer, in the way that Charlotte Brontë (Currer Bell) is not:

■ while Currer Bell analyses her own feelings, and shows uniquely what she has experienced herself and above all what she has suffered, Mrs Gaskell, removing her personality entirely, examines the problem of social issues, compresses in certain individuals the sorrows and feelings of the masses, and fixes her eyes above all on the moral problems that concern mankind as a whole.[3] □

Although the reviewer cannot entertain the idea that the female author is emotionally and subjectively involved in social issues, with which women were not supposed to have direct contact, he also contradicts his argument by praising Gaskell's nature, as evinced by her narrative. He finds, in particular, 'an infinite compassion, both tender and sweet, and an unshakeable confidence in the supreme goodness of an eternally present Providence'.[4] In order to reconcile these two positions, particularly given what he declares to be the grim truth of her depiction of Manchester, he accuses her, regretfully, of some infelicitous and discordant emotions that disrupt her narrative to its detriment:

■ With its dramatic descriptions and its stark contrasts, *Mary Barton* is the intense expression of Mrs Gaskell's thought. This direct and bold work is like the bursting out of long-restrained feeling. [. . .] [U]ltimately, it is impossible not to be aware, in some passages, of uncontrolled feelings, of an unpolished harshness, which show, in their awkward nature, the inexperience of an author writing her first work. In *North and South* . . . Mrs Gaskell gives way less to her impulses; this novel, on a related subject, is quieter, meditated at length, more accomplished, wiser, though also paler, less gripping, and one where the strong gale of passion is not felt with the same force.[5] □

The obituaries and notices that greeted Gaskell's sudden death on 12 November 1865 start the process of reviewing her literary status. Lord Houghton, writing in the *Pall Mall Gazette* on 14 November 1865, assesses her thus: 'Mrs. Gaskell, the authoress and biographer, was suddenly struck by death on Sunday last while in the act of reading to her daughters. She has thus past [*sic*] away in the midst of that domestic life out of which her literary talent grew and flourished'.[6] The assertion that Gaskell's private and domestic life nourished her fiction is based on a false account of her death: Gaskell died while talking to her daughters in their new house, bought as a surprise for their father. But the important point here is the way in which a biographical (not to say mythological) persona quickly develops a posthumous existence that finds evidence for its characterisation in the fiction, which in turn feeds the construction of the figure 'Mrs Gaskell'. The rhetorical circularity fuels responses to Gaskell's death and literary position. In addition, Houghton's assessment of Gaskell and her work as domestic, along with the other connotations such a word has (contained, private, insular, feminine), is based on the Gaskell of *Cranford*, rather than the Gaskell of *Mary Barton* and *North and*

South. Indeed, many of the assessments on her death praised her as the writer of *Cranford* and ignored her more troubling industrial fiction.

Writing in *Macmillan's Magazine* in December 1865, the critic David Masson joins the host of his colleagues who read Gaskell's fiction as a spontaneous and direct reflex of her personality, but he is careful to distinguish her work from those of other women novelists of whom he disapproves:[7]

■ [Gaskell's private life] **differed from those of most other women who write novels, in being more calm and less eventful. Neither necessity, nor the unsatisfied solitude of a single life, nor, as I fancy, an irresistible impulse, threw her into the paths of literature. She wrote, as the birds sing, because she liked to write; and ceased writing when the fancy left her. And the result of all of this was, that all of her works have, in their own way, a degree of perfection and completeness rare in these days, when successful authoresses pour out volume after volume without pause or waiting.[8]** □

Interestingly, Masson noted Gaskell's horror at the hostile reception to *Mary Barton*, and claims that this indicates a pathological feature of the woman writer: 'somehow or other, the intense personality – if I may use the word – of female nature causes women to identify their private with their literary reputations to an extent unintelligible to men'.[9] Ironically, of course, the first extract from Masson demonstrates his own investment in the creation of this female 'nature' that fuses the literary with the personal.

The following extract is taken from the French critic Louis Cazamian's *Le Roman Social en Angleterre*, published in 1903 and translated by Martin Fido into English in 1973. Cazamian's study is significant for its early attention to the social problem novel as a subgenre, which the critic approaches by setting novels by Dickens, Disraeli, Gaskell and Kingsley within a socio-political context. Cazamian's section on Gaskell absorbs the biographical criticism of his contemporary British critics, and fuses Gaskell's Christian ethics with what he sees as the typical characteristics of the middle-class clergyman's wife. Hilary Schor argues that there are two Gaskells created by literary critics: the Gaskell of the bucolic *Cranford* and the Gaskell of the social problem novel, and Cazamian is the front-runner for the latter school in this period. Attention to Gaskell's contexts and character were to be repeated throughout readings of her industrial novels until fairly recently.

■ **Between 1840 and 1850 three lady novelists, Mrs Gaskell, Charlotte Brontë, and Charlotte Elizabeth,[10] touched on the industrial question in a rather similar spirit. Mrs Gaskell's social novels are by far the** most important of this group, although her rivals' books are also of some interest historically. They all met with public approval,[11] and their similarity is evidence of their moral unanimity of the movement which was affecting the whole nation. One of the components of idealistic interventionism was exemplified better in the work of these lady novelists than anywhere else: this was the spontaneous repugnance felt by anyone of a religious disposition for an industrial system that violated scriptural teachings.

The manufacturing population of the North was predominantly Evangelical. Millowners faithfully clung to their austere, Nonconformist sects until their fortunes brought them into elegant society and into the Established Church. At the time of the Oxford Movement, the factory was the stronghold of sober, conscientiously disciplined religion. Such a faith automatically appealed to men of rigid determination, rigorous energies, and well-ordered minds. It also offered divine sanction for the strict, narrow individualism of the industrial bourgeoisie. The millowners were fortified by their personal relations with God and their severe, narrow-minded morality. And they based their sturdy respect for the rights of property on the Ten Commandments: 'thou shalt not covet thy neighbour's house, thou shalt not covet thy neighbour's wife, nor his manservant, nor his ox, nor his ass, nor any thing that is thy neighbour's'. Then they could get on with their implacable pursuit of profit, comfortably assured that their religion and conscience had nothing against it. They swept unseeing and unhearing past the silent evidence of misery around them, and the pleas of men for their charity; they were blind to any insight that had no practical use, and they braced themselves against all emotions, which they believed were dangerous. Only this radical inability to respond to any emotion, and a complete want of sympathy and understanding, can explain how men who were, in other respects, absolutely upright fought, tooth and nail[,] against the introduction of industrial legislation.

But Evangelicalism and Bible Christianity carried within themselves the seeds of a revolt against individualist morality. The teaching of the Bible might be used to sanction enlightened self-interest, but it also forbade its excessive or cruel pursuit. Evangelicalism took as its daily bread precepts like 'do unto others as you would that they should do to you'; 'thou canst not serve God and Mammon'; the parable of Dives and Lazarus,[12] and the oriental horror of the golden calf: all serve to inhibit greed, and put a check to the advance of industrial self-interest. But imagination and sensitivity would have to be revived if pious eyes were to be opened; spiritual insight and physical observation would have to become more acute if the covert class struggle was to be brought out into the familiar open terrain of tradition-hallowed morality. We know that Dickens expected no such transformation in his businessmen; nor did Disraeli expect the miracle to take place with Lord Marney. It was left to women's gentler but more impulsive imaginations to mark the link between the charitable precepts of Christianity and the duty of social responsibility. Clergy wives and daughters, drawing their sentiments from a common source, demonstrated the nature and quantity of sincere religious belief which attacked middle-class individualism from its own ranks.[13] □

After this outline of Gaskell's position in relation to the ideology she critiques – both outside the ideology, as a woman, and inside, as middle-class – Cazamian disappointingly reverts to Gaskell's personality and asserts that it directly mapped on to her narrative:

■ Mrs Gaskell wrote *Mary Barton* spontaneously.[14] It is evident that little artistic forethought went into its making. It is an overflow of sensitivity, prompted by the sort of life and experience described in the book. The kaleidoscope of familiar impressions, scenes, views, and recollected emotions keeps it going effortlessly. Mrs Gaskell instructs as painlessly as she writes. She puts down everything that Manchester has shown her in twelve years of daily life, only tinting it slightly with her own outlook. She contributes to social philosophy by giving an immediate, feminine, Christian interpretation of industrial questions. Although she read Adam Smith prior to writing *Mary Barton*, she was as little fitted as Dickens to construct an economic alternative to Ricardo. But, like Dickens, she knew how to evoke a passionate response to dismal and demanding conditions which would produce immediate action, and subsequently a new ideology.[15] □

In one of the most important early monograph studies devoted wholly to Gaskell, published in 1949, Yvonne ffrench stresses that the author's good intentions characterise *Mary Barton* and, finally, account for its flaws: she is driven by emotions, not intellect ('in a word, she felt' [p. 27]), and her sympathy is that of a detached observer characteristic of a minister's wife ('she is the interpreter of the Christian ethic' [p. 27]).[16] The contradictory gender ideology behind the analysis is telling:

■ The theme of *Mary Barton* is based on conditions prevailing among the mill-hands and operatives throughout the 'thirties: its purpose was to mediate between employers and workpeople sore with injustices they could feel but could not account for, and full of grievances they were unable to remedy. From first to last it is a social novel, with reform as its object; one of the most effective, since sincerity was its hall-mark.

To persuade the employers that the operatives had a case; to convince the operative that the employers also had their troubles; these were Mrs Gaskell's immediate aims. She set out to probe, to diagnose and to reveal; not to remedy.

The action takes place during the unsettled 'thirties. A fluent opening shows her at her ease, introducing her chief characters as they walk across the fields in the spring.

> It was an early May evening – the April of the poets; for heavy showers had fallen all the morning, and the round, soft, white clouds which were blown by a west wind over the dark blue sky, were sometimes varied by one blacker and more threatening. The softness of the day tempted forth the young green leaves, which almost visibly fluttered into life; and the willows, which that morning had had only a brown reflection in the water below, were now of the tender grey-green which blends so delicately with the spring harmony of colours.

In all rural description, and particularly of unspectacular scenes, Mrs Gaskell never went wrong. Fields, footpaths, commons and cottages are all approached lyrically, and the opening paragraph is very characteristic:

> There are some fields near Manchester, well known to the inhabitants as 'Green Heys Fields', through which runs a public footpath to a little village about two miles distant. In spite of these fields being flat, and low, nay, in spite of the want of wood . . . there is a charm about them which strikes even the inhabitant of a mountainous district, who sees and feels the effect of contrast in these commonplace but thoroughly rural fields, with the busy, bustling, manufacturing town he left but half an hour ago. Here and there an old black and white farm-house, with its rambling outbuildings, speaks of other times and other occupations than those which now absorb the population of the neighbourhood. Here in their seasons may be seen the country business of hay-making, ploughing . . .

It is easy to feel the effectiveness of this descriptive power. In this Mrs Gaskell never falters. But thereafter, the whole, top-heavy story proceeds, now rushing, now stumbling along a succession of bewildering and improbable coincidences. Apart from its sincerity and humanity, to read *Mary Barton* is to plunge into a world of melodrama.

It is not well constructed. Sentimentality cloys the characters, and turgid dialogue obscures their reality. Again and again occurs the unlikely event, until with unrelenting optimism the climax is reached with the highly melodramatic reappearance of the prostitute Esther who crawls out of her garish and teeming underworld to collapse, dying, beneath the windows of the Barton home. Humour, in this first novel of Mrs Gaskell's, is not conspicuous. No work wrung from a tormented heart to draw attention to great social wrongs could be an outlet for that exquisitely smiling muse who fortunately later reasserted her influence.

As a thesis *Mary Barton* was indicative. It showed that through industrialism society had produced sub-human living conditions for two-thirds of its population and was either unable or unwilling to remedy the causes. Mrs Gaskell's assumption was that society would be willing, if able. She finger-pointed very clearly the conclusions arrived at by the Manchester operatives that the employers were able, though unwilling. Her indications were clear and precise; her vision unclouded by bigotry or prejudice. She was neither harsh nor narrow in her views. She had studied her subject at close range; from the centre of the swaying battle. She reported truthfully, and was shocked at her own disclosures. As the wife of a minister she was drawn, a neutral, into the maelstrom of capital and labour, and from its still centre her dramatic gesture went forth.

Considered purely as a story and romance the affairs of Mary Barton and Jem Wilson are not of exceptional interest. The dominating factor is that of the gradual moral deterioration and decay of the powerfully drawn John Barton through unemployment, domestic tragedy, near-starvation and conspiracy to murder and finally to death. His career could be defined as an object-lesson in the waste of human effort through misunderstanding. Yet compared with Felix Holt there is a *naïveté* in the drawing of John Barton which points to the influence of emotional sympathy in Mrs Gaskell, rather than to an intellectual understanding of a forceful, dissatisfied nature.[17] □

This critic would rather have the Gaskell of *Cranford* and of the opening of *Mary Barton* than the social novelist she is analysing here. The structural and stylistic flaws ffrench finds in the novel, in particular melodrama, are diagnosed as feminine flaws of sentiment. Her disapproval of Esther points to ffrench's underlying concern: the limits which bound a woman writer's treatment of social problems. Although she states that Gaskell mediates between the workers and the employers, her authorial position is shaky. Gaskell's attitude is taken to be that of the neutral minister's wife and yet she is also over-sentimental and melodramatic. She has a clear ethical message and yet lacks intellectual understanding of John Barton. These contradictions come from two sources: ffrench's attempt to square the novel with the prescriptions of women's writing and her related assertion that the narrator can be identified with the author. Like many critics, ffrench astutely notes an opposition behind Gaskell's aesthetic, but her manner of interpreting the tension betrays her biographical analytical framework: 'two dominant trends in her nature control in effect her literary work: a constant attempt at reconciliation between natural escapism and the sense of moral obligation forced upon her by period, circumstances and upbringing'.[18]

The historical personage of Gaskell is firmly imprinted on the narratorial voice of her novels by David Cecil. He goes further than ffrench, however, in imagining, perhaps fantasising, that personage in his critique. As he does so, and as he grapples with the ideological contradictions inherent in a woman novelist writing about social themes, he exposes the fractures (not to say blatant inconstancies and inaccuracies) in his methodology:

■ Charlotte Brontë's admirers do not think of her as Mrs Nichols; George Eliot's admirers would wonder whom one meant if one referred to her as Mrs Cross.[19] But Elizabeth Cleghorn Stevenson is known to all the world as Mrs Gaskell. This is just as it should be. There is a great difference between her and her famous rivals: and this difference is fitly symbolised in the different form of name under which she elected to write. The outstanding fact about Mrs Gaskell is her femininity. Not that Charlotte Brontë and George Eliot are unfeminine. Charlotte Brontë indeed, emotional, illogical, exclusively concentrated on the personal, is at times distressingly the reverse. And George Eliot has only to stand forth as a teacher, to reveal how much she is a governess. But though Charlotte Brontë and George Eliot are unmistakably women, they are not ordinary women. Ugly, dynamic, childless, independent, contemptuous of the notion that women should be confined to a small area of family and social interests which was commonly regarded as the only proper province of their sex; fiercely resentful of the conventions that kept them within it – at every turn they flout the standards which were set up before the women of their day. In the placid dovecotes of Victorian womanhood, they were the eagles.

But we have only to look at a portrait of Mrs Gaskell, soft-eyed, beneath her charming veil, to see that she was a dove. In an age whose ideal of womanhood emphasised the feminine qualities at the expense of all others, she was all a woman was expected to be; gentle, domestic, tactful, unintellectual, prone to tears, easily shocked. So far from chafing at the limits imposed on her activities, she accepted them with serene satisfaction. She married young and had seven children: she performed with decorous enthusiasm the duties expected of a Unitarian minister's wife; she looked up to man as her sex's right and benevolent master. Nor were her interests incongruous with her

character and position. It is true that she was religious and philanthropic. But her religion was a simple undenominational piety,
innocent alike of mysticism and dogmatic definition; while her philanthropy was a district visitor's philanthropy – an affair of practical
individual sympathy, concerned to make the rich more charitable and
the poor more comfortable. And when she had finished with her
prayers and her personal tour of the parish, she was perfectly content
to sit down and gossip to a neighbour about marriages and clothes and
servants and children. As Trollope was the typical Victorian man, so
Mrs Gaskell was the typical Victorian woman.

This gives her books a place of their own in English literature. It is
not a place outside their period. The fact that she was so Victorian
makes her books Victorian. As much as Trollope – and as much as
Dickens and Thackeray for that matter – she admired innocence and
industry and a warm heart, disliked harshness and flippancy and
loose living. As much as they, she preferred those who were good and
let who would be clever. Her talent, too, is a Victorian talent, fertile,
intuitive, uncritical. Her rambling, unequal, enthralling novels, full of
providential chances and comic character-parts and true love
rewarded in the last chapter, are typical Victorian novels. Only with a
single difference. Her novels are Victorian novels, for the first time
transposed into the feminine key. They are *David Copperfield* and
Barchester Towers, written by a minister's wife in her drawing-room.

Now it is not to be denied that this did in some measure detract
from her stature as a novelist. For one thing, it meant that her work
was wholly lacking in the virile qualities. Her genius is so purely
feminine that it excludes from her achievement not only specifically
masculine themes, but all the more masculine qualities of thought and
feeling. She was very clever; but with a feminine cleverness, instinctive, rule-of-thumb; showing itself in illuminations of the particular,
not in general intellectual structure. The conscious reason plays little
part in her creative processes. She could not build a story round a
central idea, like Meredith, or argue from her particular observation to
discover a general conception of the laws governing human conduct,
like Thackeray. Nor could she describe intellectual characters. We are
told that Roger Hamley was a Senior Wrangler; he might be a minor
prophet for all that the quality of his mind shows itself in his conversation. Mr Hale, in *North and South,* finds himself compelled to give up
his orders owing to religious doubts. We learn in detail how this
decision affected the lives of his wife and daughter; but what the
doubts were and what there was about Mr Hale's mind which made
them so insoluble, Mrs Gaskell does not give us an idea.

Her emotional capacity is no less feminine than her intellectual.
She is not a powerful writer. She could no more express the crude, the

harsh or the violent than she could speak in a bass voice. And if the plot involves her in a situation which calls for the expression of these qualities, if Mary Barton is to bear witness at her lover's trial for murder, or Margaret Hale to confront a mob of starving cotton workers, athirst for their master's blood, Mrs Gaskell's imagination ceases abruptly to function. The characters suddenly lose life and individuality and assume the stilted postures of puppets in a marionette show.[20] □

In other words, Gaskell is castigated for not being a man. Male, and manly, novelists such as Dickens, are the standard for Cecil by which Gaskell is judged to be lacking. Although praised for being hyper-feminine (in an over-assertion of her acceptance of patriarchal norms), Gaskell, in these terms, cannot win: 'Mrs. Gaskell's femininity imposed a more serious limit on her achievement. It made her a minor artist'.[21] Her sex necessarily imposes a curfew on her activities, Cecil reasons, and this limits both her life and her narrative:

■ Confined as she was to her Victorian drawing-room, there was a great deal of the world that she could not see, a great deal highly characteristic of it; and a great deal that Dickens and Thackeray and the rest of them saw clearly. The world of common people, for instance: sometimes a decent village woman might be admitted into the drawing-room if she was in need of charity; and Mrs Gaskell sketches her in deftly enough, bobbing her respects, fumbling shyly with her apron. But the life of the poor among themselves, the teeming, squalid, vivid life of the democracy that surges through the pages of Dickens, she does not understand at all.[22] □

This charming sketch of Gaskell's domestic confinement we now know to be grossly untrue.[23] Even if we were to accept the logic of Cecil's bio-graphical analysis, such an approach ignores her extensive travelling and her active and vigorous philanthropic work, which put her in direct and sustained contact with the working class of Manchester. Ironically, it is Mr Gaskell who prefers to stay at home.[24] But Cecil's analysis is not to be thought redundant for his glaring inaccuracies and a naïve biographical approach, which, after all, is characteristic of his period. Rather, the twists and turns of his logic, as he tries to account for the contradictions within the argument, not only expose the ideology of the critic but also point to the competing ideologies within Gaskell's writing that Cecil tries to smooth over. In the following passage, Cecil attempts to account for the less feminine aspects to Gaskell's writing and ends up pronouncing *Mary Barton* and *North and South* failures because they do not fit into his notion of Victorian women's writing.

■ The moral lessons she thought important dealt with subjects outside her imaginative range. Sociological subjects for one thing: Mrs Gaskell lived a large part of her life in Manchester, during the first period of the Industrial Revolution. And she was horrified by the bad conditions in which the poor lived, and by the un-Christian spirit that possessed both employers and employed. She therefore wrote both *Mary Barton* and *North and South* in order to expose these evils and to suggest a remedy. It would have been impossible for her if she had tried, to have found a subject less suited to her talents. It was neither domestic nor pastoral. It gave scope neither to the humorous, the pathetic nor the charming. Further, it entailed an understanding of economics and history wholly outside the range of her Victorian feminine intellect. And the only emotions it could involve were masculine and violent ones. Mrs Gaskell makes a credible effort to overcome her natural deficiencies; she fills her pages with scenes of strife and sociological argument, with pitiless employers and ragged starving cotton-spinners – but all in vain. Her employers and spinners are wooden mouthpieces, not flesh-and-blood individuals; her arguments are anthologies of platitude; her riot and strike scenes are her usual feeble melodrama.[25] □

Cecil thus would have preferred *Mary Barton* and *North and South* either to have been written by a man or to have been *Cranford*. The critical response once again returns to the definition of a woman novelist and to the range of her narrative.

CHAPTER THREE

'This Unhappy State of Things':[1] Marxist Literary Criticism and the 'Social-Problem' Novel

■ Sooty Manchester [. . .] built on the infinite Abysses [. . .] and there is birth in it, and death in it; – and it is every whit as fearful, unimaginable, as the oldest Salem or Prophetic City. □

Carlyle[2]

In the 1950s, literary critics begin to take more explicit and more sophisticated notice of the novel's representation of, and contribution to, social, political and cultural issues. This had a profound impact on Gaskell studies. The Gaskell of *Cranford* – idyllic, sentimental, rural, conservative – wanes, to be replaced by the industrial, political, radical Gaskell. As literary critics absorbed and evolved Marxist interest in class struggles, Gaskell starts to lose her demeaning and unjust position, established by Leavis's *The Great Tradition*,[3] as a minor authoress. Revaluations of her industrial novels continue to assert the intrinsic realism of her narrative, but they approach its literary and political worth in very different ways from their predecessors. In addition, the re-readings place Gaskell not only in her socio-political contexts, but also in her literary milieu as critical attention shifts to the subgenre of the 'social-problem' or industrial novel. Harriet Martineau's *Illustrations of Political Economy*, Benjamin Disraeli's *Coningsby* and *Sybil*, Dickens's *Hard Times*, Charlotte Brontë's *Shirley*, and Engels's *Condition of the Working Class in Manchester* are all considered as literary precursors. But the most profound and pervasive influence is Carlyle, who provided Gaskell with a self-conscious *raison d'être*: to 'interpret and articulate the dumb deep wants of the people'.[4] From the late 1820s, Carlyle explores the 'Condition of England Question' in, for example, *Signs for the Times* (1829), *Chartism* (1839) and *Past and Present* (1843). Gaskell was indebted to him for the notion of a man's life as a poem and for his exhortation that the revolution that was threatened as a result of the workers' deep sense of injustice would only be averted when men's hearts are 'set *with* one another', an instruction that politicises sensibility.[5]

Marxist literary criticism of Gaskell's industrial novels typically values that portion of the narrative that deals directly with the social and political issues. The influential and much-cited essay by Arnold Kettle, for example, singles out the political rather than romantic elements: 'what makes *Mary Barton*, despite its weaknesses, a distinguished and still powerful novel is, above all, the presentation of John Barton'.[6] He, again like many Marxist critics, stresses how deep was Gaskell's personal commitment to the factory workers, but refuses to admit that she could entertain a political view: 'she is deeply involved [. . .] with the actual life of the people' and yet 'in her political and social *ideas* [. . .] she was a fence-sitter'.[7] What gets in the way of the author communicating her politics is her gender and class. In the following statement, Kettle argues that Gaskell's first novel is truthful and representative *despite* the author's social position:

■ As an accurate and humane picture of working-class life in a large industrial town in the forties, *Mary Barton* is without rival among the novels of the time. Elizabeth Gaskell, for all the parson's wife or district visitor flavour which, naturally enough, characterises her work, gets very deep into Manchester life.[8] □

Indeed, Kettle declares: 'the strength and weaknesses of *Mary Barton* and *North and South* are bound up with the artistic point of view of the author'.[9] This critical methodology, while invigorating Gaskell studies, remains caught up in the conventional ideology of the woman writer, who, the convention goes, can write what she knows about (and therefore the truth of Gaskell's fiction emerges from her direct experience of the poor) but cannot engage with the public sphere, and hence cannot have a political point of view.

The seminal critic of this period is unarguably Raymond Williams. In his study *The English Novel from Dickens to Hardy*, published in 1970, he sums up what by then had become the new literary orthodoxy about the key period between 1847 and 1848: 'what these months seem to mark above all is a new kind of consciousness'.[10] For Williams, this shift produced a very new type of novel that reconfigures the relationship between public and private (see the extract in the Introduction). The most significant activity of this new generation of writers, he argues, was 'the exploration of community: the substance and meaning of community'.[11] Whereas earlier critics had touched on Gaskell's representation of society, Williams stresses, indeed reiterates, community. The shift in semantics is important, signifying an intensified interest in the bonds between and within classes.

Williams's landmark *Culture and Society 1780–1950* aims to revolutionise our understanding of literature's engagement with its contexts. In particular, Williams fleshes out the significance of some key interrelated terms that entered the language, or acquired their modern meaning, at the time of the Industrial Revolution: industry, democracy, class, art and culture.[12] The relatively brief comments Williams makes on *Mary Barton* and on *North and South* have overshadowed all subsequent responses to the novels. Williams, like the critics before him, associates Gaskell herself with the authorial narrator and judges what he sees as her objective or documentary approach to be a result of her class. He compares her unfavourably, and rather unfairly, with the early work of D.H. Lawrence, who is Williams's standard empathiser with the working class.[13] Praise for the opening chapters is tempered by his damning criticism of the novel's change of direction away from John Barton to his daughter. Williams hypothesises that there was an originary narrative that revolved around the father, and he wishes this was the novel Gaskell published rather than following her publishers' stipulations and, in the end, her own instinctive distance from class issues. Towards the end of his discussion of *Mary Barton*, it becomes clear that Williams positions himself as spokesperson for and defender of the working class and, as a result, he balks at the novel's inclusion of murder perpetrated by the oppressed. This leads Williams to radically question Gaskell's commitment to realism: her class impedes her from representing the workers accurately. He sees, in *North and South*, Gaskell slipping back into the middle-class position she was more comfortable with. As a result, for Williams, this is a more accomplished but disappointing book. The importance of his critique lies in the way he opens up for analysis, diagnoses even, the reason for what he perceives to be the books' flaws, rather than merely offering a value judgement (although he does that, too). Ultimately, though, Williams imposes what he wants the industrial novel to be on to Gaskell's work. In particular, his dismissal of the narrative based around Mary Barton as melodramatic and conservative is based on a too-rigid opposition with the socio-political narrative of John Barton's story. Indeed, as he notes, that narrative is enveloped by the other's melodrama, which Williams tries to explain as the middle class's fear of working-class violence.

■ *Mary Barton* (1848)

Mary Barton, particularly in its early chapters, is the most moving response in literature to the industrial suffering of the 1840s. The really impressive thing about the book is the intensity of the effort to record, in its own terms, the feel of everyday life in the working-class homes. The method, in part, is that of documentary record, as may be seen in such details as the carefully annotated reproduction of dialect, the carefully included details of food prices in the account of the tea-party, the itemised description of the furniture of the Bartons' living-room, and the writing-out of the ballad (again annotated) of *The Oldham Weaver*. The interest of this record is considerable, but the method has, nevertheless, a slightly distancing effect. Mrs Gaskell could hardly help coming to this life as an observer, a reporter, and we are always to some extent conscious of this. But there is genuine imaginative re-creation in her accounts of the walk in Green Heys Fields, and of tea at the Bartons' house, and, again, notably, in the chapter *Poverty and Death* where John Barton and his friend find the starving family in the cellar. For so convincing a creation of the characteristic feelings and responses of families of this kind (matters more determining than the material details on which the reporter is apt to concentrate) the English novel had to wait, indeed, for the early writing of D.H. Lawrence. If Mrs Gaskell never quite manages the sense of full participation which would finally authenticate this, she yet brings to these scenes an intuitive recognition of feelings which has its own sufficient conviction. The chapter *Old Alice's History* brilliantly dramatises the situation of that early generation brought from the villages and the countryside to the streets and cellars of the industrial towns. The account of Job Legh, the weaver and naturalist, vividly embodies that other kind of response to an urban industrial environment: the devoted, lifelong study of living creatures – a piece of amateur scientific work, and at the same time an instinct for living creatures which hardens, by its very contrast with its environment, into a kind of crankiness. In the factory workers walking out in the spring into Green Heys Fields; in Alice Wilson, remembering in her cellar the ling-gathering for besoms in the native village that she will never again see; in Job Legh, intent on his impaled insects – these early chapters embody the characteristic response of a generation to the new and crushing experience of industrialism. The other early chapters movingly embody the continuity and development of the sympathy and co-operative instinct which were already establishing a main working-class tradition.

The structure of feeling from which *Mary Barton* begins is, then, a combination of sympathetic observation and of a largely successful attempt at imaginative identification. If it had continued in this way, it might have been a great novel of its kind. But the emphasis of the method changes, and there are several reasons for this. One reason can be studied in a curious aspect of the history of the writing of the book. It was originally going to be called *John Barton*. As Mrs Gaskell wrote later:

Round the character of John Barton all the others formed them-selves; he was my hero, *the* person with whom all my sympathies went.

And she added:

The character, and some of the speeches, are exactly a poor man I know.

The change of emphasis which the book subsequently underwent, and the consequent change of title to *Mary Barton*, seem to have been made at the instance of her publishers, Chapman and Hall. The details of this matter are still obscure, but we must evidently allow some-thing for this external influence on the shape of the novel. Certainly the John Barton of the later parts of the book is a very shadowy figure. In committing the murder, he seems to put himself not only beyond the range of Mrs Gaskell's sympathy (which is understandable), but, more essentially, beyond the range of her powers. The agony of con-science is there, as a thing told and sketched, but, as the crisis of 'my hero; *the* person with whom all my sympathies went', it is weak and almost incidental. This is because the novel as published is centred on the daughter – her indecision between Jem Wilson and 'her gay lover, Henry Carson'; her agony in Wilson's trial; her pursuit and last-minute rescue of the vital witness; the realisation of her love for Wilson: all this, the familiar and orthodox plot of the Victorian novel of senti-ment, but of little lasting interest. And it now seems incredible that the novel should ever have been planned in any other way. If Mrs Gaskell had written 'round the character of Mary Barton all the others formed themselves', she would have confirmed our actual impression of the finished book.

Something must be allowed for the influence of her publishers, but John Barton must always have been cast as the murderer, with the intention perhaps of showing an essentially good man driven to an appalling crime by loss, suffering, and despair. One can still see the elements of this in the novel as we have it, but there was evidently a point, in its writing, at which the flow of sympathy with which she began was arrested, and then, by the change of emphasis which the change of title accords, diverted to the less compromising figure of the daughter. The point would be less important if it were not characteris-tic of the structure of feeling within which she was working. It is not only that she recoils from the violence of the murder, to the extent of being unable even to enter it as the experience of the man conceived as her hero. It is also that, compared with the carefully representative character of the early chapters, the murder itself is exceptional. It is true that in 1831 a Thomas Ashton, of Pole Bank, Werneth, was murdered under somewhat similar circumstances, and that the Ashton family appear to have taken the murder of Carson as referring to this. Mrs Gaskell, disclaiming the reference in a letter to them, turned up similar incidents in Glasgow at about the same time. But in fact, taking the period as a whole, the response of political assassination is so uncharacteristic as to be an obvious distortion. The few recorded cases only emphasise this. Even when one adds the cases of intimidation, and the occasional vitriol-throwing during the deliberate breaking of strikes, it remains true, and was at the time a subject of surprised comment of foreign observers, that the characteristic response of the English working people, even at times of grave suffering, was not one of personal violence. Mrs Gaskell was under no personal obligation to write a representative novel; she might legitimately have taken a special case. But the tone elsewhere is deliberately representative, and she is even, as she says, modelling John Barton 'on a poor man I know.' The real explanation, surely, is that John Barton, a political murderer appointed by a trade union, is a dramatisation of the *fear of violence* which was widespread among the upper and middle classes at the time, and which penetrated, as an arresting and controlling factor, even into the deep imaginative sympathy of a Mrs Gaskell. The fear that the working people might take matters into their own hands was widespread and characteristic, and the murder of Harry Carson is an imaginative working-out of this fear, rather than any kind of observed and considered experience.

The point is made clearer when it is remembered that Mrs Gaskell planned the murder herself, and chose, for the murderer, 'my hero, *the* person with whom all my sympathies went'. In this respect the act of violence, a sudden aggression against a man contemptuous of the sufferings of the poor, looks very much like a projection, with which, in the end, she was unable to come to terms. The imaginative choice of the act of murder and then the imaginative recoil from it have the effect of ruining the necessary integration of feeling in the whole theme. The diversion to Mary Barton, even allowing for the publishers' influence, must in fact have been welcome.

Few persons felt more deeply than Elizabeth Gaskell the sufferings of the industrial poor. As a minister's wife in Manchester, she actually saw this, and did not, like many other novelists, merely know it by report or occasional visit. Her response to the suffering is deep and genuine, but pity cannot stand alone in such a structure of feeling. It is joined, in *Mary Barton*, by the confusing violence and fear of violence, and is supported, finally, by a kind of writing-off, when the misery of the actual situation can no longer be endured. John Barton dies penitent, and the elder Carson repents of his vengeance and turns, as the sympathetic observer wanted the employers to turn, to efforts at improvement and mutual understanding. This was the characteristic humanitarian conclusion, and it must certainly be respected. But it was not enough, we notice, for the persons with whom Mrs Gaskell's sympathies were engaged. Mary Barton, Jem Wilson, Mrs Wilson, Margaret, Will, Job Legh – all the objects of her real sympathy – end the book far removed from the situation which she had set out to examine. All are going to Canada; there could be no more devastating conclusion. A solution within the actual situation might be hoped for, but the solution with which the heart went was a cancelling of the actual difficulties and the removal of the persons pitied to the uncompromised New World.

North and South (1855)

Mrs Gaskell's second industrial novel, North and South, is less interesting, because the tension is less. She takes up here her actual position, as a sympathetic observer. Margaret Hale, with the feelings and upbringing of the daughter of a Southern clergyman, moves with her father to industrial Lancashire, and we follow her reactions, her observations and her attempts to do what she can. Because this is largely Mrs Gaskell's own situation, the integration of the book is markedly superior. Margaret's arguments with the mill-owner Thornton are interesting and honest, within the political and economic conceptions of the period. But the emphasis of the novel, as the lengthy inclusion of such arguments suggests, is almost entirely now on attitudes *to* the working people, rather than on the attempt to reach, imaginatively, their feelings about their lives. It is interesting, again, to note the manner of the working-out. The relationship of Margaret and Thornton and their eventual marriage serve as a unification of the practical energy of the Northern manufacturer with the developed sensibility of the Southern girl: this is stated almost explicitly, and is seen as a solution. Thornton goes back to the North

to have the opportunity of cultivating some intercourse with the hands beyond the mere 'cash nexus'.[14]

Humanised by Margaret, he will work at what we now call 'the improvement of human relations in industry'. The conclusion deserves respect, but it is worth noticing that it is not only under Margaret's influence that Thornton will attempt this, but under her patronage. The other manufacturers, as Thornton says, 'will shake their heads and look grave' at it. This may be characteristic, but Thornton, though bankrupt, can be the exception, by availing himself

of Margaret's unexpected legacy. Money from elsewhere, in fact – by
that device of the legacy which solved so many otherwise insoluble
problems in the world of the Victorian novel – will enable Thornton,
already affected by the superior gentleness and humanity of the South,
to make his humanitarian experiment. Once again Mrs Gaskell works
out her reaction to the insupportable situation by going – in part
adventitiously – outside it.[15] □

One of the first critics to address *Mary Barton* and *North and South* as
members of a particular subgenre of the novel, termed variously industrial or social-problem novels,[16] is Kathleen Tillotson. In *Novels of the
Eighteen-Forties*, she moves away from the constricting biographical criticism of her predecessors, and determines to draw on biographical
material only as a last resort: 'my subject is English novels – not English
novelists'.[17] The limitations of biographical critical practice were evident
in the previous chapter: the critic directly maps a supposed biographical
personage on to the fiction, under the assumption that life mirrors art
and that the woman novelist can write only autobiographically. In moving away from this school of analysis, Tillotson insists that: 'Mrs.
Gaskell's novels need contain no projection of herself; she was not a discoverer, but was writing of what had long been sadly familiar'.[18] The
danger with such an approach, however, is that it continues to map a
Victorian ideology of women's writing on to Gaskell's fiction. Gaskell's
novels not only contain no projection of the author, no autobiographical
element, but the novelist is so removed from the text that the narrative
exhibits a hyperimpartiality that, paradoxically, removes it from all its
contexts, including the social issues that Tillotson addresses.

■ The same social conditions [in *Mary Barton*], and something of the
same anxiety about them, inspired *Sybil* and *Yeast* and *Alton Locke*; but
Mrs. Gaskell differs from Disraeli and Kingsley in having no axe to
grind. A wider impartiality, a tenderer humanity, and it may be a
greater artistic integrity, raise this novel beyond the conditions and
problems that give rise to it.[19] □

This remark is immediately followed by Gaskell's equivocal statement
from the Preface that 'I know nothing of Political Economy, or the
theories of trade. I have tried to write truthfully'. By taking this statement, which uses Victorian gender ideology of female creativity as a
cover for her social critique, Tillotson has her critical cake and eats it too.
Her analysis refuses to accept the biographical personage of Gaskell as
sole agent behind, and through, the narrative; and yet Tillotson still
keeps in play the Victorian construction of the woman writer as totally
removed from her socio-political environment. In other words,

Tillotson's analysis is based on the premise that *Mary Barton* is so removed from its author that it is totally objective, takes no sides, and refuses to project Gaskell's own point of view. So much so, that the socio-political context that the book engages with is emptied from the text. Tillotson is not able to imagine an adequate contextual framework after she has discarded the biographical. It's not surprising, then, that she returns to the author as agent at the end of her chapter on *Mary Barton* while simultaneously removing a political agenda from the narrative. In the gendered logic of Victorian ideologies of creativity, a woman would not be capable of writing outside her limited, domestic, emotional experience. If the novel has a socio-political theme, it is a by-product of the author's personal and emotional attachment to her subject. It is an effect not a purpose:

■ It would be better then to remove from *Mary Barton* the old tag of 'novel with a purpose', implying some social, extra-artistic purpose. It was indeed, more perhaps than any other of her time, a novel with a social *effect*; but Mrs. Gaskell wrote, then as always, not with her eye on the effect, but as one possessed with and drenched in her subject.[20] □

But, despite these flaws, Tillotson is an astute commentator of *Mary Barton*'s investment in industrial fiction of the 1840s, and her close analysis of the narrative offers a fruitful guide to Gaskell's social criticism. Here is Tillotson's chapter in full.

■ 1

Mary Barton [. . .] is the outstanding example – outstanding in merit as in contemporary fame – of a kind of novel which first clearly disengaged itself in the forties: the novel directly concerned with a social problem, and especially with the 'condition-of-England question'; and because it transcends that kind; alike in motive and effect, it is far more than a 'tract for the times'. The same social conditions, and something of the same anxiety about them, inspired *Sybil* and *Yeast* and *Alton Locke*; but Mrs. Gaskell differs from Disraeli and Kingsley in having no axe to grind. A wider impartiality, a tenderer humanity, and it may be a greater artistic integrity, raise this novel beyond the conditions and problems that gave rise to it.

I know nothing of Political Economy, or the theories of trade. I have tried to write truthfully. . . .[21]

In the fifteenth chapter, after a tentative and unwonted excursion on the possible causes of the strike, she concludes with relief, 'so much for generalities. Let us now return to individuals.' It is partly because it is a novel which starts from 'individuals' that *Mary Barton* stands out from the run of 'novels with a purpose'. It is not less truthful than others of its kind, nor less passionate; but it is also, as befits a woman's novel, more purely compassionate; 'the poetry is in the pity.' But there is no patronage or condescension towards suffering. The denizens of the 'other nation' are neither harrowing victims nor heroic martyrs; they are shown in their natural human dignity, as Wordsworth might have shown them had he fulfilled his promise to make 'authentic comment' on 'sorrow barricaded evermore within the walls of cities'.

It was that sorrow which effectively awoke the writer in the Unitarian minister's wife. That is not to say that we directly owe to it her later masterpieces, such as *Cousin Phillis* and *Wives and Daughters*; but *Mary Barton* was the novel she felt compelled to write, whose instant popularity smoothed her whole subsequent literary career, and the work which set free her powers. Not itself a great novel, it is the first novel of a great novelist; and the progress is an understandable one, if we agree with the young Henry James that we have here to deal with a novelist whose 'genius' was 'so obviously the offspring of her affections, her feelings, her associations . . . so little of an intellectual matter . . . little else than a peculiar play of her personal character'.[22]

Mary Barton was like *Vanity Fair* in bringing its author her first fame in early middle age; unlike it, in being the work of a comparatively unpractised writer. The author's three stories in *Howitt's Journal*, 1847–48,[23] preceded it in publication, but probably not in composition; the much earlier verses 'Sketches among the Poor',[24] written with her husband, were intended to inaugurate a series 'in the manner of Crabbe . . . but in a more seeing-beauty spirit'; they were not followed up, though the germ of Alice Wilson may be found there. Her self-discovery as a writer is part of her personal life. She was 'cradled into' novel-writing 'by wrong', and learnt in suffering; first her own suffering in the loss of a child, which sharpened her fellow feeling with the sufferings of the Manchester poor. She had known her material for twelve years, ever since her marriage brought her from the country to the industrial city; her novel 'grew up . . . as imperceptibly as a seed germinates in the earth.'[25] When the millworker answered her attempts at comfort with 'Have you ever seen a child clemm'd to death?' the words struck home. She had seen her only son die of scarlet fever; in the grief that followed she had turned to thoughts of the country and the past and had begun to write 'a tale . . . of . . . more than a century ago . . . on the borders of Yorkshire'.[26] But now she put it aside:

I bethought me how deep might be the romance in the lives of
some of those who elbowed me daily in the busy streets of the
town in which I resided. . . .

She wrote in order

to give utterance to the agony which, from time to time, convulses
the dumb people; the agony of suffering without the sympathy of
the happy, or of erroneously believing that such is the case.
    The prevailing thought in my mind when the tale was silently
forming itself . . . was the seeming injustice of the inequalities of
fortune.[27]

The year was 1845,[28] when the events of the years 1839–42, in which
the story is set, were still painfully near in memory. Whether from
uncertainty or domestic distraction,[29] she seems not to have finished it
until 1847; at the close of that year, after other publishers had rejected
it, John Forster read it for Chapman and Hall and recommended publication. In 1848 its substance had a renewed topicality;[30] Mrs.
Gaskell, who always combined something of the serpent's wisdom
with the dove's innocence, insinuates this timeliness throughout her
preface, and concludes by remarking that her impression 'has received
some confirmation from the events which have so recently occurred
among a similar class on the Continent'. The reviews caught the hint,
and the anonymous 'tale of Manchester life', by one who knew
'nothing of Political Economy', became required reading for all
thoughtful persons. It was reviewed less as a novel than as a document; its truth and justice, its social moral were emphasised:

It embodies the dominant feeling of our times – that the ignorance,
destitution and vice which pervade and corrupt our society must
be got rid of. The ability to point out how they are to be got rid of,
is not the characteristic of this age. That will be the characteristic of
the age that is coming.[31]

The reviewer is not ironical. The necessary step was the tearing of the
iron curtain between the two Nations; and this step was within the
power, perhaps even was peculiarly the role, of the novelist – as the
construction of blueprints for reform was not. The first step was for
those who knew the other nation to build up pictures in the comfortable reader's mind, to haunt his imagination and harry the social
conscience. This was, indeed, only incidental to Mrs. Gaskell's desire
to promote understanding; but it was the main effect. The lesson was
rhetorically rammed home by the reviewer in *Fraser's*:[32]

[This is] the life-in-death – life worse than many deaths, which now besets thousands, and tens of thousands of our own country-men . . . when people on Turkey carpets, with their three meat meals a day, are wondering, forsooth, why working men turn Chartists and Communists.

Do they want to know why? Then let them read *Mary Barton*. Do they want to know why poor men . . . learn to hate law and order, Queen, Lords and Commons, country-party and corn-law leaguer, all alike – to hate the rich, in short? Then let them read *Mary Barton*. Do they want to know what can madden brave, honest, industrious North-country hearts, into self-imposed suici-dal strikes, into conspiracy, vitriol-throwing, and midnight murder? Then let them read *Mary Barton*. . . . Do they want to get a detailed insight into the whole science of starving . . . ? Let them read *Mary Barton*. . . .

The occasional adverse criticism, of the 'Unfair to Mill-owners' order (as in the *Manchester Guardian* and the review by William Rathbone Greg)[33] is itself a tribute to the novel's power; and though she disclaimed a knowledge of political economy, she aroused the political economists to approach her as an apt pupil.[34] Many shades of opinion are represented in the letters she received,[35] from Samuel Bamford, the veteran Radical (testifying to the novel's truth from his own experience – 'of John Bartons I have known hundreds'), from Ashley Cooper (later Lord Shaftesbury), Lord Brougham, Cobden, Bright, Lord Lannsdowne, Sydney Herbert, and Edwin Chadwick; from Dickens, Maria Edgeworth, and Carlyle. William Delafield Arnold wrote to say that it was being widely read in India, where its lessons were needed; and that it was a work of which his father would have approved.

Sybil, three years earlier, had met no such wide and warmhearted response, although its great phrase, 'the two nations', had run through the country and had perhaps prepared the ground; Disraeli's reputa-tion both as society novelist and ambitious politician may have blunted his social message; and though he is more than either of these in *Sybil*, his motive and approach are still limiting. A modern reader turning to these two novels as sociological documents may be struck by the way their evidence confirms and supplements each other – like the Prologues of Chaucer and Langland; but the evidence reaches us differently. The centre of Disraeli's novel is Egremont, the theme is his enlightenment as to the 'condition of England'; he is the discoverer of the 'other nation', and a projection of the author. Mrs. Gaskell's novel need contain no projection of herself; she was not a discoverer, but was writing of what had long been sadly familiar. As one of her more thoughtful critics[36] has said, Disraeli knew his material 'as a traveller knows the botany of a strange country', she 'as an ardent naturalist knows the flora of his own neighbourhood'. More, he was a traveller who travelled deliberately in order to write; and something calculating, almost inhuman, at least journalistic, clings to his report. It does not satisfy Charlotte Brontë's standards:

> To manage these great matters rightly they must be long and practically studied – their bearings known intimately, and their evils felt genuinely; they must not be taken up as a business matter and a trading speculation.[37]

Take Devilsdust, the child who defied in infancy 'starvation and poison', and even the usual baby-farm expedient of sending him 'out in the street to "play", in order to be run over'; who slept at night 'with a dungheap at his head and a cesspool at his feet', and at the age of five, when all his companions were corpses, graduated into a factory.[38] A terrible story, but its force is lessened by its not being concerned with a character in whom we are asked to take any human interest, and by being narrated, not shown. It could equally be a case-history – and an extreme, not a representative, case, selected with a manifestly propagandist purpose. The grimmest episode in *Mary Barton*, John Barton's visit to the Davenport family, dying of fever in their cellar dwelling, could easily have been merely documentary and detachable;[39] instead it is made an essential stage in Barton's experience, part of the warp of the novel. As often with Mrs. Gaskell's descriptions, it makes its effect by slow persistent accumulation; the reader is enmeshed in its detail before he is aware, and engaged as a complete human being, not a politician or philanthropist. The reader's response to Devilsdust and to the tommy-shop is simple and immediate: these conditions are wrong and should be altered by legislation. No one would belittle the value of such stimulus; but the only reason why it should be made through a novel is that it will reach a wider audience. The sufferings of the characters in *Mary Barton* evoke this response and something more. The Davenports could have a better drained and ventilated dwelling and law or charity should see that they do not starve because the mill is closed: but with John Barton we are left aware of

> how small, of all that human hearts endure,
> That part which laws or kings can cause or cure.

Not small indeed, but not all; beneath this is the hard core of irremediable suffering 'permanent, obscure, and dark', in John Barton's sense of the mysterious injustice of man's time-bound existence. To counteract this there must also be a reconciling power; the sense that 'we have all of us one human heart'. *Mary Barton* is a tale of Manchester life, of the Manchester that Engels saw, in whose poorer quarters the infant mortality was sixty per cent; it was also the Manchester of the opening chapters of *Past and Present* –

> sooty Manchester, it too is built upon the infinite abysses!

'It too'; 'Birmingham people have souls'. Manchester life is the life of men and women stirred by the primary human affections, and made in the divine image. On this simple intuition the novel is built.

2

It has therefore a more complex unity than that of social purpose, a unity rather of theme and tone. But first of all, it has the unity of a single character; the character of the title as originally planned[40] – *John Barton*. He is central both to the mere narrative, and to the theme of class antagonism; both reaching their climax in the eighteenth and exactly half-way chapter, 'Murder'. But he is also bigger than the events, even than the clashing social forces which they represent; rebelling against more than society; marked with the same tragic irrationality as Michael Henchard, Mayor of Casterbridge. Emphatically he is not put forward as a type of the working classes – Mrs. Gaskell herself protested against such critics as Greg; nor is his story simply (as some reviewers thought) a moral fable showing why working men turn Chartists and assassins; it is the timeless history of how a man full of human kindness is hardened into (and by) hatred and violence. This defines the rising curve of the story; one point,[41] for instance, is clearly plotted in the third chapter, when on his wife's death the author says that

> One of the ties which bound him down to the gentle humanities of earth was loosened.

We watch others loosen, as his experience – the strike, its typical consequences in the Davenports' starvation and fever, the employers' arrogant isolation, the failure of the petition – seems to show that the world reckons them as of no account. But, as he says on his deathbed after he has confessed the murder, 'all along it came natural to love folk, though now I am what I am . . . I did not think he'd been such an old man – Oh! that he had but forgiven me.' And even as he lies there, his enemy Mr. Carson sits in his library over the family Bible, unable to hate his son's murderer so vehemently now that he has seen him – 'something of pity would steal in for the poor, wasted skeleton of a man'. He does forgive, and John Barton dies in the arms of the man whose son he has murdered. And this points to the book's true theme: not this or that feature of industrial society is being criticised, but its whole principle, excluding any human contact between masters and men; and the hope of betterment lies not in this or that reform, but in the persistence, against all odds, of humanheartedness. It is as simple, and as remote from 'political economy' as that; the moral content of *Mary Barton*, as distinct from all its accretion of specific, documentary detail, is also that of *Dombey and Son* and of *Past and Present*. 'What's money? It isn't cruel, is it?' 'Isolation is the sum-total of wretchedness to man. . . . It was not a God that did this: no!' 'John Barton's overpowering thought . . . was rich and poor; why are they so separate, so distinct, when God has made them all? It is not His will that their interests are so far apart. Whose doing is it?'[42] It is through John Barton, his experience, his honest, confused reflections, his deterioration and his fateful actions, that Mrs. Gaskell gives 'utterance to the agony which . . . convulses the dumb people; the agony of suffering without the sympathy of the happy'.

3

Mary, John Barton's daughter, who gave the book its perhaps more marketable title,[43] nevertheless appears less prominently even than Florence Dombey; and like her, she subsides at times into the novel-heroine of the period – though the greater freedom of her class gives her more scope for action. Her emergence as active and heroic heroine after the murder, in her sensational pursuit of the missing witness in order to prove Jem Wilson innocent, makes her dominate the narrative for the latter half of the novel; but her relation to its theme seems too weakly developed. The rivalry of her two lovers, the master and the man, and her vacillation between them, her relation to her father, the threatening parallel between her and Esther, all have thematic possibilities that are only roughly suggested. It may be a concession to novel-convention that Mary alone of the working-class characters usually speaks ordinary English, not dialect; but it has its dangers. 'Now I scorn you, sir, for plotting to ruin a poor girl!'[44] flattens a climax of the narrative into a stage situation and is far removed from the Old Testament dignity of John Barton's utterances. Mary draws her importance from the story, where John Barton gives out strength to it; in her alone of the characters one sees the prentice hand. She could not have been a Margaret Hale; but she might have been a Sylvia Robson.[45]

4

More is contributed to the unity of the novel by what is indicated in its sub-title – 'a tale of Manchester life'. It is the diversity and density of Manchester life, and the figure of John Barton rising craglike above it, that is built up before our eyes in the slow-moving expository opening chapters. They needed to be slow, because of the novelty of the material; they needed also to be reassuring.[46] The author had to enlist the reader's sympathy for her hero; she could not abruptly introduce him as a Trades Union man, a Chartist, an advocate and perpetrator of violence; and it would indeed be foreign to her purpose, which is not to demand approval or condemnation, but interest and understanding. With instinctive craftiness, she does not at once demand sympathy for hardship, but gently engages the reader's participation in a simple family outing to Greenheys Fields [sic] and a north-country high tea in a basement kitchen.[47] The contrasts are so far unsensational; but there is light and shade – the back-to-back houses with their open drains, the firelit glow of the interior and the clever contrivances of small-scale housekeeping; the ripples of domestic gossip meeting sudden conversational rocks, and making us aware of such past events as little Tom's death and Esther's disappearance. John Barton's outburst, rooted in its context in the first chapter, gives out the theme and forecasts his relation to it:

> 'Thou never could abide the gentlefolk', said Wilson, half amused at his friend's vehemence.
>
> 'And what good have they ever done me that I should like them?' asked Barton, the latent fire lighting up his eye . . . 'Don't think to come over me with the old tale, that the rich know nothing of the trials of the poor. I say, if they don't know, they ought to know. We are their slaves as long as we can work; we pile up their fortunes with the sweat of our brows; and yet we are to live as separate as if we were in two worlds. . . .'[48]

Precarious present happiness, shadowed by past and future, is the 'note' of the opening chapters. But, though precarious, it yet recurs and persists, not for all characters, but as an uncovenanted hope; throughout the tribulations of the narrative, we are kept aware of another world than Manchester, another world than the two worlds of rich and poor. Its light falls on Greenheys Fields, on the recollected Cumberland childhood of old Alice (a fully substantiated 'poor Susan'), on a chance-met child's face in the street, the blind girl's singing, Job Legh's absorption in his collection of insects, Mary's desperate courage at the trial, her face haunting an onlooker like 'some wild sad melody, heard in childhood'. Its broader radiance is perhaps best seen in a passage which may at first sight seem an excrescence, an interlude; in the chapter later called 'Barton's London experiences'.[49] John Barton has returned from London, and tells Mary, Job, and Margaret the story of the Chartists' march through the West End with their petition, in ironic juxtaposition to the carriage procession for the Queen's drawing-room. The actual rejection of the petition is too bad to be spoken of:

> 'I canna tell of our down-casting just as a piece of London news. As long as I live, our rejection that day will bide in my heart; and as long as I live I shall curse them as so cruelly refused to hear us; but I'll not speak of it no more.'
> So, daunted in their inquiries, they sat silent for a few minutes.

The social point has been made (the description of the march is full of bitter detail) and there a propagandist might stop. But equally a part of Mrs. Gaskell's world view are 'the gentle humanities of earth'. From them springs the transition:

> Old Job, however, felt that someone must speak, else all the good they had done in dispelling John Barton's gloom was lost. So after a while he thought of a subject, neither sufficiently dissonant from the last to jar on the full heart, nor too much the same to cherish the continuance of the gloomy train of thought.
> 'Did you ever hear tell', said he to Mary, 'that I were in London once?'

There follows the story of how many years ago he planned a Whitsuntide visit to his married daughter in London, only to hear from her father-in-law that both she and her husband were stricken with fever. The two men had gone to London together, to find daughter and son dead, leaving a young infant; then he tells at length, in garrulous yet reticent Lancashire style, of their journey north with the child, and all their bewildered expedients. Falling into that context, this narrative, with its basis of hardship, the implicit tenderness of the two men's purpose, and the comic awkwardness of the situation, is more than a temporary relief to gloom. There is no simple contrast; Job Legh's experience shares the common ground of poverty with John Barton's grievances, but its unembittered tone supplies an unconscious corrective, a suggestion of values beyond the frustrations of political action. And because it is something past and safely lived through, it stands for hope.

That funeral cost a mint o' money, but Jennings and I wished to do th' thing decent. Then we'd the stout little babby to bring home. We'd not overmuch money left; but it were fine weather, and we thought we'd take th' coach to Brummagem, and walk on. It were a bright May morning when I last saw London town, looking back from a big hill a mile or two off. And in that big mass o' a place I were leaving my blessed child asleep – in her last sleep. Well, God's will be done! She's gotten to Heaven afore me; but I shall get there at last, please God, though it's a long while first.

The babby had been fed afore we set out, and th' coach moving kept it asleep, bless its little heart. But when th' coach stopped for dinner it were awake, and crying for its pobbies. So we asked for some bread and milk, and Jennings took it first for to feed it; but it made its mouth like a square, and let it run out at each o' the four corners. 'Shake it, Jennings', says I; 'that's the way they make water run through a funnel, when it's o'er full; and a child's mouth is broad end of the funnel, and th' gullet th' narrow one.' So he shook it, but it only cried th' more. 'Let me have it', says I, thinking he were an awkward oud chap. But it were just as bad wi' me . . . Well, poor babby cried without stopping to take breath, fra' that time till we got to Brummagem for the night [a chambermaid feeds and quiets the child]. It looked so quiet and smiling, like, as it lay in her arms, that we thought 'twould be no trouble to have it wi' us. I says 'See, Jennings, how women folk do quieten babbies; it's just as I said.' He looked grave; he were always thoughtful-looking, though I never heard him say anything very deep. At last says he – 'Young woman! have you gotten a spare nightcap? . . . Th' babby seems to have taken a mind to yo', and may be in th' dark it might take me for yo' if I'd getten your nightcap on . . . .' Such a night as we had on it! Babby began to scream o' th' oud fashion, and we took it turn and turn about to sit up and rock it. My heart were very sore for the little one, as it groped about wi' its mouth; but for a' that I could scarce keep fra' smiling at th' thought of us two oud chaps, th' one wi' a woman's nightcap on, sitting on our hinder ends for half the night, hushabying a babby as wouldn't be hushabied.

They tramp through another day and night, and next day are helped by a cottage woman who has lost her own child.

'Last look I had o' that woman she were quietly wiping her eyes wi' the corner of her apron, as she went about her husband's breakfast. But I shall know her in heaven.'

He stopped to think of that long-ago May morning, when he

had carried his grand-daughter under the distant hedgerows and beneath the flowering sycamores.

'There's nought more to say, wench,' said he to Margaret, as she begged him to go on. 'That night we reached Manchester, and I'd found out that Jennings would be glad enough to give up babby to me, so I took her home at once, and a blessing she's been to me.'

The return to the present, to the grown grand-daughter, and John Barton with his daughter asleep at his knee, is unstressed; no moral is drawn; it is the reader, rather than John Barton, who is effectively reminded of 'the gentle humanities'. In the next chapter, the present closes over him; its opening words are 'Despair settled down like a heavy cloud'. As a Chartist delegate and Trades Union man, he can find no work; his rooms are stripped to buy food:

> He would bear it all, he said to himself. And he did bear it, but not meekly; that was too much to expect.[50]

The ninth chapter points the significance of Job Legh, who is more than a minor character; he is the point of rest in the narrative, and in the theme, the embodiment of 'the gentle humanities of earth' and of the practical possibilities of the Christian ethic. Almost inactive in events until then, it is thus appropriate that it should be he who appeals for Mr. Carson's forgiveness, he who presses home the social and spiritual lesson after John Barton's death: 'I'm clear about this, when God gives a blessing to be enjoyed, He gives it with a duty to be done; and the duty of the happy is to help the suffering to bear their woe.'

A novelist of narrower purpose might have didactically emphasised the difference between Job Legh and John Barton. But Mrs. Gaskell holds the balance fairly between John Barton's bitter protest and Job Legh's acceptance of his lot; resignation to the power of the masters and to the divine will are not confused. The lesson that Job Legh presses home is that of John Barton's terrible act, without which Mr. Carson's eyes could not have been opened, and for which the masters must share the responsibility. Even by Job, John Barton's failure as a Christian is almost extenuated:

> 'You see he were sadly put about to make great riches and great poverty square with Christ's gospel. . . . For he was a loving man before he grew mad with seeing such as he was slighted, as if Christ himself had not been poor'[51]

whereas Mr. Carson's failure provokes the severest of the author's rare comments:

> Oh! Orestes! you would have made a very tolerable Christian of the nineteenth century![52]

She makes no equivalent condemnation of the murder; and Job's summing up emphasises the chain of cause and effect:

> 'The masters has it on their own conscience, – you have it on yours, sir, to answer for to God whether you've done, and are doing all in your power to lighten the evils, that seem always to hang on the trades by which you make your fortunes. . . . John Barton took the question in hand, and his answer to it was NO! Then he grew bitter and angry, and mad; and in his madness he did a great sin, and wrought a great woe; and repented him with tears as of blood, and will go through his penance humbly and meekly in t'other place, I'll be bound. . . .'[53]

5

These two men, John Barton and Job Legh, may perhaps stand not only for different yet related aspects of 'Manchester life', different responses to life's hardships, but for the defiant courage and persistent loving-kindness that are seen now colliding, now co-operating, in all Mrs. Gaskell's novels. Courage to give utterance to unfamiliar points of view – that of the workman driven to violence; of the stern self-made factory owner; of the seduced girl and the parson who protects her; but always with the purpose, unconscious perhaps, of promoting sympathy, not sharpening antagonisms; between regions, classes, sexes, generations; on the quiet assumption that to know is to understand, to forgive, and even to respect.

Not even George Eliot shows such reverence for average human nature as Mrs. Gaskell; and this is evident from her earliest work. It helped to teach her the art which her later novels perfected; helped to guide her instinctive tact in avoiding the over-emphases of sentimentality and sensationalism, even in situations that tempt towards them. For she accepts, and not ruefully, the ordinariness of people and the dailiness of life. Already in her first novel the minor characters (such as the boy Charley, Mrs. Wilson, Sally Leadbitter) are solid and distinct; each character, however small, has its scale of moral values, and its social medium; all are closely associated with the domestic detail of their surroundings. (Her explicit descriptions are mainly of what people use or make themselves at home in.) This unheightened truthfulness establishes confidence, so that we are ready to accept her 'big scenes' – the chase down the Mersey, the murder trial; like the bank failure in *Cranford*, they seem simply emergencies which must occasionally arise in ordinary life and which test character. And more: this almost pedestrian truthfulness is already accompanied by something spacious: her common flowers of human nature are rooted in earth, but over them arches 'the divine blue of the summer sky'.[54]

It would be better then to remove from *Mary Barton* the old tag of 'novel with a purpose', implying social, extra-artistic purpose. It was indeed, more perhaps than any other of the time, a novel with a social effect; but Mrs. Gaskell wrote, then as always, not with her eye on the effect, but as one possessed with and drenched in her subject:

> I *can* not (it is not *will* not) write at all if I ever think of my readers, and what impression I am making on them. 'If they don't like me, they must lump me', to use a Lancashire proverb. It is from no despising my readers. I am sure I don't do that, but if I ever let the thought or consciousness of them come between me and my subject I *could* not write at all.[55] □

John Lucas's important essay, 'Mrs Gaskell and Brotherhood', takes Tillotson to task on a number of points. His discussion compares Gaskell with the approach of Kingsley and Disraeli and is based on the premise 'that the flaws inherent in the genre of the social-problem novel are a direct result of the novelists' failure to deal really honestly with the social experiences their novels are intended to portray. Instead they rely on stock political attitudes to bridge all imaginative lacunae'.[56] The obvious problem with Lucas's approach, of course, is his understanding of what dealing 'really honestly' would be like, his consequent grasp of realist fiction (which includes the notion that art equals life), and his assumption (manifest in the passage below) of what would be conscious and unconscious in the author's attitude to social issues. In the following extract from his essay, he engages with Tillotson, Williams and Gaskell's contemporary reviewers in an analysis of the author's uncomfortable treatment of painful class issues.

■ If we turn directly from Kingsley and Disraeli's novels to *Mary Barton*, we encounter so striking a difference that we shall be tempted to overpraise Mrs Gaskell's first novel. For the strengths of *Mary Barton* lift it quite clear of the other novels, and Mrs Gaskell rarely falls into the sort of pits Disraeli and Kingsley dig for themselves. She does not repeat Disraeli's mistake of trying to fuse noble labourers with labouring nobility, nor, at her best, is she guilty of the unintelligent sentimentality which allows Kingsley to recommend the working-class to a middle-class reading public on the grounds that, contrary to appearances, their interests are the same. The truth is that Mrs Gaskell is not interested in the idea of brotherhood that Kingsley half dared to believe existed, and which Disraeli probably knew did not. If she can be said to believe in the idea at all, it is not as a conscious thesis to which her characters are bent, but as something which can be sensed in the imaginative exploration that presupposes their autonomous existence. But that, it should be obvious, is a very different sort of brotherhood, one indeed that wrecks the hopes on which the other concept is built.

Since what I am here saying may seem to inflate the novel's reputation dangerously, it is well to add a note of caution. George Eliot's claim that Mrs Gaskell is not a classic needs to be challenged, but not on the strength of *Mary Barton*. In the final reckoning the achievement of this first novel is a fairly modest one; the real wonder is that it should exist at all. For though Mrs Gaskell is a middle-class liberal who from the evidence of most of her published comments did not consciously chafe at her political creed, her novel really does have to do with working-class individuals and their environment, and not with the middle class or nobility in disguise. At least not at its best. But perhaps inevitably there are moments when she tries to evade the starker implications of her exploration by falling back on comforting attitudes. And yet the very ease with which these moments can be detected is itself proof of her customary integrity; at their truest, her characters are shaped largely by, and exist within, a precisely realised world in which the keynote is provided by grinding toil, poverty, death, and a persistent, scarcely subdued, reek of hopelessness.

The really disturbing centre of the novel, as most commentators have noticed, is not Mary herself but her father. Mary Barton, indeed, seems to owe a great deal of her prominence to the wishes of Mrs Gaskell's publishers, Chapman and Hall, that the novel should have a love-story running through it. Much of this is detachable and is certainly peripheral to the novel's real concerns, which are well enough indicated by the fact that its first title was *John Barton*. [. . .] The novel's real strengths are clustered around him, and Mrs Gaskell's triumph with him is the more remarkable in that he challenges all the ideas to which, as a middle-class liberal undertaking a social-problem novel, she holds.

To say that may well appear to beg the question. Did Mrs Gaskell undertake anything of the kind? On the evidence of her preface to *Mary Barton* the answer would have to be no, for there she goes out of her way to insist that 'I know nothing of Political Economy, or the theories of trade.'[57] It is enough to convince Mrs Tillotson. For her 'the same social conditions, and some of the same anxiety about them, inspired *Sybil* and *Yeast* and *Alton Locke*; but Mrs Gaskell differs from Disraeli and Kingsley in having no knife to grind.'[58] But as we all know now, the important thing is to trust not the teller but the tale, and the undeniable fact is that there *are* occasions when Mrs Gaskell retreats from her sensitive exploration of Barton's life to attitudes about him; and such occasions are further marred by a moralising that is strangely superficial, and frequently inapplicable. It may well be that she felt Barton would so soon offend her audience and alienate their sympathies that she forced herself to explain or interpret his behaviour in a manner that damages the fine integrity of his presentation. But there also comes a point where Barton is put beyond even *her* sympathies, making the possibility of moralising still more explicit. Something else will have to be said about this, but for the moment it is more important to insist on just how splendidly she does manage with Barton.

Essentially he is representative of the working men who during the 1830s and 1840s, as they became increasingly self-conscious of the total condition in which they lived, began to probe for its causes and enquire into its justness. Barton questions the inevitability of his sufferings, and the system that imposes them; and for this he is made to suffer still more. Because of his Chartist allegiances he is thrown out of work and blacklegged by all employers: the wages of resistance is poverty and death. Mrs Gaskell's is by no means a diagrammatic or external statement of what happens to her hero; one of the very best things about *Mary Barton* is the feel of poverty as its consequences eat into a man, and the sense of the surrounding, ubiquitous city, which imposes hideous conditions on a life from which there is no easy escape. There is then a real temptation for Barton to give in, to accept the system in the hope of living less miserably. So his refusal to do this has a stubborn integrity that is only occasionally upset by Mrs Gaskell's prim interpolations, asking forgiveness of his sins. Barton's bewilderment at the injustice of the social system in which he finds himself, the gradually hardening knot of his own bitterness, and the impulse towards a violent reaction, all spring organically from his situation. And so do his finer qualities. Mrs Gaskell is very good at showing how difficult it is for any human assertions to struggle against the overwhelming power of poverty, and her art is at its best in the moments which show that the smallest gesture of human decency is, for Barton and his friends, likely to be a considerable triumph over conditions which require selfishness as the best hope for survival.

To put the matter like that is to see just why Barton is the novel's disturbing centre. Certainly it explains why he so disturbed the critics. Indeed, it would be nice to provide a *sottisier* of reviews of *Mary Barton*, merely to show the comedy of their attempts to find new and legitimate grounds for the liberal conscience, either by trying to reason with Barton (several reviewers adopt a 'look here, old chap, this isn't going to get you anywhere' tone) or by distorting the novel until it fits a picture on which that conscience can bear to gaze. But to do this is beyond the scope of the present essay, and I must restrict myself to two reviews, which suggest well enough the difficulties reviewers found themselves up against. The first comes from *The New Monthly Magazine and Humourist*:

> The authoress professes to have nothing to do with political econ-omy or the theories of trade, she says that she merely wishes to impress what the workman thinks and feels, but she allows the discontented to murmur in prolonged strains without an attempt to chasten the heart or correct the understanding. Barton rails at all capitalists as being so only through the toil of the poor. This would be staunch communism. There surely must be capitalists or the condition of the poor would be worse than ever. We are told in scripture that the poor shall never cease out of the land, but we are also taught that their expectation shall not perish, and that those who trust, shall be fed and delivered out of affliction. Further than this we are told that the person of the poor should be no more respected than that of the rich should be honoured, and while it is sinful to oppress and a duty to assist, so also the poor that will not bear rebuke, their poverty is their destruction.[59]

The riches of this piece are wellnigh inexhaustible, but two points deserve special attention. One is that the review is an extreme example of the unease which the novel caused, and which was principally owing to the imaginative power that went into the presentation of Barton. You can feel the reviewer struggling against being swept away by the power, clutching feebly at the straws of communism and the need for capitalists, and then sensing deliverance as he grasps at scripture. The tone steadies, the sentences lengthen, there is a fine bravura about the last words, and a generous magnanimity in the earlier reassurance: 'those who trust, shall be fed and delivered out of affliction.' Only, unfortunately, and this is the other point, it is quite irrelevant to the novel, in which the family which dies most horribly in a slum cellar – of typhoid brought on by prolonged starvation – are the Davenports, who are good Methodists. The points are obvious ones, but that is because of the obviousness of the reviewer's evasions.

The other review is an altogether more serious affair. It was pub-lished in the *Westminster Review*, and is the longest and most considered of all contemporary criticisms of the book. It begins by noting that *Mary Barton* 'embodies the dominant feeling of our times – a feeling that the ignorance, destitution and vice which pervade and corrupt our society must be got rid of. The ability to point out how they are to be got rid of, is not the characteristic of this age. That will be the characteristic of the age which is coming.'[60] As Mrs Tillotson says of this:

> the reviewer is not being ironical. The necessary step was the tearing of the iron curtain between the two Nations; and this step was within the power, perhaps even was peculiarly the role, of the novelist – as the construction of blueprints for reform was not. The first step was for those who knew the other nation to build up pictures in the comfortable reader's mind, to haunt his imagination and harry the social conscience.

Yet the odd fact is that *Mary Barton* does construct blue-prints for reform or, since that puts the matter a little too flagrantly, it recommends. And what interests me about the reviewer's comment is that in his total impression of the novel that is quite forgotten. His responsiveness to *Mary Barton*'s embodying 'the dominant feeling of our time' is such that he cannot take at all seriously the novel's recommendations; and in this he is right, since without doubt they are mere paper boats, sunk under Mrs Gaskell's weighty realisation of the industrial world. It is therefore natural that he should concentrate on this, and much the largest part of his article is taken up with a discussion about John Barton. But here again odd things happen to the reviewer's memory.

To begin with, he says of Barton that

> In the commencement of the tale he is full in work, with high wages, and possesses a comfortable home. But in possessing that comfortable home, like too many around him (including other portions of society as well as the mere day-labourers), the enjoyment of the present is alone well attended to; while the provision for a continuation of even moderate enjoyment for the future, seems to be scarcely heeded.

Now these sentences quite blunt Mrs Gaskell's sharp insights, and they do it by a mixture of facts which are true to the novel, together with some illegitimate deductions from the facts which are made to seem equally factual by the quasi-paratactical syntax.[61] So though it is quite right to say Barton is in full employment, to add that he gets high wages is a deduction from that true fact, not another fact taken from the novel, even though that is how it reads. And to then state that Barton possesses 'a comfortable home' is to make the comfort dependent on his high wages; you tend to read in 'therefore'. But this is quite improper, as a glance at the novel will confirm. True, the Barton home has a certain comfort, but this is emotional rather than material. The warmth of family feeling manages to minimise the lack of soldier comforts, a far different matter from pretending that a comfortable home is owing to the Bartons being comfortably off.

But I don't want to accuse the reviewer of seeking to muddle his audience, rather I think he confuses himself; but the way he does so is highly revealing. For the whole point of the muddle is that it helps him to turn away from the force of Mrs Gaskell's work, and this becomes startlingly clear when he goes on to reprimand Barton for attending to the present alone rather than providing for 'even moderate enjoyment of the future' (if he's comfortably off, of course he can manage that). Here, then, is part of the episode with which the novel opens. The Bartons, out for a Sunday walk, have met the Wilsons, and invite their friends home for tea.

> Then came a long whispering, and chinking of money, to which Mr and Mrs Wilson were too polite to attend; knowing, as they did full well, that it all related to the preparations for hospitality; hospitality that, in their turn, they should have much pleasure in offering. So they tried to be busily occupied with the children, and not to hear Mrs Barton's directions to Mary.
>
> 'Run, Mary dear, just round the corner, and get some fresh eggs at Tipping's (you may get one a-piece, and that will be five-pence), and see if he has any nice ham cut, that he would let us have a pound of.'
>
> 'Say two pounds, missis, and don't be stingy,' chimed in the husband.
>
> 'Well, a pound and a half, Mary. And get it Cumberland ham, for Wilson comes from there-away, and it will have a sort of relish of home with it he'll like, – and Mary . . . you must get a pennyworth of milk and a half loaf of bread – mind you get it fresh and new – and, and – that's all, Mary.'
>
> 'No, it's not all,' said her husband. 'Thou must get sixpennyworth of rum, to warm the tea; thou'll get it at the "Grapes". And thou just go to Alice Wilson . . . and tell her to come and take her tea with us; she'll like to see her brother, I'll be bound, let alone Jane and the twins.'

The reviewer's rebuke to Barton shows very plainly that he is relying on the liberal remedy of thrift to see a person through even the worst situations, and since *Mary Barton* is pretty firm in showing the hopelessness of this he has to convert the facts before the remedy can apply. But even if it could in Barton's case – and there is no solid evidence of a supply of money that would last any length of time – the fact is that self-help would merely destroy the comfortable home, because it would squeeze out all the decency and generosity of spirit that manage to survive in the Barton household. So the reviewer's advice to all future Bartons is yet another way of trying to hedge round the truths of the novel.

> I must, therefore, provide against the ignorance and imprudence of my employer. He may over-engage himself at one time, and subsequently be obliged to dismiss a portion of his labourers, or become insolvent, and be obliged to shut up his works. Folly, similar to this, may prevail among others. My duty to myself commands me to acquire, by saving a capital for myself – a duty which every well conducted labourer can perform.

Mrs Tillotson says that *Mary Barton* was reviewed 'less as a novel than as a document; its truth and justice, its social moral were emphasised'. But what she does not say, though it strikes me as more important, is that the chief reason for the novel's being reviewed as a document is that its truth and justice and social moral could be not only emphasised but questioned. It is easier to argue with a document than a novel, for the truths of the latter are not open to the techniques by which the worth of documents can be examined. That is why the reviewer's advice to Barton must strike us as ludicrously beside the point when we are faced with the scene which presents his attending to the 'enjoyment of the present'. On the other hand, what the scene does show – and finely – is the struggle there has to be for gestures of human decency to survive. Mrs Barton's anxiety about money ought to win the reviewer's plaudits, but though we may well feel sympathy for what causes it we are unlikely to think of her caution as virtue overruled by culpable extravagance. And at one point the reviewer himself is forced to acknowledge the imaginative power of Mrs Gaskell's treatment of Barton:

> That John Barton should have had the discontent, engendered by want, increased to hatred towards the class of rich employers, is not strange nor forced. The patience and long suffering of the industrious poor, left in the ignorance which we see, are more strange than the conclusions to which John Barton arrives, and which lead him, an unwilling agent, step by step, to the crime. . . .

That moment of insight is not sustained, and before the end of the review there is more haranguing and advice; yet the fact it is there at all suggests how the strength of *Mary Barton* can break through the most determined resistance. More particularly, it is because Barton is so satisfactory a fictional creation that he is disturbing as neither Alton Locke nor 'Bishop' Hatton could be; and only by backing away from what actually is in the novel could reviewers accommodate him to the world of cliché in which Disraeli and Kingsley's workmen move.

There is not the space to examine in detail the justness of the *Westminster Review*'s critic's admission that Barton's progress towards hatred 'is not strange nor forced'. One instance must do, and I choose it because it also suggests where Mrs Gaskell fails. Barton and Wilson go to the help of the Davenport family, who are living in terrible squalor since the dying husband has been for so many weeks out of work and there is no money for food or medicine. The approach to the Davenport's [*sic*] living quarters is described in this way:

> It (the road) was unpaved: and down the middle a gutter forced its way, every now and then forming pools in the road with which the street abounded. . . . Our friends were not dainty, but even they picked their way, till they got to some steps leading down to a small area, where a person standing would have his head about one foot below the level of the street, and might at the same time, without the least motion of his body, touch the window of a cellar [. . .] in which a family of human beings lived. It was very dark inside. The window-panes of many of them were broken and stuffed with rags, which was reason enough for the dusky light that pervaded the place even at mid-day. After the account I have given of the state of the street, no one can be surprised that on going into the cellar inhabited by Davenport, the smell was so foetid as almost to knock the two men down. Quickly recovering themselves, as those inured to such things do, they began to penetrate the thick darkness of the place, and to see three or four children rolling on the damp, nay, wet brick floor, through which the stagnant, filthy moisture of the street oozed up; the fire-place was empty and black; the wife sat on her husband's lair, and cried in the black loneliness.

As soon as he sees the family's condition Barton goes home and takes his remaining few valuables to pawn; and with the money he buys some necessaries for them.

So far the episode is pretty well a conventional matter. And in addition there are elements of an amateurishness in the initial description suggesting at the very least that Mrs Gaskell is a little unsure of her audience's response: 'after the account I have given of the state of the street, no one can be surprised', reads very much like a defence against charges of improbability. It also makes the description seem little more than factual reportage on the lines of *Sybil*. True, there are occasional felicities, as in that quiet, un-ironic phrase 'a family of human beings'. Un-ironic, because the note is one of wondering acceptance: it could have been a family of rats, but it is a family of human beings. The addition of 'human beings' tells you much more than the word 'family' could; don't we expect the family to be human? But answer the question too contemptuously in the negative, and you find yourself implying an ironical attitude which so easily becomes the mark of feeling good about your protest against conditions in an industrial society. Irony in this sort of context is nearly always a defence, a retreat from honest exploration; it is a sealing-off of imagination. It seems to me a test of Mrs Gaskell's quality that she avoids this, as Disraeli, for example, does not; his descriptions of Wodgate in *Sybil* frequently make use of an irony to which only a much better work would earn the right.

But when this is said, it still remains true that there is little in what we have so far been given of this episode to distinguish it from conventional treatment. It is only when we consider how it might continue that we begin to see where the difference lies. What we could expect is that Barton's money would see Davenport through his illness and save his family; and the implication would be that working-class people were capable of sufficiently helping each other through an inexhaustible fund of good-natured generosity.

It hardly needs saying that in *Mary Barton* matters are very different: Davenport does die, and his family continues to suffer, so that Barton's money is wasted (whether the *Westminster Review* critic ought to regard his action as culpable because he is 'scarcely heeding' future needs, is a nice point). In addition, Mrs Gaskell lets us into how Barton thinks of his action and what caused it: 'Barton's was an errand of mercy: but the thoughts of his heart were touched by sin, by bitter hatred of the happy, whom he, for the time, confounded with the selfish.' Later, as he and Wilson watch over the dying man, Barton curses God for being 'th' masters' father', and Wilson rebukes him,

> 'Eh, John! donna talk so; sure there's many and many a master as good or better nor us.'
> If you think so, tell me this. How comes it they're rich, and we're poor? I'd like to know that. Han they done as they'd be done by for us?'
> But Wilson was no arguer; no speechifier, as he would have called it.

No trace of a thesis there, but a grittily attentive rendering of two men plunged in discussion, one trying to reconcile himself by clichés to an intolerable situation, one in a rage of indignation against it. Their being 'right' or 'wrong' is not at stake, what matters is the insight we are offered into how the system they encounter distorts their lives and thoughts; indeed, it is the helpless inadequacy of their words that makes the episode so moving. Neither cliché or argument will make sense of their experience. It is so even more remarkably in Barton's next speech, where the cliché of argument takes on an especial poignancy; it is revivified by the bitterness of personal utterance. At such moments you realise how fine Mrs Gaskell's understanding is, not so much of the intricacies of radical thought as of the way in which a man like Barton will cling desperately to its more elegant phrases, hoping that they will somehow light a way through the muddle he finds so bafflingly impenetrable.

> 'You'll say (at least many a one does) they'n getten capital an' we'n getten none. I say, our labour's our capital, and we ought to draw interest on that. They get interest on their capital somehow a' this time, while ourn is lying idle, else how else could they all live as they do? Besides, there's many on 'em has had nought to begin wi'; there's Carsons, and Duncombes, and Mengies, and many another, as comed into Manchester with clothes on their back, and that were all, and now they're worth their tens of thousands, a'getten out of our labour; why the very land as fetched but sixty pounds twenty year agone is now worth six hundred, and that, too, is owing to our labour: but look at you, and see me, and poor Davenport yonder; whatten better are we? They'n screwed us down to th' lowest peg, in order to make their great big fortunes, and build their great big houses, and we, why we're just clemming, many and many of us. Can you say there's nought wrong in this?'
>
> 'Well, Barton, I'll not gainsay ye. But Mr Carson spoke to me after th'fire, and says he, "I shall ha' to retrench, and be very careful in my expenditure during these bad times, I assure ye"; so yo see th' masters suffer too.'
>
> 'Han they ever seen a child o' their'n die for want o' food?' asked Barton, in a low, deep voice.

It seems to me possible to allow for some flaws here – the last five words, for instance, could be wished away – and still find this an astonishingly fine achievement. Mrs Gaskell is not putting words into Barton's mouth when she has him say that 'our labour's our capital', because the phrase is so properly available to what he wants to communicate – which in the end is not so much an argument as a protest. The word 'Besides' introduces not another phrase in the argument but another aspect of the grievance he knows is just but not how to justify.

He casts around for the right clue, picking up fragments of his experience and one after the other throwing them away because they cannot help him. That is why his appeal to Wilson, 'Can you say there's nought wrong in this?' is so touching; all sense of argument has got lost in the deeper, more personal sense of unaccountable injustice. So with Wilson's answer, and Barton's counter-question. What each says is true, but the two truths do not supplement each other, not even cancel each other out; they merely make the muddle more overwhelming. It is the anger and bitterness, the sense of muddle which reason cannot cope with and which makes truth seem useless, that force themselves out into Barton's speech, making it credible and moving as no speech in *Sybil* or *Alton Locke* could be.

Yet even so there is in this fine scene something that hints at a failure on Mrs Gaskell's part. It comes out in her mentioning that Barton's thought 'were touched by sin'; the inadequacy of that comment rivals the inadequacy of some of her hero's. The judgement feels so irrelevant, so trifling; and I think it can be accounted for if only we grasp that Mrs Gaskell finds the muddle every bit as overwhelming as do Barton and Wilson. Like them she wants to make sense of it, but unlike them she finds the way to understanding made out of liberalism generously tinged with Christianity. In itself this is not remarkable; it was the way many took. But *Mary Barton* is a remarkable novel because it so powerfully suggests the guilt at which all liberalism must eventually connive, and which therefore requires Mrs Gaskell to put it behind her with a resoluteness for which few liberals would feel the need: that the happy *may* be the selfish; that her religion *may* be for the masters only; that caring for individual freedom *may* mean caring for the freedom of a relatively few individuals: it is from the shocked recognition of such possibilities that Mrs Gaskell finally turns away. So it is that trying as honestly as she can to present the denseness and bewildering complexity of the industrial experience, and for that very reason finding it bearable only as it can be accounted for, she produces moments in the novel where interpretation usurps and contradicts imaginative exploration, and the 'truths' of liberalism become the novel's lies. Most troublingly this is the case with the murder of the manufacturer Carson's son, and what stems from it.

There can be little doubt that Mrs Gaskell always intended the murder to happen, even though it would be bound to put great strain upon her claim that Barton was '*the* person with whom all my sympathies went'. And undoubtedly she does her best to make it seem fitting. In particular, she makes the victim the son of a bullying manufacturer and the would-be seducer of Mary; and the *Westminster Review* critic spotted the implications of this: '[Carson's morals] are only of, and for, a class . . . a beauty in humble life might – without any blot on

his class-character, detriment to his station, or remorse to his conscience – be made to serve the purpose of his mere animal indulgence
. . . Class-morality naturally made him thoughtless of the feelings of
those not of his rank . . .' So in having Barton kill him Mrs Gaskell
closes the circle of moral retribution with a neatness that recalls
Carlyle's grim pleasure in pointing out that the widow of the Glasgow
slums 'proves her sisterhood; her typhus-fever kills them: they actually
were her brothers, though denying it'. Indeed, so positively does Mrs
Gaskell appear to accept the proof of brotherhood that she has the
elder Carson forgive his son's murderer and plan to become a more
considerate employer.

So far so good. But, as Raymond Williams has quite rightly
noticed, the trouble with the murder is that it is so unrepresentative an
act for a novel whose focus is predominantly representative; it is
altogether too exceptional. And in addition it seems an exceptionally
crude way of representing class conflict. Where I disagree with
Williams is in his explanation of why Mrs Gaskell falls back on the
murder: 'the real explanation, surely, is that John Barton, a political
murderer appointed by a trade union, is a dramatisation of the *fear of
violence* which was widespread among the upper and middle classes at
the time, and which penetrated, as an arresting and controlling factor,
even into the imaginative deep sympathy of a Mrs Gaskell' (Williams'
italics). I think not. True, as we have seen in *Sybil* and *Alton Locke*, fear
of such violence was widespread, and it may even be the case that Mrs
Gaskell was partly conditioned by it when she came to deal with the
murder; but that is not the central reason for the violence. It seems to
me that she finds the murder necessary, because by means of it she can
simplify a complexity which has become too terrific for her to accept
consciously. Her mind shuts out the awareness of a muddle so colossal
that it defeats the explanations of her social creeds, and so she
attempts to impose order by turning to murder, where a neat pattern
can realise itself: class antagonism producing a violence from which
springs reconciliation. It is far too simple, principally because the
antagonism is *reduced* to a matter of individual violence, so that though
the pattern itself is intendedly representative it is fashioned out of
quite arbitrary material.

Mrs Gaskell may, however, have been additionally persuaded to
adopt it, since it has the apparent advantage of disposing of Barton. I
put the matter callously, and that is as it should be, for there *is* something callous in her attempt to write him off. The word seems an odd
one to use about her, but her treatment of her hero justifies it. For
Williams, 'she recoils from the violence of murder, to the extent of
being unable even to enter it as the experience of the man conceived as
her hero.' Again, this seems to me not the whole truth. It is not so

much that Mrs Gaskell is unable to enter the experience as that she sees she does not need to; Barton's act means that she need no longer take him seriously. More and more he has been leading her to an understanding of the limitations of her consciously held beliefs, but now she can stand back and judge him, as she had earlier when she noted that 'his thoughts were touched by sin'. As soon as Barton commits murder he becomes at best an object of pity; and that phrase fairly suggests the position of superiority to which Mrs Gaskell retreats. She can now take up an attitude to Barton.

Mrs Gaskell, then, profits from the murder in two ways, though at the cost of damaging all that is best in her novel. Because of Barton's act she can simplify the issues *Mary Barton* has been exploring, and she can also dismiss from serious attention its disturbing centre. I do not say that this latter gain had always been intended, in fact I am certain that the murder must have come as a tremendous relief to her, since it offered the way out of her problem with Barton, his so awkwardly leading her to the exposure of false hopes she dared not abandon. It is these which are meant to be realised by the consequences of the murder. Carson's forgiveness and vow of reform seem to represent a triumph for the best hopes of liberalism. Mrs Tillotson, seizing on the detail of Barton's dying in Carson's arms, says: 'and this points to the book's true theme: not this or that feature of industrial society is being criticised, but its whole principle, excluding any human contact between masters and men; and the hope of betterment lies not in this or that reform, but in the persistence, against all odds, of humanheartedness.' But this is a grotesquely inadequate hope in terms of the novel itself. For one thing, even if Carson's reform is genuine it is a purely individual matter, whereas one side of Mrs Gaskell certainly hopes it will emerge a general recommendation. For another, it *is* only one side of her, and the shallower, interpretative side, at that. The side which is truer to the novel knows that such a resolution is impossible, and indeed at the very end of *Mary Barton* all the main characters are sent off to Canada to make a fresh start, and so are given a purely fortuitous, and individual, release from a context which had been shown to be so inescapable. As Williams remarks, there is at this point 'a kind of writing off, when the misery of the actual situation can no longer be endured'. Human heartedness indeed! If only the matter were *that* simple, Mrs Gaskell's liberalism need not have been in conflict with all that is finest in her novel.[62] □

In Lucas's monograph study of industrial fiction, he devotes the first two chapters to a discussion of Gaskell's work. Despite, in the second chapter, comparing her with Engels[63] and suggesting that her experience of the working class was more real, because more familiar, in the first chapter

Gaskell is castigated for ignoring the context to *Mary Barton* and *North and South*:

■ [. . .] she hopes that the problems can somehow be detached from their context and so made to appear contingent rather than inevitable. The result is that two otherwise fine novels are weakened by their author's readiness to slacken her realistic grip on probabilities in order to make room for some convenient liberal pieties; we are offered an entirely ahistorical view of change as being able to accommodate and reconcile conflicting interests and energies. At its crudest (and such a view hardly ever rises above such crudeness) this comes down to suggesting that master and man will learn to understand, respect and even love one another. Barton and Carson, Higgins and Thornton: they are to stand as a general and generous statement about enlightened relationships in an industrialised society. [. . .]

But it will not do. In the novels Mrs Gaskell has to fudge the important issues she herself has raised. It may of course be that Higgins and Thornton will come to understand one another – though Mrs Gaskell is a good deal more convincing when she writes of their misunderstandings, and it may be that Margaret will come to understand the North. But such understanding amounts to little more than an impotent recognition that this is the way things are – master stays master, man stays man; and for Mrs Gaskell to suggest that it amounts to any more than that is silly. Besides, as soon as Thornton and Higgins arrive at their highly unlikely friendship they cease to be representative figures and drop into eccentricity. Limited and atypical reconciliations cannot be given the type of representativeness that Mrs Gaskell desperately hopes will accompany the vast social changes many of whose effects she so finely studies.[64] □

Arthur Pollard's monograph of Gaskell's novels heavily stresses the personal factor in *Mary Barton*. The narrative 'is not about industrial conditions, but about people living in those conditions'.[65] The truth of the story compels because of her own personal contact with the working class: 'the book's imaginative energy is nourished on close experience, deep sincerity and immense compassion'.[66] He finds the novel full of authentic details: 'she is aware of background and history. She can suggest so much of this by a single remark. It is the effect of intimacy. She knows the type of people she is writing about'.[67] Pollard's particular blend of biographical criticism, attention to social issues, and interest in details places him in a curious position looking back to earlier author-orientated studies of Gaskell, and forward to the new historicist interest in contextual detail.

Most post-Marxist critics of Gaskell feel the need to reclaim her from the negative or unrepresentative assessments of predecessors. This is certainly true of Coral Lansbury's monograph, which seeks to rescue Gaskell as an avant-garde writer and social prophet:

■ Long before it became the popular avocation of social historians, Elizabeth Gaskell was writing histories of the 'common people', describing how it felt to be poor, what it meant to be denied work and opportunity in an affluent society, and the means whereby the workers would eventually forge the trades-union into a hammer to smash the interlocking ranks of class and privilege. She also stated that the trades-union would become as oppressive and inherently conservative as the society that had forced it into being. As she remarked of the Camorra in 'An Italian Institution', movements that arise in violent opposition to a society all too often become mirror images of that society.[68] □

Lansbury gives a useful analysis of how Gaskell's Unitarianism equips her for such a project, explaining how religious, social, cultural and gender concerns are part of Gaskell's religious background. Unfortunately many attempts to reclaim Gaskell's contexts have tended to elide Unitarianism, which in particular provides a useful framework for exploring the inter-linked concerns of class and gender in Gaskell's fiction. The following description of what it means to be a Unitarian, and how it inflected Gaskell's worldview, is important for its emphasis on the radical nature of her religion, which provides a corrective to the views of critics such as Raymond Williams, who declare that Gaskell's interest in socio-political issues is hampered by her background and class.

■ To be born a woman in the Victorian era was to enter a world of social and cultural deprivation unknown to a man. But to be born a woman and Unitarian was to be released from much of the prejudice and oppression enjoined upon other women. Elizabeth Cleghorn Gaskell was born on September 29, 1810, at Cheyne Walk in Chelsea into a double tradition of Unitarianism. Her father, William Stevenson, had been a Unitarian minister for a time, but forsook the pulpit when he could not reconcile his faith with the acceptance of fees for preaching. A man of diverse talents, he worked as a farmer and as editor of *The Scots Magazine*; he also wrote a number of historical articles for *The Edinburgh Review* and *The Monthly Repository*, the main Unitarian journal of the day. Never poor but always pressed for money, Stevenson grate-fully accepted the post of Keeper of the Records to the Treasury and held that position with distinction until his death in 1829. William Stevenson married a woman from a family with even longer Unitarian traditions. The Hollands had been active in political and religious reform since the eighteenth century, and Elizabeth Holland came from the Cheshire branch, from a family that was related in turn to the Darwins, the Wedgwoods, the Turners and Dr Peter Gaskell, the medical and social reformer.

Unitarians married more to find partners of like mind than for reasons of property or political advantage. They were a singular and distinct community in Victorian society, unaffected by the crises of faith that shook so many Christians and produced among them a profound and lasting pessimism. Claud Welch correctly describes the Victorian mind as being 'characterised by uncertainty and doubt',[69] but this is not the mood of Unitarians. Their theology was an optimistic affirmation of man as a rational being who could ultimately attain a perfect state in this world without recourse to marvels and miracles. To the nineteenth century they brought a doctrine of rationalism that spoke in terms of the enlightenment of the preceding century. Further, they were untouched by the struggle between science and Christian doctrine. Indeed, in the contest between the apes and the angels, they gladly espoused the cause of the apes as further proof of man's capacity to evolve by reason and by will. For many Christians the Unitarian was the arch apostle of heresy, the one member of the Christian community who was beyond redemption. One of the most popular Methodist hymns was an appeal to the 'Triune God', imploring him to expel the Unitarian fiend and 'chase his doctrines back to Hell'.[70] If Elizabeth Gaskell was born to a heritage of political and social reform, and a passion for individual liberty and justice, she also knew that she belonged to 'a sect everywhere spoken against'.[71] John Priestley regarded this as a statement of fact; he also saw it as a challenge.

The Unitarian rejected the divinity of Christ and with it belief in the Trinity. For men like Priestley and Theophilus Lindsey the Trinitarian formula was an impossible one, and in consequence, the doctrine derived from it was equally invalid. Christ was a man, albeit the best of men, and could not be worshipped. Socinus had rejected the doctrines of original sin, eternal punishment and the atonement, but he saw Christ as quasi-divine and thought it was permissible for him to be made the object of prayer. The Unitarians of the nineteenth century rejected even this limited form of worship as blasphemous and continually emphasised the simple humanity of Christ, his witness to the truth, and his death because of that witness. If many Christians regarded the Unitarians as heretics, more thought of them as less a religious sect than a political group, radical in temperament, reformers by design. It was difficult for a practising Unitarian to dissociate himself from social and political life. He was committed to social involvement as the visible expression of his faith. The Duke of Wellington despised Unitarians as atheists, and Lord Ashley saw them as lost souls, but despite persecution and derision they contrived to become leaders of reform, scientists, manufacturers, merchants and politicians.

Education was the right of every being, male or female. When James Anthony Froude was appointed as tutor to the children of Samuel Darbishire, the wealthy Unitarian solicitor of Manchester, he was told that there was to be no distinction between the education of his sons and daughters. Unitarian schools flourished and their teaching methods of making learning a pleasure by means of games and dramatised scenes in the classroom were the most advanced of the century. The ideal was not the moulding of Christian gentlemen but the creation of individuals who would each in his and her own way find fulfilment as an active member of society. There is no record of Elizabeth Gaskell having been beaten as a child or at school. Reason and the birch could not exist together in the schoolroom according to Unitarian practice. If an adult was a rational being, then a child was only slightly less so, and no one had ever beaten understanding into a human being. Naturally, with these views, the Unitarians were to be leaders in the movement for women's rights. Eliza Fox, Barbara Bodichon, Harriet Martineau, Emily Shaen and Florence Nightingale were all Unitarians of varying degrees of faith. Of course, those degrees were never characterised since that would have necessitated an abridgement of individual liberty. Essentially, Unitarianism was a paradox, a collectivist movement in praise of the individual.

It was the incorrigible optimism of the Unitarian that most offended his fellow Christian. In the face of slums and poverty, crime and prostitution, the Unitarian maintained his faith in progress and perfectibility, in the power of reason to effect change. Naturally inclined towards Utilitarianism, a number of Unitarians became fervent statisticians, veritable Gradgrinds of religion in their insistence upon facts. William Gaskell was one of the founders of the Manchester Statistical Society and Florence Nightingale's genius for accountancy made her a revolutionary force in the Army Medical Service. Sustaining their life and work was their belief in the natural goodness of man. Theophilus Lindsey did not deny the existence of sin but declared emphatically that God 'never ordains or permits evil but with a view to the production of a greater good, which could not have existed without it'.[72] King David committed murder and sinned greatly when he took Bathsheba as his wife, but the fruit of that union was Solomon. Unitarians were always careful to distinguish between the evil engendered by society and the suffering that men saw as evil but which was, in effect, part of God's plan for greater goodness.

The only safe path to follow in life was one of absolute truth. For a man to lie was to obscure God's design for a world of virtue and knowledge. Truth to a Unitarian was the torch that would eventually illuminate the whole of mankind. Much of the abrasiveness people felt in the company of Unitarians was a result of their custom of speaking honestly. Because they could still believe, despite the problems of a new industrial society and the challenge of science, they were both the envy and the outrage of their day. It was not difficult for a Unitarian scientist like Charles Lyell or an industrialist like John Fielden to find a harmony between their work and their religion. Yet the fact that they remained so composed when the citadel of faith was crumbling around them seemed contrary to all sense of propriety. Froude found them infuriating. It was unsettling for the author of *The Nemesis of Faith* to find himself surrounded in Manchester with unfailing kindness and a certain indifference to his religious conflicts. Carlyle was converting many to religious despair, but Unitarians were not numbered among his disciples.[73] Almost in hysteria, Froude wrote: 'we hate Manchester – Manchester in any form – Unitarian Manchester most of all. Vulgar and insolent: as they practise little virtue among themselves, so they pretend to even less than they possess, by the gracelessness of their manner; and when we leave the place, which we shall do in the summer, we shall leave it without breaking any ties except such as one might form with a prison cell.'[74] Froude and his wife had been frequent visitors to the Gaskell home, but Elizabeth Gaskell found it easier to maintain a friendship with Charlotte Froude, Kingsley's sister, than with her husband.

The insistence upon action, the refusal to take refuge in metaphysics or doctrine, was as trying for most Christians as it was for Froude. In 1801 the Unitarian John Cartwright met William Wilberforce, the Evangelical, in Westminster, and the exchange between them summarised the fundamental difference in religion between the two men. Cartwright recalled: 'among other friendly expressions, he [Wilberforce] said he hoped we should meet in a better world: I answered that *I hoped we should first mend the world we were in.*'[75] Elizabeth Gaskell never doubted that she was born with the right and the ability to change society. Her novels and her life as a woman and social reformer were expressions of this theology of optimism. She was a religious writer, but her religion was at variance with most contemporary attitudes. Religious doubt is generally taken as an indication of some complexity of thought, while faith is regarded as the attribute of an unthinking mind. But the Unitarians confound this easy generalisation. Elizabeth Gaskell's religion was as closely reasoned as the denial of faith by Froude and Ruskin, but it was they who spoke to their age and found a sympathetic response. Elizabeth Gaskell has been consistently misunderstood because insufficient attention has been paid to her religion, and what it meant to be a

Unitarian, isolated and privileged, dedicated to the principle of individual independence and yet determined to ameliorate society.[76] □

Another study of Gaskell's fiction published in the same year as Lansbury's also insists upon the author's break with tradition, but it is a radicalism of a genteel kind: 'like the primitive in other arts, she virtually unconsciously creates an unobtrusive, wholly invigorating and wholly beneficial revolution'.[77] W. A. Craik thus recirculates the gender ideology of women's creativity that Gaskell was working within and against, for, by claiming that her fiction is unconsciously radical and that the revolution is politely feminine (if robustly medicinal), Gaskell is absolved from stepping outside the proper domain of the female novelist. Craik's comments on *Mary Barton* in the following extract emphasise the vacuum that Gaskell works within and highlights generic innovations and complexities as faults:

■ Elizabeth Gaskell is apart from novelists of her time, as well as social reformers. She is a 'primitive', working out her own art and craft of the novel for herself, enlarging and perfecting it in the course of her career, very much independently of novelists before her, and those around her. Naturally, therefore, she blunders, she sometimes lacks assurance, she sometimes over-emphasises. These faults of a beginner are most visible in *Mary Barton*, as is another fault of a very interesting kind. Elizabeth Gaskell shows she is aware that she is learning her craft, by the way that in some parts of this novel she depends on and uses the traditional material of the novel, such as the love story of a young heroine, the subject of seduction, sensational and improbable happenings, and a test of heroism for her central characters. *Mary Barton* suffers from being an amalgam of what can be seen as two distinct novels, one of them a quite original tragic novel, the other a much more conventional one which, though in many ways congenial and suited to her, is yet a sign of depending on what she knows will be acceptable to a novel-reading public. The tragic novel concerns John Barton, driven by his sense of justice, his loyalties to his fellow mill-workers and to his Trade Union, into the extreme act of murdering his employer's son; through it Elizabeth Gaskell explores his social problem of the struggles between masters and men. It has its end in the superb reconciliation between the broken and dying Barton, and the father of the murdered man. The theme is great enough for a novel and gives enough scope on its own, as the wiser Elizabeth Gaskell of *Sylvia's Lovers* – her great and achieved tragic novel – would have known. Her second story is that of John's daughter Mary, the much more orthodox heroine, who hesitates between her real love, the workman Jem Wilson, and the dazzling wealthy lover

Harry Carson; who, rejecting the one, on the murder of the other suffers the terrible dilemma of having to save Jem from being hanged, without revealing her father's guilt. This exciting plot, with the capacity for a (qualified) happy ending, is both more conventional and more sensational. Providing a study of the moral and spiritual growth of a young girl, it suits its author, and it provides some of the novel's finest scenes. Yet undoubtedly the two stories are too much for a single work, and account for many of its incidental failures in emphasis and proportion. Yet *Mary Barton* is an exciting whole, for its originality of subject matter, of character, and of methods, and impressive for the unobtrusive assurance of its writer, not least when she appears quite unaware that what she is doing is wholly new.[78] □

By terming *Mary Barton* 'primitive', this assessment positions the novel outside its socio-political contexts, as well as its literary contexts. Although eager to stress the narrative's naivety, evinced by the assertion that Gaskell was not influenced by her precursors, Craik also paradoxically declares the text to be derivative, adopting stock features of the novel because of Gaskell's creative immaturity. Another problem with Craik's approach is the insistence that *Mary Barton* is seen as two novels, one tragic (and original) and the other melodramatic (and staid). More recent critics have come to question, as we shall see in chapters four and five, whether these two competing narratives can be kept so separate.

Towards the end of the period covered in this chapter, critics start to pay attention to the neglected tradition of women's writing and to the place held by Gaskell in that tradition. Elaine Showalter's *A Literature of Their Own* is the most important of these early feminist reclamations of women's literary history. She places the history of women's writing into three phases: the 'Feminine' (1840–1880), characterised by an imitation and internalisation of the dominant androcentric norms; 'Feminist' (1880–1920), in which period there was a protest at the standard norms and an advocacy of the rights of women; and 'Female' (from 1920), a period of women's self-discovery, which achieves a new intensity with the Women's Liberation movement in the 1960s. Gaskell is firmly entrenched in the first category not only by virtue of her historical positioning, for Showalter concedes that the phases may overlap, but by virtue of her conservative acceptance of patriarchal norms. Of Margaret Hale's gift of money to Thornton, Showalter declares, rather ironically given that this is the period of Marxist interest in class and social tensions that symbolically fracture economic exchange: 'to get a great deal of money and give it to a man for his work was the feminine heroine's apotheosis, the ultimate in the power of self-sacrifice'.[79] It was left to the next decade of feminist responses to trace the complex interconnections of Gaskell's class and gender concerns.

CHAPTER FOUR

Feminist Neglect and Feminist Celebration: the 1980s

■ Mrs. Gaskell has done what neither I nor other female writers in France can accomplish – she has written novels which excite the deepest interest in men of the world, and which every girl will be the better for reading. □

George Sand in conversation to Lord Houghton[1]

Witty, brilliant, provocative George Sand summarises the ambivalence of feminist readings of Elizabeth Gaskell over 100 years later, in the 1980s. While the Gaskell recovered by the Marxist critics is indisputably a socio-political novelist, dealing with matters which 'excite the deepest interest in men of the world', she nevertheless provokes the impossible mixture of neglect, censure and celebration from feminist critics. Of course, feminist literary criticism is not, and should not be, a homogeneous orthodoxy, but few Victorian women writers have produced such a mixed response. Sand's final comment, for me, holds the answer: 'every girl will be the better for reading [Gaskell]'. This could mean two things: Gaskell's novels, in the way that they deal with matters that excite 'men of the world', 'better' female readers because of their analyses of issues pertaining to the public sphere, issues not normally considered suitable for female readers. But the bettering of *girls* also suggests something rather more conservative: novels that educate the impressionable about feminine matters, something suitable and safe for girls to read. Indeed, these two responses to Gaskell's industrial fiction can be found in the feminist literary criticism of the 1980s, in particular, as the extract from Davis in the Introduction argues, the response to Gaskell's treatment of the private sphere of motherhood and domesticity. As Schor points out, such major studies as Sandra Gilbert and Susan Gubar's *The Madwoman in the Attic*, published in the late 1970s and heralding the new Anglo-American feminism, ignore or diminish Gaskell. As we have seen at the

close of the previous chapter, Elaine Showalter's *A Literature of Their Own*
dismisses, if not disparages, Gaskell. As an unravelling of Sand's comment suggests, the reason for feminist ambivalence towards Gaskell's
industrial fiction is the now familiar crux in the history of its reception:
whether the novels are conservative or subversive of dominant patriarchal norms. While the extracts in this chapter do not chart the neglect
towards or silence about Gaskell, they have been chosen with a view to
providing a flavour of the diversity of feminist responses to the
public/private, conservative/subversive issues, and to providing a flavour
of the way in which such issues are elucidated by the growing tendency
towards contextual or new historicist readings.[2]

Published as part of the important and revisionary Key Women
Writers series, Patsy Stoneman's analysis of Gaskell's fiction is one of the
earliest to challenge Marxist criticism. She declares her determination to
consider both the industrial and domestic aspects of the novels as inter-
acting, thus revising previous models of reading that addressed either
one or the other.[3] Stoneman's particular case against Marxist criticism of
Gaskell is its neglect of gender. In the extract below, she explains how
class and gender are interrelated and argues that *North and South* provides a more sophisticated model of that interaction than *Mary Barton*:

■ Lying is done with words, and also with silence.[4]

With *Mary Barton, North and South* is now the most widely read of Gaskell's
works, and we owe its modern rehabilitation to the Marxist critics of
the 1950s, who saw its significance as an 'industrial' or 'social problem'
novel. This critical mediation, however, means that we now receive
the text together with a consciousness of its short-comings in Marxist
terms: its parent-child analogy for class relations obscures the economic source of class opposition in the appropriation of surplus value,
and its 'resolution' is a marriage which at best seems a symbolic reconciliation and at worst a romantic diversion from the industrial theme.

I want to argue, however, that the novel only appears inadequate
because of the assumption underpinning Marxist theory that work
relations alone provide the fundamental structures of society. Feminist
theory affirms that gender relations are at least of equal, if not primary,
importance and that any intelligent analysis of society or literature
must orientate itself on not one but two axes of explanation. In
Elizabeth Gaskell's novels the gender perspective is strongly present,
but has been discounted because it does not take the recognisable
feminist form of concern for women's rights but instead rises from
what Temma Kaplan calls 'the bedrock of women's consciousness . . .
the need to preserve life'.[5]

The parent-child analogy for class relations, while inaccurate in economic terms, is powerfully suggestive in gender terms as an ambivalent model for relationships between unequal partners, implying the divergent possibilities of (maternal) nurturance and (paternal) authority, and many Victorian thinkers apart from Elizabeth Gaskell attempted to solve class conflict by integrating these parental qualities into a benevolent authority. The resulting term, 'paternalist', which is often used dismissively of Elizabeth Gaskell's 'industrial' novels, only properly applies, however, to *Mary Barton*.

Because *Mary Barton* stresses the 'feminisation' of working-class life [. . .], it tends to collapse together the axes of class and gender, seeing female/nurturing/working-class as a 'package' in opposition to male/authoritarian/middle-class. The inference from this assumption is that class problems can be solved in gender terms by 'maternal' fathers who see that 'the interests of one [are] the interests of all.'[6] Although this solution expresses the spirit of female, working-class nurturance, however, it is embodied in men: the reformed capitalist Carson and the incipient capitalist Jem Wilson.

North and South offers a sharper analysis by seeing class and gender as axes which intersect rather than coincide. Its male protagonists of both classes are shown as conditioned by masculine codes of conduct which privilege aggression and inhibit tenderness, rendering the notion of the 'benevolent father' suspect. Moreover, the novel recognises class struggle as the product of economic conflicts of interest which are not resolvable, though they can be ameliorated, by benevolence. Whereas *Mary Barton* reaches a solution more symbolic than material, which paradoxically excludes the working-class heroine, *North and South* reveals a situation which requires the active and continuing mediation of its heroine to affirm 'the need to preserve life' in a class struggle expressed in terms of masculine aggression.

Margaret Hale's achievement of this role is, however, impeded by the disabling ideology of 'separate spheres', and her relationship with Thornton exposes how each is inhibited from full humanity by codes of conduct which effectively rest on lies. While Thornton enacts the 'masculine lie' that judgement must not be swayed by sentiment, Margaret acts the 'feminine lie' that modesty overrides all other virtues. Their relationship, which conventional criticism reads as a 'romance plot' offering a false 'resolution' to the 'industrial theme', thus proves to be an essential analysis of the ideologies which structure industrial organisation, dictating why, among other things, class struggle is always aggressive. The mutual partial emancipation from gender ideology is offered not as a resolution of class conflict but as a necessary step in a political reorientation which would give higher priority to human need and ensure, minimally, that class struggle is conducted in terms of political debate rather than physical warfare.[7] □

The Marxist interest in capitalist economic structures translates, for some feminist critics in this period, into a concern with woman's role in the commodity culture of the literary marketplace. Terry Lovell's discussion of Gaskell in *Consuming Fiction* directly and self-consciously engages with Marxist interpretation, in particular that of Raymond Williams. Like Stoneman, Lovell adds feminism to the Marxist interest in class issues and, also like Stoneman, she attempts to recuperate aspects of Gaskell that Marxist critics have disparaged or ignored. Influenced by Mary Poovey's important study *Uneven Developments*, Lovell sees the enabling potential of Victorian middle-class domestic ideology as a position from which Gaskell can empathise with the oppressed working class. But her project admits to ambivalences, and the way in which Lovell opens these ambivalences out for analysis shows how fruitful directly confronting them can be. Indeed, Lovell argues that ambivalence is an intrinsic characteristic of the Victorian novel as a commodity in the literary marketplace: '[the Victorian novel] depended on profitability, but its rationale was literary value. Insofar as intellectual and literary production took a commodity form, it tended towards the denial of its own commodity status'.[8] The manifestation of a novel's oscillating position within and without the marketplace affects its content as women writers wrote within and against the dominant commodity culture. As Schor notes, Lovell confronts the problem of the subversive text as it 'reproduces middle-class woman's relationship to a patriarchal capitalism, "but the relationship it reproduced is a deeply ambivalent one, which protested while it submitted. It may be read as conciliatory, reconciling women to their own subordination. It may also be read as reproducing and reinforcing women's characteristic fears of male domination, their resentment against it, and wish to escape it."'[9] Lovell's analysis of *Mary Barton* frames itself around these issues.

■ Realism versus Melodrama

Elizabeth Gaskell's fiction is almost entirely innocent of irony at the expense of men, or 'the male regime'. Rather her work illustrates another option open to middle-class women and writers in the negotiation of domestic ideology. In her writing she gives the feminine role and identity pivotal importance in the construction and maintenance of social life. This strategy is common in woman-to-woman genres [such as soap operas], and Gaskell's novels share some features of these forms. *Mary Barton* finds its place within the great tradition by virtue of its descriptive realism in introducing the author's middle-class readers to the living conditions of the working class. Its central concern is *the* social problem of her time, the 'condition of England' question. But her novel is usually also seen as flawed by a retreat into melodrama.

Certainly it has a highly melodramatic plot. It shares what Ien Ang has called 'the tragic view' of today's television soap operas.[10] There are nine deaths, if my tally is correct, in the course of its pages, one of which is murder. Another victim, Aunt Esther, supplies the secondary theme of the fallen woman become prostitute. The narrative is about family relationships as much as it is about the relationship between masters and men, and it offers the familial model as the potential basis for reconstituting the latter on a sound footing.

But the family is the site, above all, of great suffering and great sacrifice on the part of its female members, and it is this which gives the book its resemblance to today's soaps. The women of the family learn to endure and to forbear. They spend much of their time waiting. The heroine alone is offered the opportunity to display her heroism as she initiates the search for Will Wilson which terminates in the exciting chase after his departing vessel in the waters of Liverpool. Her success saves her lover, Jem, from death by hanging for a murder he did not commit. She is even allowed an almost unprecedented privilege in the modest and chaste heroine — that of publicly declaring her love for Jem, which he learns of for the first time as she gives her testimony from the witness box.

Raymond Williams's analysis of *Mary Barton* has coloured most subsequent left interpretations of this novel.[11] He categorises it as an industrial novel, and locates its best moments in its documentary realism: 'the really impressive thing about the book is the intensity of the effort to record, in its own terms, the feel of everyday life in the working-class homes.'[12] The shift into melodrama he dismisses as '. . . the familiar and orthodox plot of the Victorian novel of sentiment . . .'[13] He explains this shift in terms of contradictory 'structures of feeling' which inform the novel – on the one hand, sympathy with the suffering of the working-class, and on the other, fear of violence. Yet the melodrama is pervasive, and does not depend entirely on the uncharacteristic political murder. The incidents of family suffering are the very stuff of women's melodrama, including many contemporary soaps. But the novel lacks, of course, soap opera's open-ended structure.

Woman-to-Woman: Woman-to-People

A second difference between the two may be located in a difference of address. Today's soaps are predominantly woman-to-woman forms. *Mary Barton* is a woman-to-people/men. It addresses men as well as women, and in this case, quite crucially, the former. Gaskell published this her first full-length novel anonymously. But her feminine authorial identity was quickly perceived by at least one eminent reader. Thomas Carlyle wrote to her in 1848, 'Dear Madam, (For I catch the treble of that fine melodious voice very well) . . .'[14] But the reader addressed and whom she was most anxious to meet, was male: the manufacturing employer, the 'master'. She was deeply concerned about their response to the book.

The feminine persona of the author is established in many of the direct authorial interventions which litter her narrative. She has a recurrent refrain, her disclaimer of any knowledge of political economy. As author, she claims the right to speak not from knowledge of 'the facts' but from an identification with the feelings of an oppressed and suffering workforce. In so doing, she claims a woman's privilege. In fact Gaskell was an intelligent woman whose wide reading included works of political economy which she claimed in her authorial role not to comprehend. But it would be presumptuous in a woman to speak authoritatively in a woman's voice of such matters. Where she could legitimately speak was of course from sympathetic feeling, and this is what she chose to do, at the cost of playing down her own intellect.

However, while the address is from a feminine position, the subject matter of the novel places it firmly in the public domain. Yet the novel is remarkably lacking in any scenes which are set in the public world of paid work and politics in spite of its concern with the relationship between masters and men. The book is almost entirely enacted in terms of the effects of this relationship upon personal and family lives. John Barton's visit to London with the chartists is told off-stage, and there is but a single scene of direct confrontation between masters and men which provides the motivation for the killing of Henry Carson. So though the original title as Williams points out, was to have been 'John Barton', '. . . *the* person with whom all my sympathies went . . .',[15] yet the change which foregrounds the daughter at the expense of the father is, in some respects, appropriate. For it is women and their suffering in the family which provide the angle of vision in a melodramatic plot in which that suffering can take tangible and heightened forms such as the brain fever suffered by Mary upon Jem's acquittal. It is this angle of vision on the condition of England question which legitimates Gaskell's authority to speak, to write in her authorial persona as educated, womanly sympathiser, first hand observer although an outsider, of the suffering of the working class.[16] □

Other feminist readers of Gaskell articulate the radical aspect of her novels by deploying alternative and revised models of Victorian femininity. Rosemarie Bodenheimer, for example, engages with the ideology of plot in industrial fiction by women. She asserts strongly, as do all critics cited in this chapter, that Gaskell's novels are not failed attempts to empathise with the working class, nor are they attempts to impose a fictional solution onto the social problems they represent. For Bodenheimer, these charges that were made against Gaskell by Marxist critics are based on inaccurate assumptions about realist fiction.[17] Bodenheimer's analysis of *North and South* is important for its attention to the novel's literariness as both a reflection and product of the ideology Gaskell critiques. The study compares *North and South* with two of its most significant literary precursors, Fanny Trollope's *Michael Armstrong, the Factory Boy* (1840) and *Jessie Phillips: A Tale of the Present Day* (1844), together with Charlotte Brontë's *Shirley* (1849).[18] Bodenheimer argues that Trollope inscribes what she terms 'the romance of the female paternalist': 'this story pattern places active paternalist interventions in the hands of middle class heroines while assigning proprietorship of "the system" to male manufacturers'.[19] Such plot lines are, Bodenheimer argues, a 'fantasy of intervention without power' for, while the heroine perceives class injustice and is empowered enough by her insight to intervene to save a few individuals from the working class, she does not reform the system. Instead, the heroine's success is a symbolic romance and marriage at the novel's conclusion. While Trollope's version of this 'romance' becomes melodrama, Brontë complicates and undermines the plot and Gaskell radically revises it. Not only does this radical revision grant the heroine, Margaret, a conflicted agency that immerses her in the spheres from which she should be excluded, but it allows the representation of the working class to escape from the stale oversimplifications that trip up so many industrial novels.

■ While paternalistic images of the working class necessarily alternate between the obedient, deferent worker and the violent, rebellious mob, Gaskell turns the working class into an autonomous arena in which issues of authority and dependence must play themselves out. Inverting conventional representations of unions as virtuous but hapless masses manipulated by self-serving leaders, she creates in Nicholas Higgins an intelligent, idealistic, and flexible union leader whose plans for a peaceful strike are undermined by desperate members such as John Boucher. The revision alters the almost universal identification of striking and violence in earlier industrial fictions. In *Mary Barton* Gaskell herself made a more conventional move from a strike action to the melodramatically plotted murder of a millowner's son; in *North and South* the violence born of starvation – a stone throw – is overt, public, and unpremeditated.[20] □

In another departure from earlier responses to Gaskell, Bodenheimer argues that the contradictions inherent to *North and South* are not failures but productive confusion:

■ revising paternalistic images of government, views of the working class, and the separate woman's sphere, Gaskell's narrative is itself an enactment of the experimental social activity it recommends, for it takes us through a gradual breakdown of traditional ways of thinking about society and the confusion generated by the process of working toward new ones.[21] □

Bodenheimer pays attention to the place of Gaskell's fiction within a female genealogy of writing, specifically her response to Charlotte Brontë's *Shirley*, which shaped the writing of *North and South* and, shortly afterwards, Gaskell's decision to write Brontë's biography after her death.[22] Another significant, dynamic and painful literary influence on *North and South* is Dickens's *Hard Times*. Jerome Meckier charts their difficult and complicated relation to each other through their serial publication as Gaskell attempts to revise, correct and parody the negative and satirical representation of her rival's (and indeed editor's) industrial Manchester. Although Meckier usefully outlines the literary contexts to *North and South*, his discussion begs many feminist questions:[23]

■ Mrs. Gaskell's ambition is to deride Dickens repeatedly, extensively, and as soon as possible. But the hasty revaluation takes a chance analogous to the risk that popular dramatists had run, earlier in Dickens's career, by staging a novel before it completed its serial publication. [. . .] Similarly, Dickens could disarm revaluative parody of his satiric vision by lessening the discrepancy between his critique and a rival's premature retaliations.

'Parody' derives from the Greek parõidia, the counter-ode or satyr play put on by the same actors – now in grotesque costume – who had just appeared in a more serious drama. Dickens's rivals pretend that his satirical novels are no more realistic in their representation of Victorian prospects than the counter-odes of classical theatre; the problem is that works they see as lopsided have usurped the place that truer, more complex assessments of life should occupy. Thus Bounderby, a grotesque version of a Manchester manufacturer, misleads a public that has yet to see Thornton. Dickens's rivals reverse Athenian practice by concocting a new form of parody to supply the more ennobling works that once took precedence. These correctives – parodies or truthful redoings of Dickens's counter-odes – are to bring about renewed confidence in man and society.

But if the parodist fires before the target exists in final, printed form, later developments may accidentally if not consciously defuse revaluation. Using truth to undercut falsity means parodying a parody: negating a negative to return to something more constructive. This proves dangerous when works like *Hard Times* and *North and South* appear in quick succession and deal with similar locales. If the revaluing novelist revises too soon or too thoroughly (or both, in Mrs.

Gaskell's case), the revaluation process automatically threatens to reverse itself. A kind of double vision results in which the novel being corrected also seems to be parodying its corrector.[24] □

The major extract from this section is taken from Catherine Gallagher's *The Industrial Reformation of English Fiction 1832–1867*. Gallagher adopts an historicist approach that is arguably the most sophisticated and influential of post-Marxist critiques from the 1980s and that looks towards the extracts discussed in chapter five. While not explicitly positioning herself as a feminist literary critic, Gallagher's approach builds on the feminist rereadings of Gaskell in order to present her inconsistencies and formal multiplicities in *Mary Barton* as intellectually complex and creatively fruitful. In the Introduction, Gallagher outlines her argument 'that narrative fiction, especially the novel, underwent basic changes whenever it became a part of the discourse over industrialism'.[25] The strength of this chapter on *Mary Barton* is its negotiation of Gaskell's intellectual heritage, discussed in terms of the tensions between causality and conscience in the novel and its impact on literary genre, in particular the relationship between melodrama and tragedy. The chapter on *North and South* is also recommended for its reading of family and society.

■ As in the *Religion of Causation*, Man seemed to be crushed into a mere creature, so it was on his behalf that remonstrance broke forth, and, at the bidding of Channing, the *Religion of Conscience* sprang to its feet. However fascinating the precision and simplicity of the Necessarian theory in its advance through the fields of physical and biological law, it meets with vehement resistance in its attempts to annex human nature, and put it under the same code with the tides and trees and reptiles. Our personality . . . is sure to recover from the most ingenious philosophy, and to re-assert its power over the alternatives before it . . . ; and the second period of our theology is marked by this recovered sense of Moral Freedom.
James Martineau, 'Three Stages of Unitarian Theology'

No one seems to see my idea of a tragic poem; so I, in reality, mourn over my failure.
Elizabeth Gaskell, Letter to Edward Chapman

When Elizabeth Gaskell wrote *Mary Barton* (1845–47), many Unitarians were revising their theories about free will. In those years James Martineau was trying to start what he later called the 'second period of Unitarian theology,' the period in which 'moral freedom' was emphasised. James Martineau, Harriet's younger brother, was the most influential English Unitarian theologian in the nineteenth century. In their early childhood he and his sister Harriet established a profound emotional and intellectual bond that remained unbroken throughout their youth.

It was James who suggested she read Priestley, but once Harriet had arrived at her 'grand conviction'[26] of Necessarianism, she took every possible opportunity to impress the doctrine on her brother. According to James, Harriet dominated him intellectually throughout their adolescence and early adulthood. Describing their conversation while on a walking tour of Scotland in 1824, he reminisced:

> My sister's acute, rapid, and incisive advance to a conclusion upon every point pleasantly relieved my slower judgement and gave me courage to dismiss suspense. I was at that time, and for several years after, an enthusiastic disciple of the deterministic philosophy . . . yet not without such inward reserves and misgivings as to render welcome my sister's more firm and ready verdict.[27]

Harriet managed to suppress James's 'inward reservations and misgivings' until after she became a well-known writer. R.K. Webb reports that in 1832 James still shared her views, and Harriet expressed the hope that James might also share her work of improving mankind: he by 'lofty appeals to the guides of [Society], I by being the annalist of the poor'.[28]

As this proposed division of labours indicates, Harriet was conscious of certain intellectual and temperamental differences between herself and her brother, even while they espoused the same philosophy. She thought her own talent lay in logical cause-and-effect analysis, while his consisted of eloquence and intuition. In time the differences Harriet perceived in their modes of thinking developed into a philosophical disagreement that separated the intellectually intense siblings for life. As James recalled:

> While she remained faithful through life to that early mode of thought, with me those 'reserves and misgivings', suppressed for a while, recovered from the shock and gained the ascendancy. The divergence led to this result, – that while my sister changed her conclusions, and I my basis, we both cleared ourselves from incompatible admixtures, and paid the deference due to logical consistency and completeness.[29]

Harriet's Necessarianism finally led her to accept 'free thought'; all organised religious practice came to seem incompatible with the logic of her determinism. James, on the other hand, rejected Harriet's basis, her 'Religion of Causality', and reached down to the 'springs of a sleeping enthusiasm' for a religion that could carry him 'from the outer temple of devout science' to an inner conviction of the 'greatness of human capacity, not so much for intellectual training, as for voluntary righteousness, for victory over temptation'.[30]

The change in James both symbolised and helped to bring about a vast transformation in the Unitarian Church. William Ellery Channing, the American Transcendentalist, converted James to the doctrine of a 'free ideal life . . . which we know is in subjection to nothing inflexible'.[31] Channing's idea of the human will had been inspired by the writings of Coleridge, and James, in his turn, set about transforming English Unitarianism from a 'Religion of Causality' to a 'Religion of Conscience', emphasising voluntary righteousness. He was not the first English Unitarian to believe in free will; Priestley's determinism had been modified and even opposed by many Unitarian theologians of the early nineteenth century. Indeed, Harriet Martineau's extreme Necessarianism was somewhat anachronistic in the 1830s, for by that decade most Unitarians either ignored the issue or settled for a moderate determinism. James Martineau's version of Transcendentalism, however, strongly insisted on the idea of free will, giving it a new emphasis within Unitarianism. Although James was not the acknowledged leader of the English Unitarians until later in the century, during the 1840s and 1850s his thought was a powerful intellectual stimulus that led to the de-emphasis of 'scientific' explanations of behaviour and a new stress on the other side of Unitarianism – its exhortations to moral exertion.

Although Elizabeth Gaskell and her husband, William, stayed within the old school of Unitarianism on most issues and made no decided moves towards Transcendentalism,[32] they were well acquainted with James Martineau. William Gaskell was a Unitarian minister and a colleague of Martineau's at Manchester New College in the 1840s, and their exposure to Martineau's brand of Unitarianism might easily have served to strengthen Elizabeth Gaskell's interest in the issue of moral responsibility. Moreover, in 1845, at the very time when she first began writing *Mary Barton*, she was deeply influenced by a close friend of Martineau's. Although not himself a Unitarian, Francis Newman, brother of John Henry Newman, associated almost exclusively with Unitarians in the 1840s, and on many issues his thinking closely resembles James Martineau's. Like James Martineau, Newman made much of man's 'higher nature', his free moral life. Rejecting the psychological materialism of Priestley and Harriet Martineau, he argued that 'human intelligence is a result of other intelligence higher than itself – is not a source, or a result, of what is unintelligent'.[33]

To Elizabeth Gaskell in the mid-1840s, Francis Newman seemed a living saint. She claimed to have hung on his every word, and it is quite probable that an 1844 booklet of his, *Catholic Union*, was an important source of inspiration for *Mary Barton*. This booklet, together with a series of lectures given in 1846, clearly reveals Newman's belief in a transcendent 'moral energy'.[34] These works also, however, contain reminders of Unitarian's earlier determinism, for in them Newman paradoxically insisted that morality does not exist in a realm apart from social and economic necessity. Thus he believed economic and spiritual issues interpenetrated one another, and like Gaskell in *Mary Barton*, he treated radical working-class movements sympathetically: Communism is called 'one mode in which human nature is crying out for a new and better union than has yet been achieved'.[35] Although he strove to affirm the independence of the human spirit, he continually reversed himself and implied that spirit is chained to matter, that it does not exist in a separate realm of freedom: 'to the support of moral energies', he wrote, 'certain material conditions are required'.[36]

Elizabeth Gaskell absorbed this ambivalence about moral freedom not only from the works and conversation of Francis Newman, but also from the whole context of Unitarian intellectualism that surrounded her. The Unitarianism that shaped her perceptions was thus a different religion in several important respects from that which nurtured Harriet Martineau. Of course, because Gaskell's social experience also differed markedly from Martineau's, the dissimilarities in the two women's outlooks cannot be attributed solely to their religious beliefs. Nevertheless, important differences in their fiction can be traced to their disparate attitudes toward causality and free will. Martineau believed that Providence worked through natural laws that precluded human free will, whereas Gaskell, without abandoning the idea of Providence, tried to make room in her fiction for moral freedom. Gaskell's use of causality, like that of many other thoughtful Unitarians of the 1840s, was less consistent than Martineau's. It was, however, her very inconsistency, her refusal to be tied down to a single explanatory mode, that marked Elizabeth Gaskell's advance over Harriet Martineau in the craft of novel writing.

To move from the *Illustrations* to *Mary Barton* is to leave behind the narrowness of a unicausal interpretative scheme. The wider range of explanations available to Gaskell partly accounts for our sense that she is a more realistic novelist than Harriet Martineau. As James Martineau wrote, breaking away from the Necessarian doctrine constituted 'an escape from a logical cage into the open air'.[37] And as he further pointed out, the escape entailed perceptual and stylistic changes: 'I could mingle with the world and believe in what I saw and felt, without refracting it through a glass, which construed it into something else. I could use the language of men – of their love and

hate, of remorse and resolve, of repentance and prayer – in its simplicity'.[38] The firm reliance on what is vividly seen and an expanded
use of the simple 'language of men' are the hallmarks of Gaskell's realism. The 'real' reality for her does not lie behind human behaviour in
a set of scientific laws; it is on the very surface of life, and although it
is often obscured by conventional modes of perception, it can be
adequately represented in common language. Indeed, Gaskell specifically objected to the kind of abstract language used by Harriet
Martineau: she believed that presenting people as embodiments of
labour and capital could only hide their true natures and the underlying motives of their actions.

In one important respect, however, Elizabeth Gaskell must be considered Harriet Martineau's heir: she intended John Barton's story, the
story of a working man, to be a tragedy. 'I had so long felt', she wrote in
a letter, 'that the bewildered life of an ignorant thoughtful man of strong
power of sympathy, dwelling in a town so full of striking contrasts as
this is, was a tragic poem, that on writing he was my "hero"'.[39] In several
ways John Barton is a more successful working-class character than
Martineau's William Allen, for many of Allen's characteristics seem
inappropriate to a worker. His heroism relies, for example, on an
elevated style of speaking, while Barton's tragic heroism gains
poignancy from his working-class dialect. Adhering closely to classical
models, Martineau presents Allen as far superior to other members of
his class: she stresses how unusual his forbearance and intelligence
are, and even makes him the victim of striking workers. Barton, on the
other hand, is presented as a typical worker. Indeed, his typicality is
precisely what makes his story an important one to tell: 'There are
many such whose lives are tragic poems', Gaskell wrote, 'which cannot take formal language'.[40] Moreover, Gaskell did not adopt the
reversed chronology of Martineau's fiction, her tendency to reveal the
ending at the beginning of the story, destroying suspense and preclud-
ing catharsis. In fact, Gaskell believed that the ordering of events was
a major flaw in Martineau's work; she complained about one of
Martineau's books that 'the *story* is too like a history – one knows all
along how it must end'.[41] Gaskell's own story, although it makes John
Barton's decline seem inevitable, is not 'like a history': she maintains
suspense and seeks an intense emotional reaction from the reader.
Barton has neither of Allen's defences against suffering: he lacks both
foreknowledge and stoicism. Barton thus seems more unequivocally
victimised than did Allen.

Yet when the book came out, Gaskell complained that no one
seemed to see her idea of a tragedy. She concluded that she had failed
but could not identify the source of her failure. Her confusion is not
surprising, for there are many ways in which Gaskell undercut her

own intended tragic effects. One of these, a relatively minor one, reminds us again of the religious kinship between Gaskell and Harriet Martineau: the providential resolution of John Barton's story partly mitigates his tragedy. Although moral freedom was an increasingly important idea in Unitarian theology in the 1840s, Gaskell was still writing within a teleological tradition. John Barton feels responsible for his crime, but in the end the very intensity of his remorse leads to both his own and his enemy's spiritual regeneration. There is not even a hint of possible damnation in the novel: evil is eventually self-effacing and productive of good, although sin is not explicitly ordained by God. The close of Barton's life, therefore, hardly appears to be tragic; his life veers from its tragic course in the final episode, and readers are apt to agree with an early reviewer who complained that the ending was a religious homily, 'twisted out of shape, to serve the didactic purpose of the author'.[42]

Long before the story's close, however, Gaskell's ambivalence about the tragedy she was writing manifests itself in the book's formal eclecticism, an eclecticism that cannot be traced simply to the contradiction between tragic and providential perspectives. For tragedy and theodicy both contain explanatory systems; both trace cause and effect. A dominant impulse in *Mary Barton*, however, is to escape altogether from causality, to transcend explanation. *Mary Barton* expresses both stages of Unitarianism of the 1840s; it was inspired by both the 'Religion of Causality' that Harriet Martineau advocated and the 'Religion of Conscience' that her brother eloquently preached. It contains, therefore, an ambivalence about causality that finds its way into Gaskell's tragedy and creates an irresolvable paradox there: Barton's political radicalism is presented both as proof that he is incapable of making moral choices and as an emblem of his moral responsibility. The author consequently seeks refuge from the contradictions of her tragedy in other narrative forms, primarily melodrama and domestic fiction. The resulting formal multiplicity is most apparent in the first half of the book. Only in the second half, after the tragic action is complete, does she temporarily achieve a kind of generic consistency by retreating into the domestic mentality of her heroine. However, because the major action of these chapters is the suppression of the tragic narrative, the book seems to divide into not merely separate but mutually exclusive stories. In the conclusion, when the narrator must return to the subject of John Barton, she seems to have abandoned any attempt to give a consistent explanation of his development. Instead, we are given several stories that mix social criticism with religious homily, and we are then assured that, after all, causal interpretations are irrelevant to the story's meaning.

Gaskell's inability to commit herself to a causal scheme leads, therefore, to formal inconsistencies, but it also leads to a high degree of formal self-consciousness. Although she does not find a narrative form that satisfactorily reveals the reality of working-class life, she does identify several conventional genres that hide the reality. Her attempt to render the truth is beset by irresolvable difficulties, but some relief, some certainty, is secured in attacking what is obviously false. Thus *Mary Barton* is partly about the ways in which narrative conventions mask and distort reality; form becomes content by this process. But the criticism of false conventions does not succeed in deflecting attention from the absence of a stable, self-assured narrative posture. Rather, it makes us more acutely aware of that absence simply by emphasising the issue of genre. Thus, in the very act of trying to evade certain narrative responsibilities, the book becomes peculiarly self-regarding.

Gaskell's use of contrasting narrative forms is one of the most interesting and overlooked features of *Mary Barton*. In a sense, the first half of the novel is about the dangers inherent in various conventional ways of organising reality. The two most obviously false and destructive conventional perspectives on the novel's action are the sentimentally romantic and the farcical. The narrator herself never adopts these modes; rather, they enter the narrative as the distorted literary viewpoints of a few characters. Esther and young Mary hold the sentimental perspective; Sally Leadbitter and Harry Carson hold the complementary viewpoint of farce. Gaskell is careful to point out that the sentimental perspective originates in literature; Mary's 'foolish, unworldly ideas' come not only from her Aunt Esther's talk about 'making a lady' of her, but also from 'the romances which Miss Simmonds' young ladies were in the habit of recommending to each other'.[43] And although the narrator excuses both Esther and Mary on the grounds of their youth, she indicates that their conventional literary delusions are truly pernicious. Esther's elopement ruins her and apparently also contributes to the death of Mary's mother, and Mary's desire to marry a gentleman brings her and almost all of the other characters in the book 'bitter woe' (p. 80).

The complement to these sentimental notions, the convention that they play into and that makes them dangerous, is farce. Both Sally Leadbitter and Harry Carson see their lives and the lives of others as farce. Sally becomes a *farceuse* because she cannot be a sentimental heroine. Being 'but a plain, red-haired, freckled, girl', she tries to make up for her lack of beauty 'by a kind of witty boldness, which gave her, what her betters would have called piquancy' (p. 132). Sally is a working-class version of the witty female rogue: 'considerations of modesty or propriety never checked her utterance of a good thing' (p. 132). Her vision is entirely comic; it excludes any serious thought about the consequences of Mary's flirtation with young Carson at the same time that it denied the very possibility that Mary's romantic fantasies might be sincerely held: 'Sally Leadbitter laughed in her sleeve at them both, and wondered how it would all end, – whether Mary would gain her point of marriage, with her sly affectation of believing such to be Mr Carson's intention in courting her' (p. 180). Harry Carson, of course, shares this farcical perspective on Mary's actions. Both he and Sally imagine her to be a character in their own farcical world – a 'sweet little coquette' (p. 181), 'a darling little rascal' (p. 181) with an 'ambitious heart' (p. 183). For Sally and Harry Carson, this characterisation gives a conventional authorisation, indeed a conventional imperative, to Mary's seduction.

Moreover, Mary's is not the only reality that the farcical perspective distorts: everything that enters Sally's or young Carson's purview becomes comic material. Sally is always 'ready to recount the events of the day, to turn them into ridicule, and to mimic, with admirable fidelity, any person gifted with an absurdity who had fallen under her keen eye' (p. 133). The ability to mimic 'with admirable fidelity' is also a talent, indeed a fatal talent of Harry Carson. Young Carson's farcical vision leads him to caricature not only Mary, but the whole of the working class as well, and as Gaskell points out, these comic caricatures both mask and perpetuate working-class suffering. In her exposition of the dangers inherent in farcical distortions, the author brings together the sexual and social themes of the novel: both Mary and the delegation of striking workers are victimised by Harry Carson's conventional blindness.

If working-class women are seducible 'little rascals' for Harry Carson, working-class men are clowns. Young Carson exhibits his blindness to the human reality of working-class men on several occasions (for instance, in his treatment of Mr Wilson, in his interview with Jem, and in his obstinate behaviour at the negotiating table), but the conventional attitude that motivates his behaviour is most clearly expressed in the action that precipitates his murder. He is killed for making a joke, for attempting to transform a workers' delegation into a troop of Shakespearean clowns:

> Mr Harry Carson had taken out his silver pencil, and had drawn an admirable caricature of them – lank, ragged, dispirited, and famine-stricken. Underneath he wrote a hasty quotation from the fat-knight's well-known speech in Henry IV. He passed it to one of his neighbours, who acknowledged the likeness instantly, and by him it was sent round to others, who all smiled and nodded their heads. (p. 235)

The caricature, tossed away by Carson but retrieved by a curious member of the worker's delegation, so enrages John Barton that he conspires with the ridiculed workers to kill the caricaturist. It is significant that the fatal joke is as much Shakespeare's as it is Carson's: that fact emphasises the unreal, literary nature of Carson's perception. It also stresses how deeply entrenched the farcical distortion of working-class life is in English culture. Carson's destructive use of Shakespeare reminds Gaskell's readers that although they have the best precedents for laughing at rags and tatters, they must now free themselves from the conventional association between 'low' characters and comedy.

But the whole incident raises another question: what new associations should replace the old? It is quite clear that Gaskell intends to expose the dangerous falseness of both sentimental romance and farce; but the ground of her exposition, the narrative mode that she adopted because she believed that it did reflect working-class reality, is difficult to identify. Most literary practices calling themselves realistic rely on contrasts with other, presumably false and outdated narrative perspectives. In *Mary Barton* Gaskell purposely sets up false conventions for contrast, thereby calling attention to her own narrative method as the 'true' perspective. The problem is that she then has trouble fixing on any one narrative mode; the ground of the contrast continually shifts in the first half of the book while the author searches for a mode of realism adequate to her subject matter. Thus, in her attempt to juxtapose reality and these false conventions, Gaskell employs several alternative narrative modes: tragedy, melodrama, domestic fiction, and finally religious homily.

The most obvious realistic contrast to both the sentimentality of Esther and Mary and the farce of Sally Leadbitter and Harry Carson is the tragedy of John Barton. Barton is the most active and outspoken adversary of both of these false conventions. It is from his perspective that we first see Esther's romantic folly; the story of the girl's elopement is completely contained within John Barton's gloomy interpretation of it: 'bad's come over her, one way or another' (p. 46), he tells his friend Wilson. And his interpretation, of course, immediately undercuts all the story's romance. Moreover, his version of Esther's story makes it merely a part of a larger social tragedy. It includes the girl's social determinism: factory work, he is convinced, led to Esther's downfall by making her recklessly independent and giving her the means to buy finery. As Barton tells Esther's story, he reveals his perspective on the relationship between the classes, a perspective that is itself tragic and productive of tragedy. He opposes Esther's romantic dreams not only because they are dangerous, but also because he hates the class she wishes to join. Barton's is a completely polarised view of social reality: only rich and poor seem to

exist, and the rich are the constant oppressors of the poor. The ubiquitous slavery metaphor makes its appearance here, attesting to Barton's
radicalism, his polarised social vision, and the determinism that
informs his thinking:

> 'We are their slaves as long as we can work; we pile up their for-
> tunes with the sweat of our brows; and yet we are to live as
> separate as Dives and Lazarus, with a great gulf betwixt us: but I
> know who was best off then,' and he wound up his speech with a
> low chuckle that had no mirth in it. (p. 45)

Even this closing reference to heavenly justice is a gloomy prophecy of
revenge, not a joyful anticipation of saintly rewards.

Barton's tragic perspective, therefore, contrasts sharply with
Esther's and, later, with Mary's romantic fantasies. Moreover, his
interpretation is corroborated by the plot itself; he is correct to note
that Esther's romantic dreamworld is really a disguised stage for
tragedy. Barton's relationship to the farcical viewpoint is similar:
again he opposes it energetically, and again in his opposition he
speaks the truth. In fact, in the most decisive moment of his own
tragedy, Barton contrasts Harry Carson's caricature, his fixed, farcical
representation, with the tragic reality that lies behind the convention-
ally ludicrous appearance:

> 'it makes my heart burn within me, to see that folk can make a jest
> of earnest men; of chaps, who comed to ask for a bit o' fire for th'
> old granny, as shivers in the cold; for a bit o' bedding, and some
> warm clothing to the poor wife as lies in labour on th' damp flags;
> and for victuals for the children, whose little voices are getting too
> faint and weak to cry aloud wi' hunger.' (p. 238)

Through Barton's eyes we see behind the cartoon images of the ragged
men to the suffering of thousands of helpless people. The delegates
caricatured by Harry Carson are tragic; they are compelled to strike by
their noblest characteristics: their sympathy with and sense of responsibility to their hungry dependants. But Carson's Shakespearean joke
attempts to freeze the imagination at the level of appearances, where
the workmen become a troop of clowns. In Falstaff's speech, alluded
to but not quoted, they are 'good enough to toss; food for powder, food
for powder; they'll fill a pit as well as better. Tush, man, mortal men,
mortal men'. Such dehumanisation obscures the tragedy, making it
perfectly appropriate that the story's central tragic action should be the
destruction of this *farceur*, the murder of Harry Carson. Thus farce,
the mask of tragedy, becomes its stuff, just as Falstaff's callous speech

trails off into a sad and even levelling refrain: 'Tush, man, mortal men, mortal men'.

Tragedy, then, is the immediate realistic ground against which both romance and farce are contrasted. But the narrative method of this novel cannot be called tragic. As we will see, tragedy is forced to compete with other realistic forms in the book's first half, and in the last half it is present only as a suppressed reality. By examining the part of the story that Gaskell specifically intended as tragic – John Barton's own story – we can see why the author continually shifted to other modes of narration. For John Barton's tragedy is self-contradictory. Because she draws on both traditional ideas of heroic character and on determinist, Owenite ideas of character formation, the author encounters a paradox as she attempts to trace a continuous line of tragic development.

The causality Gaskell attempts to trace follows a traditional tragic pattern; it is the result of the interaction between the character's heroic actions and external circumstances. As Gaskell told a correspondent after the book's publication, her original intention was to show the operations of inner and outer causes in the destiny of a Manchester weaver:

> I can remember now that the prevailing thought in my mind at the time . . . was the seeming injustice of the inequalities of fortune. Now, if they occasionally appeared unjust to the more fortunate, they must bewilder an ignorant man full of rude, illogical thought, and also full of sympathy for suffering which appealed to him through his senses. I fancied I saw how all this might lead to a course of action which might appear right for a time to the bewildered mind of such a one.[44]

This was, she said, her original 'design': the very qualities that made Barton a hero, his thoughtfulness and sympathy, were to combine with external circumstances to produce a tragic action.

Thus tragic design is certainly apparent in John Barton's story. We are often reminded by both Barton's speeches and the narrator's characterisations of him that his love for his family and his sympathy for the suffering poor cause his hatred of the rich. His unselfishness is emphasised repeatedly; he feels angry not on his own behalf, but on behalf of those who are weaker and poorer. The need to stress Barton's heroic unselfishness determines many of the plot's details; it is significant, for example, that he is not one of the workers caricatured by Harry Carson. His rude thoughtfulness, his desire to understand the suffering he sees, is a second admirable trait contributing to his downfall. Barton is the only character who consistently seeks causes for the world's phenomena, but his analyses are marred by his ignorance, by the fact that his understanding is circumscribed by his limited experience.

Gaskell carefully shows how these qualities of mind are impressed with a tragic stamp by external circumstances, by what comes to Barton 'through his senses'. The links in the tragic chain are clearly identified and labelled: his parents' poverty, his son's death, his wife's death, the trade depression and the consequent suffering of neighbours, his trip to London, his hunger, his opium addiction. Each of these incidents or circumstances is noted by the narrator as yet another cause of Barton's bitterness. The account of his wife's death, for example, concludes with the gloss: 'one of the good influences over John Barton's life had departed that night. One of the ties which bound him down to the gentle humanities of earth was loosened, and henceforward the neighbours all remarked he was a changed man' (p.58). The story of his son's illness and death also ends with emphasis on its consequences: 'you can fancy, now, the hoards of vengeance in his heart against the employers' (p.61).

Even the narrative's disavowals of Barton's ideas and feelings are intended to contribute to his story's tragedy. Remarks such as 'I know that this is not really the case [that the workers alone suffer from trade depressions]; and I know what is the truth in such matters: but what I wish to impress is what the workman feels and thinks' (p.60) may seem annoying intrusions to twentieth-century readers, but they were designed to keep the nineteenth-century readers' own opinions from interfering with their ability to follow Barton's tragedy. The disavowals are there to prevent the reader from becoming distracted by the issue of whether or not Barton's ideas are objectively true; Barton, we are told in these asides, reached the wrong conclusions, but the circumstances of his life did not allow him to reach any other.

Their very inevitability, however, creates a problem for the author. Unlike Harriet Martineau, Gaskell is not able to rest comfortably with the determinism she traces. Two obstacles present themselves: first, her idea of heroism entails moral freedom; and second, Gaskell's and Martineau's determinisms are of very different kinds. Martineau's does not explain the development of the protagonist's character. William Allen is a fully formed hero at the story's outset; the development of his character is unexplored and irrelevant to the story. He is a heroic, working-class *homo economicus* whose actions may be explained by his character, but whose character is not itself tragically determined. Gaskell's tragic vision, on the other hand, encompasses the formation and deformation of John Barton's character. Her social determinism is, in this sense, closer to Charlotte Elizabeth Tonna's than to Harriet Martineau's. Both use Robert Owen's brand of social theory, showing how the worker's environment and experiences shape his moral being. But unlike Tonna, Gaskell wishes to show us a worker who is a hero, not a monster; she wishes to give us a tragedy, not a freak show. As she traces Barton's inescapable decline, a decline that entails moral degeneration, she risks reducing him to a character without a will. In the words James Martineau uses to describe the effects of Necessarianism, she almost 'crushes' him 'into a mere creature' with her causation.

Gaskell, then, was writing partly in the determinist tradition as it had been adapted by critics of industrialism, but her writing was also infused with the new Unitarian emphasis on free will. Consequently, a tension approaches until it finally emerges as an observable contradiction Barton has come to advocate. His radical ambition to become a shaper of society, to cast off the role of a passive creature, acts as a magnet that draws both poles of the author's ambivalence about freedom toward one paradoxical centre. The paradox is most clearly visible in the narrator's very last expository attempt to explain the causality of John Barton's story:

> No education had given him wisdom; and without wisdom, even love, with all its effects, too often works but harm. He acted to the best of his judgment [*sic*] but it was a widely-erring judgement.
>
> The actions of the uneducated seem to me typified in those of Frankenstein, that monster of many human qualities, ungifted with a soul, a knowledge of the difference between good and evil.
>
> The people rise up to life; they irritate us, they terrify us, and we become their enemies. Then, in the sorrowful moment of our triumphant power, their eyes gaze on us with a mute reproach. Why have we made them what they are, a powerful monster, yet without the inner means for peace and happiness?
>
> John Barton became a Chartist, a Communist, all that is commonly called wild and visionary. Ay! but being visionary is something. It shows a soul, a being not altogether sensual; a creature who looks forward for others, if not for himself. (pp. 219–29)

All the elements of the tragedy are present in these metaphorical exchanges. Barton represents the uneducated, who are collected into the image of Frankenstein's tragically determined, larger-than-life monster. Then the monster, defeated and gazing at us, shrinks back to the dimensions of John Barton, the unselfish visionary. But these smooth metaphorical transitions do not quite cover the passage's central paradox: the 'actions of the uneducated' grow out of their soullessness, their incapacity to make moral choices. Barton became a 'Chartist, a Communist', a visionary in consequence of this soullessness. But the metaphor is too harsh, too denigrating to the hero, and the narrator pulls back and reverses herself: 'But being visionary is something. It shows a soul'. Suddenly John Barton's rebellious actions, instead of showing him to be a creature 'ungifted with a soul', become the proof that he has a soul, the emblem of his humanity and his moral freedom. His heroism is saved, but only at the expense of the causality implied by the Frankenstein metaphor, a causality that traces Barton's crime to 'us'.

We can argue, therefore, that the paradoxical nature of Gaskell's tragic vision forces her to abandon it in the novel's second half. Even in the first half of the book, though, the narrator never confines her own view to this tragic dynamic, dangerous as it was to the very idea of moral freedom. Instead, she juxtaposes three 'realistic' narrative modes in the book's early chapters: tragedy, melodrama, and a working-class domestic tale. The presence, indeed the competition, of the melodrama and the domestic tale allows two things. First, the author is able to avoid her tragic responsibilities, which are too contradictory to fulfil successfully; these other modes distract attention from and obscure the problematic causality of John Barton's story. Second, the presence of the melodrama, in particular, allows Gaskell to extend her critical exploration of conventional ways of interpreting reality.

Gaskell's use of melodrama is skilful: she first invites us into a melodramatic narrative, sets up melodramatic expectations, and then reveals that melodrama is a mere conventional distortion, a genre inappropriate to modern reality. Critics have claimed that *Mary Barton* becomes melodramatic with the death of Harry Carson, but this for-mulation is backwards. The first half of the book is much more seriously melodramatic than the second because in the first half there is a melodrama just offstage, in the wings, as it were, which threatens to take over the drama entirely. Indeed, the reader cannot initially tell whether the early chapters are part of a melodrama or some other kind of narrative. They contain many melodramatic characteristics. We view Esther's elopement not only from Barton's tragic perspective, but also through the unarticulated, excessive, grief of her sister Mary, young Mary's mother. Her grief is so excessive that it kills her, suddenly and surprisingly. It is the kind of parabolical death that abounded in nineteenth-century melodramas, and it leads into young Mary's potential melodrama – the threat of her seduction by the rakish Harry Carson. The narrator, in true melodramatic manner, continually sus-pends any resolution of Mary's fate and makes dark prognostications about it: 'Mary hoped to meet him every day in her walks, blushed when she heard his name, and tried to think of him as her future husband, and above all, tried to think of herself as his future wife. Alas! poor Mary! Bitter woe did thy weakness lead thee' (p. 80). The wholly conventional language here ('Alas! poor Mary!') leads us to expect, mistakenly, that Mary's 'bitter woe' will also be of the conventional melodramatic kind.

Although romance and farce finally do turn into tragedy in *Mary Barton*, they threaten repeatedly in the first half to turn into melodrama. Mary's renunciation of Harry Carson, her abandonment of romance, brings the melodrama even closer; for it is after his rejection that Harry Carson becomes truly villainous, indeed a potential rapist: 'from blandishments he had even gone to threats – threats that whether she would or not she should be his' (p.224). It is only after she has awakened from her romantic dream that Mary is in danger of becoming a truly melodramatic heroine: an innocent girl sexually persecuted by a villain. Indeed, Mary registers the change linguistically. As soon as she understands her true position she declares: 'if I had loved you before, I don't think I should have loved you now you have told me you meant to ruin me; for that's the plain English of not meaning to marry me till just this minute. . . . Now I scorn you, sir, for plotting to ruin a poor girl' (pp.183–84). This is not 'plain English', the language Mary usually speaks. It is popular stage English,[45] and it temporarily throws a melodramatic light across Mary's features. Harry Carson's murder, instead of beginning the novel's melodrama, effectively terminates it. In fact, as we will see, in the second half of the book melodrama joins romance and farce as an overtly discredited convention.

In the first half, however, Mary's potential melodrama competes for our attention with her father's tragedy. Through the melodramatic mode of presentation, our concern is solicited for Mary in a way that it never is for John. Indeed, Gaskell so arranges her narrative that we end up looking for the catastrophic event in the wrong plot. The melodrama of Mary's story, therefore, makes us inattentive to the threatening nature of John's career. The careful tracing of his decline does not have the interest of Mary's melodrama because we are not expecting John's story to culminate in some disastrous event. Our sense of impending catastrophe, which is essential to a tragic narrative, is misplaced in *Mary Barton*. It is attached not only to the wrong plot but also to the wrong set of narrative conventions. We mistakenly expect a melodramatic catastrophe, one arising from a simple confrontation between good and evil, but we are given a tragic catastrophe, a complexly and carefully motivated revenge murder, the outcome of an inner as well as an outer struggle. The presence of the melodrama in the book's first half, therefore, prevents us from clearly seeing John Barton's decline as the successive complications of a tragedy, and his story, with its unresolved contradictions, tends to fade into the background.

In the book's second half, most of the characters repeat our mistake. They continue to interpret the plot according to a pre-conceived melodramatic pattern, assuming that Jem killed Harry Carson. It then becomes Mary's job to discredit their conventional assumptions. To save Jem is to disprove the melodramatic interpretation of the murder. Melodrama is, therefore, explicitly consigned to the category of false conventions. It is associated with other kinds of sensation-seeking, and Sally Leadbitter is its most determined spokesperson. Because her cliché-ridden mind is only able to perceive situations in terms of popular stage conventions, after Carson's murder she moves with ease from a farcical to a melodramatic interpretation of the plot. She holds to her melodramatic version of the story even after Jem's acquittal. In explaining why Jem was dismissed from his job, she reveals the source of her opinions: 'decent men were not going to work with a – no! I suppose I mustn't say it, seeing you went to so much trouble to get up an *alibi*; not that I should think much the worse of a spirited young fellow for falling foul of a rival, – they always do *at the theatre*' (p.427; latter emphasis added). Mary, who is concerned for Jem, gasps, 'tell me all about it', and Sally continues, 'why, you see, they've always swords quite handy at them plays' (p.427).

At this point in the story, Sally's melodramatic viewpoint is relatively harmless – the basis of a joke. But the same viewpoint predominates among the spectators at Jem's trial, almost costing him his life. It is Mary's hard task to disabuse the court of the notion that Jem was a 'young fellow' who had 'fallen foul of a rival'. However, the court-room, like Sally Leadbitter, seems receptive only to melodrama; even Mary's struggle to save Jem must be rendered melodramatically before it can be admitted: 'the barrister, who defended Jem, took new heart when he was put in possession of these striking points to be adduced . . . because he saw the opportunities for a display of forensic eloquence which were presented by the facts; "a gallant tar brought back from the pathless ocean by a girl's noble daring"' (p.395). This bit of parody points up the difference between the narrative we have just read and the same facts couched in melodramatic language.

Far from being melodramatic, therefore, the last half of the book takes melodrama as its specific point of contrast. The fact that we ourselves formerly shared the melodramatic assumption, however, allows us to understand what a natural reading of the events it is and how difficult it will be to overcome. Because Mary must overthrow the assumptions not only of the other characters, but also of one of the major narrative conventions of the book's first half, we feel that her task is almost overwhelming. The drama of Mary's plight, therefore, is heightened by the narrative reversal, and the reader's interest in Mary's story intensifies.

By discrediting melodrama however, the later chapters raise the question of realistic narrative form even more insistently than do the earlier chapters. For the narrator's reversed attitude toward melodrama broadens her criticism of the conventional, a criticism that depends on a contrastingly realistic narrative ground. Again, the obvious candidate for such a ground is tragedy; the tragic interpretation of the murder is, after all, the truth that the melodramatic interpretation hides. But the tragic reality is precisely what all the actions of the book's second half are designed to conceal. The very causality that the narrator meticulously traced through the first half is hidden in the second. The events of the second half are more than an escape, an avoidance, of the tragic problem; they represent the problem's deliberate suppression.

In the second half of the book, Mary knows the truth, but she refuses to probe it, to ascertain its meaning. Instead, all her energies go into suppressing both public knowledge of her father's crime and her own consciousness of it. The 'why' of the crime, the very substance of the tragedy is not even a subject for speculation in the later chapters: '[Mary] felt it was of no use to conjecture his motives. His actions had become so wild and so irregular of late, that she could not reason upon them' (p. 301). In the chapters that are largely confined to Mary's consciousness, therefore, those that take place between the murder and Mary's return to Manchester after the trial, the narrator imposes a moratorium on reasoning about John Barton's life, on thinking about tragic causation. Mary's truth-concealing action takes the place of reason; finding an alibi substitutes for seeking the truth. Tragedy is still present as a narrative ground, but is increasingly shadowy; like melodrama, it is a genre Mary struggles against inhabiting. Thus, at precisely the moment when a stable, realistic narrative form is most needed, tragedy becomes unavailable and another genre emerges into prominence as Mary's special domain. Restricted almost entirely to Mary's viewpoint, the narrative becomes a working-class domestic tale that formally authorises the suppression of tragic causality.

Elizabeth Gaskell was a pioneer of the working-class domestic tale. In 1837 she and her husband published a sketch of working-class life, 'rather in the manner of Crabbe',[46] which tried to illustrate that the 'poetry of humble life' exists 'even in a town'.[47] Three short stories she published in Howitt's Journal share the intention of the sketch and are characterised by a wealth of domestic detail, illustrations of the charitable affection that the poor have for one another, and an emphasis on the trials and learning experiences of young women. All the women learn one thing: to do their duty, the duty obviously and immediately before them. These stories are also marked by some conspicuous absences: factories and other workplaces are alluded to but never shown, and people from other classes are almost entirely missing. The working-class domestic tales written by Gaskell combined the genres of homily and urban idyll; they were both exclusively domestic and exclusively working-class.

Much of *Mary Barton* is written in this genre. The documentary realism for which Gaskell is often praised grows out of the impulse to compile domestic details. Thus she gives us elaborate and affectionate descriptions of working-class homes, clothes, and traditions, as well as careful transcriptions of working-class Lancashire dialect. Domesticity dominates the narratives told by old Alice and Job Leigh [*sic*], narratives that are moving in the matter-of-fact spareness of their language and in the unobtrusiveness of their message: friends and family are all; duty is clear. Even Sally Leadbitter's farcical outlook is inspired by filial affection (pp. 132–33). Most of the working-class characters in the book share this domestic mentality: they think very little about the masters, they endure bad times, and they seek their satisfaction in the love of family and close friends. Margaret, Job Leigh, the Wilsons, and old Alice all belong to the domestic mode. This is the circle of duty and affection that Mary struggles to maintain.

But Mary is firmly established as a domestic heroine only after her interview with Esther, which reveals the truth about Harry Carson's murder, disabusing Mary of her melodramatic ideas. While the heroine glimpses the tragic abyss (a glimpse that speeds her on to the mental reality of a thoroughly domestic character), the narrator contrasts Mary's lot with Esther's. The contrast is explicitly between the domestic nature of Mary's working-class world and the territories of melodrama and tragedy that Esther inhabits. Just moments before, Mary believed she had driven Jem to murder; she is turned out of the Wilsons' home into the 'busy, desolate, crowded street', and her own home seems to her 'only the hiding place of four walls . . . where no welcome, no love, no sympathising tears awaited her' (p. 284). She thinks of herself melodramatically as an abandoned waif and longs for her mother, the absent centre of a lost domestic idyll. She remembers 'long-past times . . . when her father was a cheery-hearted man, rich in the love of his wife, and the companionship of his friend; – when (for it still worked round to that), when mother was alive' (p. 286). And while Mary longs, her mother actually seems to appear in the form of Esther, who had hidden her own melodrama *cum* tragedy behind the costume of a working-class wife. From Esther we get an entirely different perspective on Mary's reality; Mary, who a minute before fancied herself a pathetic creature in a comfortless room, is seen by Esther as the lucky inhabitant of 'that home of her early innocence' (p. 293). The house is Esther's 'old dwelling-place, whose very walls, and flags, dingy and sordid as they were, had a charm for her' (p. 297), and Mary now seems to be a potential mother, the woman with the power to heal: 'for [Esther] longed to open her wretched, wretched heart, so hopeless, so abandoned by all living things, to one who had loved her once; and yet she refrained, from dread of the averted eye, the altered voice, the internal loathing, which she feared such disclosure might create' (pp.294–95). The poignant and ironic contrast firmly situates Mary in the narrative space between the distortions of melodrama and the abyss of tragedy. It identifies her as a domestic heroine, one still capable of becoming 'the wife of a working-man' and thereby joining 'that happy class to which [Esther] could never, never more belong' (p.292).

The interview makes Mary a domestic heroine at the same time that it reveals the extent to which both her future and her present domestic worlds are threatened by the novel's other forms: the melo-dramatic lie that might condemn Jem and the tragic truth that might condemn her father. She emerges as a domestic heroine just in time to lock up her little house and embark on her mission to save these two men and rescue her personal life. For this reason, the events and set-tings of the book's second half are neither particularly domestic nor particularly working-class. We should not, however, let the public and adventurous events obscure the narrative mentality that pervades this part of the novel. As Kathleen Tillotson has pointed out, the thickness of domestic detail in *Mary Barton* makes its '"big scenes" – the chase down the Mersey, the murder trial . . . seem simply emergencies that must occasionally arise in ordinary life'.[48]

Mary's existence is 'ordinary', but it is also seriously threatened by the emergency she faces. A flawed social order has allowed melodrama and tragedy to break into Mary's world, and she must re-establish its domestic boundaries. Her task involved travel, public notoriety, and extraordinary events of all kinds, but these are necessary to combat melodrama, suppress tragedy, and save what little remains of her fam-ily. Mary's homelessness in the later chapters is symptomatic of the social evils the author is trying to illustrate. Mary's struggle to remain a domestic heroine is itself a social criticism with an ideal image of family life at its centre. The domestic keynote of these later chapters sounds again and again: in Mary's relationship to Mrs Wilson; in the minute but emotionally constrained accounts of Mary's tentative and fearful actions and reactions; in the descriptions of the lives and homes she encounters in Liverpool; and in the idyllic, domestic dreamworld that old Alice inhabits throughout the book's second half. Alice's reverie is both a vision of her own past and of Mary's future; Alice imagines the domestic world Mary's actions are retrieving.

For most of the book's second half, then, the domestic tale pre-dominates and suppresses the tragedy, although the two genres are complexly interrelated throughout the novel. Barton's tragedy is itself fundamentally domestic. The loss of his son is the most decisive blow against him. Domestic also is the tragic reality behind the clownish appearance of the workers' delegation, the barren rooms and the sickly wives and children that *Mary Barton* tries to expose. The book was inspired by scenes of blighted domestic life in the working class, and John Barton's narrative sketches the disastrous course that such suffering might initiate.

Although reality is always domestic in *Mary Barton*, it is by no means always tragic. Tragedy may grow out of a working-class domestic life, but it ultimately excludes that life. For the most part, *Mary Barton* is a domestic tale, not a domestic tragedy, and the two genres present mutually exclusive kinds of reality in this novel. Barton's tragic career, we are repeatedly told, increasingly takes him away from home; furthermore, most of the working-class characters, drawn in the domestic mode, are uninterested in Barton's talk about social injustice. In fact, the book's first dialogue, between Barton and Wilson, typifies the interaction between the hero and most of the working-class characters. Barton rails on for half a page against the 'gentlefolk', but Wilson cuts him short: 'well, neighbour, . . . all that may be very true, but what I want to know now is about Esther' (p. 45). This kind of exchange is repeated on other occasions with Jem Wilson and with Job Leigh; the other men all express the assumptions that are built into Gaskell's domestic convention: being too aware of social injustice only distracts one from the principal realities of family and home; conversely, home and family can protect one from the tragedy that attends class conflict.

His respondents never try to refute Barton's social analyses in these exchanges. Rather, the other men quietly recur to their private preoccupations. Thus, after John Barton tells the sad story of his London journey and concludes that 'as long as I live I shall curse them as so cruelly refused to hear us' (p. 145). Job Leigh tells his own London story, which includes his daughter's death and his retrieval of his granddaughter Margaret. The narrator confides that Job chose the domestic subject matter because it was 'neither sufficiently dissonant from the last to jar on the full heart, nor too much the same to cherish the continuance of the gloomy chain of thought' (p. 145). The domestic tale suppresses the tragedy not by explicitly denying it, but rather by ending its causality. John Barton's tragedy, as we have seen, is primarily concerned with cause and effect, with showing how and why the hero became 'a Chartist, a Communist, all that is commonly called wild and visionary'. Gaskell's domestic tales, on the other hand, aim at showing how to circumvent tragic cause-and-effect logic by simply acting, doing one's immediate duty, without stopping to ponder all of the consequences.

Inevitably, the solemn basis of tragedy is thus obscured by a flurry of activity. On learning of her father's guilt, Mary first determines not to speculate about his motives and then wades into the myriad activities of the book's second half. The causal logic of this part of the book is explicitly and enthusiastically stated by the narrator in the first person:

> Oh! I do think that the necessity for exertion, for some kind of action . . . in time of distress, is a most infinite blessing. . . . Something to be done implies that there is yet a hope of some good thing to be accomplished, or some additional evil that may be avoided; and by degrees the hope absorbs much of the sorrow. (p.301)

Thus action itself disproves inevitability: it gradually absorbs the tragic causality at the same time that it keeps that causality from emerging into conscious, public view. John Barton dies, but he dies, as Mary wished, at home.

The domestic tale, therefore, is to tragedy in *Mary Barton* as the 'Religion of Moral Freedom' was to the 'Religion of Causality' in Unitarian theology in the 1840s. Gaskell could not sustain Barton's tragedy, because in doing so she risked denying his freedom, his hero-ism, even his humanity. But, as the narrator points out, action implies freedom without overtly denying the tragic causality, without provid-ing an alternative interpretation. The action in the book's second half is specifically anti-interpretative; it is designed to establish an alibi for Jem, to set up a competing version of the truth. Similarly, the tran-scendental element in Unitarianism was not so much a competing causality as it was a suspension of the older deterministic causality.

Throughout the Liverpool chapters, however, the narrator reminds us that the suspension is merely temporary, that John Barton's terrible guilt is in no way affected by Mary's adventures. We know that once the alibi is established, there will be nothing left to do but confront the awful truth. Thus Will Wilson's arrival in the courtroom produces Mary's collapse. She breaks under the pressure of the suppressed truth, the truth to which the novel must recur once the melodramatic life is overthrown. Mary's illness gives some reprieve from the inevitable confrontation with John Barton, as do old Alice's death and the settlements of numerous domestic details between Mary and the Wilsons. Each of these in its own way, however, conjures up the 'phantom likeness of John Barton' (p.414) and the problematic causality that attends his story.

Causation once again becomes an explicit theme in the book, one that haunts and perplexes the narrator. Indeed, at one point she attacks the reader for demanding causal explanations. After giving a somewhat unconvincing account of Jem's reasons for prolonging Mary's (and by extension, the novel's) separation from John Barton, she impatiently asserts that reality is not always amenable to clear cause-and-effect analysis: 'if you think this account of mine confused, of the half-feelings, half-reasons, which passed through Jem's mind, . . . if you are perplexed to disentangle the real motives, I do assure you it was from such an involved set of thoughts that Jem drew the resolution to act' (pp. 413–14). It is not, however, the reader, the threatening, sceptical, and ultimately guilty 'you' of the novel, who demands cause-and-effect logic; it is the narrative itself. In the sentence quoted above, the narrator turns the novel inward by addressing the expectations that the book itself created and declaring both her inability and her unwillingness to meet them. It is a prominently placed sentence, standing at the end of the chapter between the courtroom scene and Mary's return to Manchester; it is an expression of failure, of liberation, and of formal self-consciousness that might well be taken as a motto for the chapters that follow.

The concluding chapters of *Mary Barton* return us to the story of John; Mary continues in the domestic mode, specifically refusing to think about causes. Indeed, where her father's story should be, there is nothing but a blank in Mary's mind: 'he was her father! her own dear father! and in his sufferings, whatever their cause, more dearly loved than ever before. His crime was a thing apart, never more to be considered by her' (p. 422). The narrator, however, cannot so easily refuse to consider the causes of John Barton's suffering. Having returned to the subject, she must try to conclude it, but she faces the same bind she encountered earlier: she must indict society as the source of Barton's crime and still grant Barton his free will. Whereas her strategy in the Liverpool chapters was to suppress John Barton's story, her strategy in the concluding chapters is to tell different versions of the story. Since she has declared herself free from the necessity to 'disentangle the real motives', she allows herself the luxury of presenting an 'involved set' of interpretations without really striving after consistency. Thus the recapitulations contain elements of both social determinism and voluntarism. Finally, however, salvation comes in this novel not through retelling John Barton's story, but through making it irrelevant. All John Barton's and the narrator's explanations are for naught; his story is redeemed through the intervention of another story that makes all talk of causality superfluous.

In the terms of James Martineau's dichotomy, 'conscience' is the key word in John Barton's development after the murder, just as 'causality' had been before. The issue of John Barton's moral responsibility is partly settled by the mere description of the state in which

Mary finds him on her return home: 'he had taken the accustomed seat from mere force of habit, which ruled his automaton-body. For all energy, both physical and mental, seemed to have retreated inwards to some of the great citadels of life, there to do battle against the Destroyer, Conscience' (p.422). John Barton now has no will; he acts from 'mere force of habit'. But the intensity of his remorse implies that in the past he was free. He takes full responsibility for his crime during his interview with Henry Carson, and his remorse intensifies in the course of conversation. So that remorse might appear a completely appropriate emotion, the narrator gives an account of the murder that makes it seem almost a voluntary political act rather than a desperate crime formed by the convergence of uncontrollable indignation and intolerable suffering. The version of Barton's crime given during his interview with Carson contains a causality compatible with freedom. It contains nothing of the intense suffering of the strikers or of Harry Carson's maddening arrogance: 'to intimidate a class of men, known only to those below them as desirous to obtain the greatest quantity of work for the lowest wages, – at most to remove an overbearing partner from an obnoxious firm . . . this was the light in which John Barton had viewed his deed' (pp.435–36). This very word 'cause' takes on a new meaning in this account of Barton's story: instead of implying a set of circumstances that led up to the fatal action, it comes to denote the partisan purpose of the trade unionists, the 'cause he had so blindly espoused' (p.436).

This description of the murder as a wholly political, indeed almost unemotional, act contains a social criticism, but one that increases our sense of Barton's guilty freedom. The account allows the narrator once again to argue that domesticity is the ultimate ground of reality. John Barton's reasoning had produced the distortion of human reality that always occurs when men are severed from their domestic contexts: 'he had no more imagined to himself the blighted home, and the miserable parents, than does the soldier, who discharges the musket, picture to himself the desolation of the wife, and the pitiful cries of the helpless little ones, who are in an instant to be made widowed, and fatherless' (p.435). The analogy links Barton's failing to Harry Carson's insensitivity: each in his own way was deaf to 'the pitiful cries' of helpless relations. This plea for a more highly developed domestic consciousness is itself a species of social criticism, albeit a vague one. Barton's sin of abstracting Harry Carson from his domestic context is presented as the characteristic error of industrial society. By substituting this kind of broad criticism of an abstract and abstracting mentality for the careful descriptions of social relationships and experiences contained in earlier chapters, the author unites the classes on the basis of a shared human reality, the universal reality of family life. The account of Barton's story that emerges from the interview with Mr Carson, therefore, makes a critical point, but the point does not relieve the hero of any guilt. Indeed, it increases Barton's crimes by adding to his faults of resentment and murder the crime of insensitivity to human suffering, which was previously attributed to his masters. In this account, the murder is no longer the result but the cause of suffering:

> The sympathy for suffering, formerly so prevalent a feeling with him, again filled John Barton's heart, and almost impelled him to speak . . . some earnest, tender words to the stern man, shaking in his agony.
>
> But who was he, that he should utter sympathy, or consolation? The cause of all this woe. (p.435)

This version of Barton's story is concerned with causation, but not the kind of causation that the earlier chapters traced. In this retelling, 'cause' comes to mean political purpose, and Barton himself becomes the cause of another's suffering. Causation in this version, therefore, is compatible with conscience and its corollary, free will.

Those circumstances formerly presented as the sources of Barton's actions, however, are not completely ignored in the resolution of his story. After the unforgiving Mr Carson leaves him, Barton gives an account of his own tragedy, an account which contains a heavy dose of the social determinism of earlier chapters. From him we hear once more about the moral effects of poverty and ignorance: 'you see I've so often been hankering after the right way; and it's a hard one for a poor man to find. . . . No one learned me, and no one told me' (p.440). Ignorance and poverty are two determining circumstances, and the hypocrisy of the upper classes is a third: 'I would fain have gone after the Bible rules if I'd seen folk credit it; they all spoke up for it, and went and did clean contrary' (p.440). And we hear again about the hatred inspired by his son's death from want of medicine and proper food: 'wife, and children never spoke, but their helplessness cried aloud, and I was driven to do as others did, – and then Tom died' (p.440).

The image of Barton as a driven man, however, competes in this deathbed account with yet another characterisation, one quite new to the novel. Barton acknowledges that he is creating a new self in his story-telling; he describes the act of narration as 'wrestling with my soul for a character to take into the other world' (p.434). Although Barton's characterisation of himself has elements of social determinism, it is not completely dominated by that model of causation. Even as he recapitulates the familiar circumstance, he subtly undermines

113

their explanatory power by prefacing them: 'it's not much I can say for myself in t'other world. God forgive me: but I can say this . . .' (p. 440). This preface reminds us that John Barton's acknowledged guilt, his full moral responsibility, is the given context of his narrative; he is not rehearsing his story as a defence, as a proof of innocence. Instead, he is describing, somewhat inconsistently, the extenuating circumstances of a crime to which he has already pleaded guilty.

Accordingly, the focus of his narrative is not on the familiar circumstances of his decline, but on a new set of facts about his life, facts implying that he could have avoided his tragic course. We learn for the first time that the hero was once very devout, that he studied the Bible and tried to follow its precepts, that he even had a special comradeship with old Alice, who had tried to 'strengthen' him. His faith, however, was not strong enough to survive the corrosive bitterness of his experience; the loss of his faith, we are told, was the turning point of his career: 'at last I gave it up in despair, trying to make folks' actions square wi' th' Bible; and I thought I'd no longer labour at following th' Bible myself. I've said all this afore; may be. But from that time I've dropped down, down, – down' (p. 441). Despair, itself a sin, becomes the decisive factor in this religious account of Barton's life. The character that Barton creates 'to take into the other world' is thus a cross between the tragically determined John Barton we know and a John Barton we have never seen before, the free but erring subject of a religious homily.

The writer seems to have felt some uneasiness about introducing a completely new version of the story at such a late hour, especially one that fits imperfectly with the older deterministic version, for she has Barton suggest that 'I've said all this afore; may be'. If the sentence is meant to make the new facts seem less strange, it defeats its own purpose, for it conveys the self-conscious uneasiness of the writer by reminding us that in fact *no one* has 'said all this afore', that we are being given a new story, one that is not easy to reconcile with the old. The sentence therefore increases our awareness of the discontinuities of these last chapters.

The issues tangled in the summaries of Barton's life and crime (whether he is fully responsible or not, free or determined) are never finally sorted out. We must accept this 'involved set' of accounts, but we are also reassured that ultimately it does not matter how we interpret Barton's story. For the novel we have been reading is finally resolved by the introduction of a different book, the Bible. The narrator finds relief from the multiple interpretations of John Barton's story by superimposing the ending as well as the meaning of the Gospel onto her novel, and the meaning of the Gospel is that we need not choose among the several versions of John Barton's story.

While John Barton is recounting his failure to live 'Gospel-wise', Henry J. Carson recreates himself (in both senses of the phrase) through the other story: 'he fell to the narrative now, afresh, with all the interest of a little child. He began at the beginning, and read on almost greedily, understanding for the first time the full meaning of the story' (pp.439–40). The 'full meaning' of the story turns out to be that John Barton should be forgiven, no matter what the sources or consequences of his crime. Henry Carson comes to forgive John Barton not because he has been told the hero's own story, but because Barton's words 'I did not know what I was doing' (p.435) referred him to the Gospel story. Forgiveness is mandated by the other narrative, and all versions of John Barton's life thus become irrelevant to the novel's concluding and redeeming action: Carson's forgiveness, which is a foretaste of the Christian spirit that the narrator assures us will allow Carson to effect industrial social change.

Thus the conclusion of John Barton's story points to narrative as an instrument of God's Providence without having to sort out the tangle of its own narrative threads. In the few episodes that remain, the characters settle in Canada, and the domestic tale is finally protected by distance from the tragedy caused by industrial vicissitudes. But the final episodes fail to settle the question that the novel repeatedly raises: the question of an appropriate narrative form. It is not surprising that, in Gaskell's words, no one 'saw' her 'idea of a tragic poem', for the tragedy is even more obscured by antagonistic interpretations at the end of the novel than in the early chapters. We must therefore agree with the author's judgement that she failed to express perfectly her tragic intentions. But we must also remember that her tragic purpose contained its own contradiction, which had definite historical roots in the Unitarianism of the 1840s and in certain features of the tradition of industrial social criticism that Gaskell inherited. We should also remember that her failure is the foundation of the book's formal significance, for its very generic eclecticism points toward the formal self-consciousness of later British realism.[49] □

As the 1980s drew to a close, some feminist literary critics began to adopt more complex and sophisticated psychoanalytical readings of women's writing. This approach transforms critiques of Gaskell's *Mary Barton* and *North and South*. As we have seen, the earliest responses to these novels, by contemporary reviewers, were doubtful whether Gaskell was writing the type of fiction expected of a woman in the 1840s. The next wave of critical responses attempts to resurrect Gaskell's propriety by concentrating upon her biographical personage and representing both the author and her work as appropriately feminine. The Marxist and post-Marxist backlash forces readers to pay attention not to the conservative gentility of the fiction, but instead to the most radical changes in English society that the texts both reflect and produce. The psychoanalytical model of reading, at its best, offers an understanding of crucial psychic features of the text – such as the 'other' – as a function of social and/or linguistic structures. To date, the most influential theoretical model is an Anglo-American approach influenced by Nancy Chodorow and Carol Gilligan.[50] Future directions in criticism could fruitfully adopt a continental psycho-analytical model, which has a very different approach to the relationship between the self, language, and society.[51] Margaret Homans' ground-breaking *Bearing the Word: Language and Female Experience in Nineteenth-Century Women's Writing* devotes two chapters to Gaskell. Neither analyses *Mary Barton* nor *North and South* at length. Her discussion of Gaskell and motherhood, however, is an excellent and clear explanation of how such issues radically open up the text and suggests, tantalisingly, the exciting possibilities of psychoanalytical feminist theory that have yet to come to fruition in Gaskell studies:[52]

■ Central to Gaskell's myth of herself as a writer who put her duties as a woman ahead of her writing is the story of how she began to write seriously. In 1845 her ten-month-old son, William, died of scarlet fever, and 'it was to turn her thoughts from the subject of grief that, by her husband's advice, she attempted to write a book of some length'.[53] This work was *Mary Barton*, her first novel, published in 1848 with a preface that encodes her sacred reason for writing: 'three years ago I became anxious (from circumstances that need not be more fully alluded to) to employ myself'. Like Mary Shelley in her introduction to *Frankenstein*, Gaskell wishes to demonstrate that her writing begins safely within the bounds of a woman's duty to her family, as behaviour that the death of a son might legitimately provoke and of which a protective husband approves. Only when deprived of a woman's proper duties would she consider writing.

Yet the novel also bears an epigraph that encodes a slightly different story of origins:

Nimm nur, Fährmann, nimm die Miethe,
Die ich gerne dreifach biete!
Zween, die mit nur überfuhren,
Waren geistige Naturen.[54]

Two dead children, not one, thus make their ghostly appearance at the start of this novel. The public myth of her writing would make the death of her son be the pivotal moment of her life, yet the other death, the first death, was that of her first child, a stillborn daughter, in 1833. In 1836 she wrote a sonnet 'On Visiting the grave of my stillborn little girl.' The poem records, and by doing so enacts, the carrying out of the speaker's 'vow' never to forget this child, who was 'laid beside my weary heart,/With marks of Death on every tender part', even when another is born. 'And thou, my child, from thy bright heaven see/How well I keep my faithful vow to thee.'[55] As Gaskell's first self-consciously literary venture, though she never published it, the poem marks a different point of origin for the writer's career from that indicated by the story about the death of her son. Written during the period of the diary about Marianne, the 'living infant' who the poem asserts does not supplant the dead one, the sonnet precedes her first published work, the Wordsworthian poem 'Sketches Among the Poor' (1837), and her sketch of Clopton Hall published in 1840 in William Howitt's *Visits to Remarkable Places*. Most significantly, the first short story she wrote, in 1838, was 'Lizzie Leigh' (not published till 1851, after her reputation had already been established by *Mary Barton*), a story about mothers and daughters that hinges on the death of a little girl. The writing of this story suggests that the poem's vow not to forget the dead daughter continues to provide the impetus to write, even if the child is memorialised by a re-enactment of her death. Thus, behind the myth of the writer as mother grieving over her son and directed by her husband's wisdom, who writes novels and publishes them immediately, lies hidden another writer who grieves alone over a daughter and writes a poem and a story she is reticent to publish. It is this second writer I wish to uncover.

When Gaskell's living daughter begins to speak, as Gaskell describes it in the diary, Papa's name and the signs of Papa's arrival make up her earliest language, 'leaving poor Mama in the background'.[56] With the only partially comic exclusion of the mother from the scene of symbolic language, Gaskell's diary begins making its covert myth about the place of women in language, a myth that in the next diary entry offers as compensation for this exclusion women's traditional role as passive medium for the transmission of men's, or God's, words. Though the diary starts out by uniting mother and daughter as its fused 'subject', it also acknowledges the premise of symbolic language, that the text will have meaning only if one or the other of its subjects is dead. In these and other ways, the diary yields up to the predominant myths of language and of writing the primacy and tenacity of a mother's relation with her daughter and of the linguistic possibilities that relation might offer.

[. . .] [T]he mother's relegation to the background is the result of her being that against which a male subject and speaker must define his difference, defining her as the difference and absence that constitute symbolic language. But furthermore – and this is what is of particular relevance for our discussion of Gaskell – Nancy Chodorow

117

argues that the daughter's original, preoedipal attachment to her mother outlasts the time of the son's separation from the mother and identification with the father, because unlike the son she is never obliged to renounce the mother. Chodorow argues further that it is the desire to reproduce this early situation that causes daughters, and not sons, to grow up to want not only to bear but to rear – to 'mother' – children. Whereas sons seek representations of the mother in later romantic attachments, allowing them to keep the mother at a safe distance (and while daughters seek representations of the father in the same way), daughters seek to reproduce literally the same situation they once lived in, without wanting to distance the mother. As part of a myth of language, this desire to reproduce the mother-daughter relation, with the non- or presymbolic language that both accompanies it and is modelled on it, is the desire to write in what I have been calling a literal language. This literal language is fleetingly exemplified by the rhythmic, cadenced speech Mrs Ramsey shares with her daughter in Woolf's *To the Lighthouse*, a kind of speech that does not matter because it refers to things but rather because it reassures the daughter of her mother's presence, a presence that is not distanced by the law of the father.

However, women writers of the nineteenth-century depend too much for the legitimisation of their writing on their acceptance of the symbolic order's codes, codes that would exclude them as the silent objects of representation from writing as women, for them to see value in writing in this way as mother or daughter. Or perhaps it would be more accurate to say that those women novelists who have been accepted within the literary canon are those who have accepted these codes and write according to their identification of writing with masculinity. At the same time, the desire to retain and to reproduce something of, or like, this nonsymbolic language may entice women to value a role as bearers of language (and also bearers of children). This role has the added appeal of offering an alternative way of accommodating paternal codes. Yet situated as it is in a culture that devalues whatever women do, including motherhood, this role becomes a position of subordination, appropriated, as maternity itself is appropriated, to fill the needs of a paternal order. Women are encouraged to define themselves as mothers, yet are permitted only a narrow and subordinate role when writing as mothers. *Frankenstein* articulates a woman writer's protest against this situation perhaps the most clearly, while the Victorian novelists, especially Gaskell and Eliot, who were personally as well as culturally obliged to subscribe to the cultural mythology of woman as mother, both accede to this situation and find ways to accommodate their own writing to it. Eliot is interested in the manipulation of women's given role as bearers of androcentric language – the role that Gaskell sees as available to her as compensation for Mama's relegation to the background – to see how far women's subjection to a masculinist myth of language can yet be made to afford women speech. Gaskell, perhaps more bold in her claims for writing as a woman, is interested in recovering, however fleetingly and however coloured by its situation within the confines of the paternal order, that discourse between mothers and daughters that is lost to most women writers before the twentieth century, given up by daughters and mothers alike as the price of any sort of access to the language of fathers. That Gaskell is the least canonical of the novelists considered in this book is directly related to her claiming, however conditionally, that there might be other ways for women to write, beyond the unsatisfactory alternatives of either adopting what her culture perceived as the masculine position or of accepting the narrow definition of the mother as the servant to patriliny.[57] □

CHAPTER FIVE

Recovering Contexts: New Historicism in the 1990s

IN THE 1990s, Gaskell criticism has come into its own. The dominance of new historicist approaches has produced a wealth of work on Elizabeth Gaskell's industrial novels that aims to situate them in their cultural, historical and political contexts. Consequently, criticism rejects the traditional 'Gaskell' as either the conservative minister's wife or the radical middle-class visionary. Instead, we are offered a more vibrant and exciting Gaskell: an author whose novels are deeply imbedded in the complex and most vital issues of her day and whose inconsistencies are, rather than artistic failures, proof of her engagement with problematic and conflicting ideologies. In this and the previous decade, issues of class and gender become intertwined in an attempt to recover Gaskell's contexts, so much so that the aims of the feminist criticism often overlap with the agenda of the new historicists, and the content of chapters four and five of this Guide is determined more by chronology than by critical praxis. The extracts given here, while all broadly new historicist, would also sit comfortably under a feminist umbrella.

New historicist critiques of Victorian fiction start from the premise that the novel is an institution imbedded in a complex matrix of power relations. This approach is heavily indebted to, indeed inspired by, the work of Michel Foucault.[1] Such criticism has evolved into regarding the novel as one of an infinitude of intermeshed 'texts'. To read a novel as a text involves taking account of the other texts to which it is affianced, together with the complex power relationships that determine them. The network of texts do not, crucially, correspond to a unitary, monolithic or stable notion of history. Rather, they themselves both reflect and produce history as fragmented, displaced, and made up of multiple and unstable centres of power. The school of criticism most closely related to Foucault's work is arguably most vigorous in the Renaissance period. The Victorian novel, however, is fast becoming the focus of Foucauldian-inspired new historicist study, which is typically characterised by analyses of the sub-versions of the dispossessed or other (such as the working class, the mother, the fallen woman) that both constitute a challenge to the tradi-tional account of the novel and its history and illustrate how the nexus of power relationships operates by displacement. Such studies address hitherto forgotten or neglected aspects of fiction for feminists (such as the body, sexuality, maternity) and, for other critics, the mode of a novel's production and reception.[2]

For Hilary M. Schor, the premise of reading Gaskell is that the author herself was aware of her position as culturally, socially and politically marginalised. Gaskell empathises with others, and Schor maps out the consequent tensions that publication produces:

■ Gaskell was intensely interested in publication and in acquiring a public voice, and [. . .] her attempt to write the fiction of those denied a voice within Victorian society led her to an awareness of her own silencing, a sense of the ways that literary and cultural plots shape our understanding of our world and limit our ability to describe it. Her experiments with literary form led her to examine the central stories of her culture, particularly the inscription of woman as the (silent) other.[3] □

The following extract illustrates the attraction of detail in Foucauldian literary criticism as a method of recovering forgotten or elided contexts. Mary Ann O'Farrell's approach juxtaposes Foucault's body-orientated methodology with Roland Barthes's emphasis on pleasure and on the erotics of reading.[4] The study's focus is how the blush operates as a semiotic sign in Victorian fiction:

■ Whether understood as the effect of contagion or as effecting a polite interdiscourse between bodies, the blush's circulation between and among persons is expressive of social relation. But while it may announce most clearly the subscription of the blushing body to the code of an extensive social network, the blush in the nineteenth-century English novel can also work the work of local resistance, embodying with a flush relations – not always fully articulable in the nineteenth-century novel – that cross or evade the strictures and com-pulsions of class and gender and the marriage plot.[5] □

O'Farrell's attention to the details that other criticism has neglected makes a significant and refreshing contribution to Gaskell studies. Her chapter on *North and South* illustrates the novel's anxiety about the truth-fulness of bodily signs and the experimental attempt to replace the blush, in particular, with alternative indices of a character's psyche, such as the blunder:[6]

■ To read *North and South* in a way that is responsive to the narrative's direction of reader-identification – to read, that is, with some sympathetic access to Margaret Hale's thoughts and feelings – is to read a story propelled by Margaret's vexations and frustrations in the face of perceived misunderstanding. Margaret understands her blunders as obstacles imposed by a resistant world (which she largely conceives of as the industrial Milton-Northern), obstacles that are themselves resistant to removal and clarification. And Gaskell's use of Margaret's blunders in some way supports that understanding. Margaret's difficulty in making herself clear – in blush or in language – supports a vision of the world as denying her access to expressivity and usurping her right to be read accurately, to be understood. At one moment in the text, Margaret's embrace of this vision will seem to offer all the pleasures afforded by resigned abjection and apocalyptic vindication. When Mr Bell dies, Margaret thinks about his death as, among other things, a loss of the means by which Thornton might have learned 'the simple facts' (p.505) that would dispel his suspicion of her virtue (a blunder with respect to reader sympathy, that version of Bell's loss): 'she must just submit, like many another, to be misunderstood; but, though reasoning herself into the belief that in this hers was no uncommon lot, her heart did not ache the less with longing that some time – years and years hence – before he died at any rate, he might know how much she had been tempted' (p.506). Margaret's submission to misunderstanding as an existential condition prepares for her the way either brilliantly to be read or felicitously to be misread. Within just seconds or sentences after her offer of a loan, potentially a great blundering offence to Thornton's pride, Thornton warns Margaret (in pre-Harlequin language, 'panted out the words'): 'take care. – If you do not speak – I shall claim you as my own in some strange presumptuous way. – Send me away at once, if I must go; – Margaret! –' (p.529). Margaret assents as rapidly to Thornton's strange and presumptuous yet also simply accurate conflation of financial 'proposal' (p.529) with erotic proposition, and consents to marry him.

The triumphant conversion of this blunder into success is Gaskell's recuperation of the novel she has written as a festival of error. Gaskell's fantasy of characterological legibility fades fast into a recognition that somatic legibility implies the possibility of misreading, and that a system of legibility based in bodily involuntarity and figured by the blush depends upon the illogic of seeking fixity through instability. The blush, ostensibly the source of fixity through legibility, proves itself dramatically the site of misprision and blunder; in a climactic scene from Gaskell's novel, the blush proves sometimes not even reliably to be a blush.[7] When Thornton sees Margaret walking, far from home, in the evening, with a young man Thornton does not know to be her brother, Thornton's reading of Margaret's position as compromised is wrought in part by the effects of light. Standing still, standing together with clasped hands, one (Frederick) reading the other's face 'with wistful anxiety' (p.331), Margaret and Frederick look like lovers, for Thornton, in part because 'the setting sun fell in their faces', colouring and coupling them with a tell-tale but not somatic blush. The blush of the setting sun, the product of Gaskell's imaginative manufactory, thus renders Margaret's body and Frederick's liable to the likelihood of what makes Gaskell nervous – semiotic failure and semiotic excess.[8] □

Another very different new historicist approach to lies and silences in *North and South* is taken in Catherine Barnes Stevenson's recent article. Stevenson is interested in the novel's mode of production and distribution to explain the novel's investment in blunder, lies and silence. Macherey's formulation of a book's speech is Stevenson's starting point:

■ The speech of a book comes from a certain silence . . . a ground on which it traces a figure. . . . In order to say anything, there are other things *which must not be said*. . . . What the work cannot say is important, because there the elaboration of the utterance is acted out.[9] □

Spiralling out from Macherey, Stevenson locates as the silences (and deceptions) in *North and South* the fact of women working for money as factory workers and authors, and through this forbidden narrative she links together Gaskell's ambivalent attitude towards women workers (as writers and as factory hands), her troubles with Dickens during the serial publication, and the novel's representation of Bessy Higgins.

■ The Problematics of Women's Speech

Bessy Higgins, the text's representative woman worker, has 'secured the right not to work' only through fatal disability. The iconic figure of the disabled mill girl, the victim of the unhealthy working conditions in the factories, was a familiar one to Victorian readers of blue books on factory conditions or of Charlotte Tonna's works. As Catherine Gallagher observes, advocates of The Ten Hours Movement focused on the sufferings of young girls (who were of course assumed to be weaker and more passive than their male counterparts) in order to generate support for legislative intervention on behalf of all workers who were thereby assumed to be feminine and defenceless.[10]

Initially at least, Bessy also evokes that favourite Victorian senti-mental fantasy – the young dying woman. But, although she is pale, sickly, weak, and obsessed with images of heaven, Bessy is neither a little Nell, a Sarah Green, nor a Helen Fleetwood. She is rebellious, angry, unpredictable, articulate, curious. 'I want to know so many things, and am so tossed about wi' wonder', she exclaims to Margaret.[11] Like Jane Eyre she longs for wider vistas: 'I've always wanted to get high up and see far away, and take a deep breath o' full-ness in that air' (p.144). Having dutifully worked to support her family, she confesses that 'I've longed for to be a man to go spreeing' (p.185). In a moment of rage at the inexplicable pain of her life she lashes out at Margaret: 'I could go mad and kill yo' I could' (p.145).

Although she is crippled by lung disease that 'smothers' her, mak-ing breathing and talking difficult, Bessy nonetheless is gifted with enough breath to speak long and eloquently about her situation. Not only does she voice her own anger and frustration, she also acts as the narrator of her family's history and the sole voice in the novel that actually describes working conditions in the factory (ch. 13). She articulates the psychological costs of working-class anger against injustice. Moreover, she tries to find patterns that make experience comprehensible and bearable. Unable to accept her life and its meaning-less suffering, Bessy turns to the mysterious prophesies of the Book of Revelation. In his study of popular millenarianism, J.F.C. Harrison comments on the psychological appeal of this way of thinking: 'the search for meaning, in both personal experience and the world at large, usually found expression in some kind of eschatology'.[12]

The mill girl then is a story-teller, perhaps even a kind of author. After Chapter 13, the authorial dimension of Bessy's character becomes even clearer. Gaskell could not bring herself to write of a mill girl actually at work (in *Mary Barton*, remember, Esther 'goes astray' as a result of her job in the mill, which itself is never described, and in *North and South* the youngest Higgins girl is kept out of the factory at all cost). Yet, through the figure of the mill girl, Gaskell seems to have embodied some of her frustrations with her own work situation. Like an author, Bessy has created Margaret in her imagination before even meeting her: 'I ha' dreamed of yo', long afore ever I seed yo'' (p.200), and she even seems to have a privileged knowledge of the develop-ment of the plot of the novel: Bessy alone anticipates that Margaret will 'sin' in the future (p.188). Like Gaskell who claimed to 'speak out' in her works,[13] Bessy makes heroic attempts to speak. At the same time that narrative authority accrues to her, however, Bessy ironically begins to rely more and more on the Book of Revelation as an author-itative guide to understanding experience. In this instance we see the seeds of a conflict that will be [sic] become full-blown later in the novel: the imaginative authority of woman's speech is curtailed by the 'authorities' – social, divine, literary – that would shape and control that speech. Her powerful, visionary speech is soon curtailed since she literally loses all her breath approximately half-way through the novel.

Curtailing Women's Words: The Serialisation of *North and South*

Significantly, Bessy's increasing resemblance to an author and her silencing follow hard upon the opening salvo in the battle between Gaskell and Dickens over the length, shape, and content of the manuscript which was to be serialised in *Household Words*. The only one of Gaskell's novels to be published as a weekly serial (appearing between September 1854 and January 1855), *North and South* had to be produced on a tight schedule under Dickens's firm expectations about the length and format of each instalment. In June 1854 Elizabeth Gaskell submitted the first thirteen chapters to Dickens, receiving back a letter critical of the length and shape of the text. In the very next section of her manuscript, Gaskell introduced elements into Bessy's character to make her resemble an author and then killed her off (ch. 25). At this point, the text begins to register some of the problems and tensions arising from its mode of production. The editor of *Household Words* wanted to control the length of the story and its division into parts in order to maximise his profits; the author, on the other hand, fought to maintain control over her work by resisting editorial pressure to condense and restructure the text.

Macherey observes that a text is determined not by 'the history of literary production, . . . the means of . . . [its] own realisation', but also by 'the formal function of the writer and . . . the problems of his individual existence' (p. 53). *North and South* certainly bears traces of the struggle over its serialisation and also of the ideological conflicts that any mid-Victorian writer who was also a wife and a mother had to negotiate. These conflicts are simplified and imaginatively reconstructed by Gaskell in the novel itself as the struggle between personal freedom to work/speak/write and the 'authorities' which would constrain and silence female self-expression. The complicated story of *North and South*'s production as a text provides valuable evidence about how Gaskell came to construct her dilemma in this way and consequently how the representations of Bessy Higgins and Margaret Hale manifest the irreconcilable conflict which structures the text.

Annette Hopkins and Dorothy Collin have chronicled the relationship between Gaskell and Dickens and have analysed the economic and literary forces at work in their dispute over the serialisation of *North and South*.[14] The enormous commercial success of the 'Cranford Papers', irregularly serialised in *Household Words* (1851–1853), led Dickens to solicit further contributions from Mrs Gaskell: he claimed she could not 'write too much' for him.[15] From the beginning of her association with *Household Words*, however, Gaskell seems to have had some doubts about her ability to write to Dickens's formula for serialisation. Her reservations arose both from a sense of her inability to accede to the journal's restrictions on length and her commitment to domestic responsibilities.[16]

Writing in February 1854 to urge Gaskell to produce a new work for his magazine, Dickens tried to allay her fears. After encouraging her to 'write it in your own way',[17] Dickens offered to 'make . . . little suggestions' about the chapter breaks so essential to his concept of serialisation. In June, the first batch of manuscript covering chapters one to thirteen was sent to Dickens. His response was critical: he urged Gaskell to condense; he suggested ways of dividing the text for *Household Words*; he offered to take an active part in shaping her text for publication. 'These Nos.', he wrote, 'would sometimes require to be divided again into two chapters, and would sometimes want a word or two of conclusion. If you could be content to leave this to me, I could make those arrangements of the text . . .'[18] But he warned: 'I am bound to put before you my perfect conviction that if it did not [divide well], the story would be wasted – would miss its effect as it went on – *and would not recover it when published complete*'.[19] He asserted that his suggestions could not be 'disregarded without injury to the book' and certainly to his sales as well.

By July 1854, Gaskell had completed the novel through chapter twenty-three and submitted the manuscript to Dickens. The relationship between author and editor had clearly grown tense. She apparently had balked at her editor's offer to shape her text and add his own words, for Dickens had to write to her denying 'any ambition to interpose my own words of conclusion to any of the divisions. I merely wished to smooth everything for you'. As his letters to friends and to his sub-editor indicate, Dickens was growing increasingly angry about the manuscript. Because of erroneous calculations, Dickens had underestimated the space Gaskell's manuscript would occupy when set in type for *Household Words*. When he realised the actual length of the still incomplete manuscript, Dickens peremptorily insisted, in Annette Hopkins's words, 'on compression of manuscript, at whatever artistic cost, to meet the requirements of space and pattern'.[20] He fumed to his sub-editor Wills about the 'tediousness' of Gaskell's text and the imminent disaster it would bring to *Household Words*.

Since Gaskell's letters to Dickens have been lost, her exact responses to her editor's demands during the tense summer of 1854 can only be deduced from Dickens's end of the correspondence. It seems clear, however, that she turned a deaf ear to many of his requests: in the margin of one of the letters in which he claims 'this is the place where we agreed that there should be great condensation and considerable compression', Gaskell wrote 'I've not a notion what he means'.[21] Not only did she ignore his demands for condensation and resist his offers to 'make . . . arrangements of the text' and provide 'a word or two of conclusion',[22] Gaskell also seems to have questioned Dickens's proposals for advertising the new serial. His response to her lost letter suggests that Gaskell was concerned about the 'propriety' of the publicity he might choose: 'I should propose to advertise the story, exactly as I allowed my own stories to be advertised; and I assure you that I have a very considerable respect for my art and a very considerable respect for myself'.[23] Implicit here is Gaskell's fear that Dickens's desire for commercial success might lead him to represent her inappropriately before the public.

Clearly, the dispute between author and editor illustrates Dickens's desire to have absolute editorial control over submissions – a desire which manifested itself in 'extensive – and drastic' revisions of his contributors' texts.[24] In addition it might betray jealousy on Dickens's part about a work that covered some of the same ground as his own *Hard Times*. He wrote to his sub-editor that 'if we put in more, every week, of *North and South* than we did of *Hard Times*, we shall ruin *Household Words*. Therefore, it must at all hazards be kept down'.[25] When he did publish it, he placed it in a subordinate position: instead of being the showcase piece which led each weekly issue as *Cranford* and *Hard Times* had been, *North and South* was 'sandwiched somewhere in the middle'.[26]

For Gaskell herself, this story can be read as a commentary on the limitations of her ability to construct a rapid-paced plot suitable for serialisation, or it can be interpreted as a tale about her growing sense of professional identity and strength which made her 'unwilling to obey the rules of the game' established by Dickens.[27] From a feminist point of view this struggle manifests the 'strong reservations' that Gaskell felt about 'the power relations involved in writing for male editors'.[28] More than this, however, Gaskell's refusal to maim her text by condensing it or shaping it according to some pre-determined formula can be read as a defensive ploy in a war over words that enacted a sexual politic. For the sake of profitability of his magazine Dickens wished to alter the contours, rhythms, and climaxes of Gaskell's leisurely text, reshaping it to conform to a rapid-paced, climactically structured, eight-columned format. In resisting Dickens's demands,

Gaskell was fighting male authority (which had control of the means of production) for the right to spin out her own story as she saw fit. But of course, there was a limit to how far she could take her rebellion if she wanted to see her text in print.

During these months of tension (late July to October 1854), Gaskell was working on the section of the manuscript in which Bessy is permanently silenced and Margaret tells the lie that brings her shame. Her letters to female friends give voice to the anger and frustration that she was feeling during this period. She told Eliza Fox in vivid language of the physical toll that the struggle over the novel's composition had taken: 'I've been as nearly dazed and crazed with this c-, d- be h- to it, story as can be. I've been sick of writing, and everything connected with literature or improvement of the mind; to say nothing of deep hatred to my species about whom I was obliged to write as if I loved 'em . . .'[29] It is surely significant that in penning her frustration with her manuscript she employs the initials of the man who was the source of this frustration, Mr. 'C.D.' (In an 1859 letter to Smith, Gaskell actually refers to Dickens this way.)[30] Although Gaskell and her friends were quick to blame Dickens, and even in the case of Catherine Winkworth to put an explicitly sexual construction on the conflict,[31] Gaskell's response is symptomatic, I would argue, not simply of a bad relationship with an editor but also of the demands of the mode of production of this work.

Feltes, citing Marx, argues that the nineteenth-century writer 'whether genius or hack, presented him- or herself to the publisher, as did any other worker in the capitalist mode of production, as the "owner of nothing but his labour-power"'.[32] The literary text 'newly defined as a commodity [was] newly available as the locus of surplus value' (p.96). Although writing was a more 'respectable' form of employment than factory labour, Gaskell, like Bessy Higgins, was nonetheless a paid woman worker whose family relied on her earnings. Just as the mill girl laboured in the carding room in order to generate the profits for the 'master', so the writer of serialised fiction laboured to produce text that would boost the circulation and profits of a magazine's owners. As Collin observes, Dickens's eagerness to have Gaskell write for *Household Words* was fuelled by his desire for 'commercial success: when he found a rich vein he exploited it to the utmost'.[33] Furthermore, Bessy sacrificed herself for the comfort of her family: 'Mary's schooling were to be kept up, mother said, and father he were always liking to buy books, and go to lectures o' one kind or another – all which took money – so I just worked on . . .' (p.147). So too Gaskell complained to her daughter Polly – during the months that she was working on this section of the novel – that she needed to 'scrubble up money' to pay for domestic expenses.[34] Although her working situation was not comparable in literal detail to that of the mill girl, Gaskell used the plight of Bessy to encode some of her own frustrations with a situation which placed conflicting demands on her and within which she began to see herself as unjustly exploited.[35] □

Barbara Leah Harman's *The Feminine Political Novel in Victorian England* contains a chapter on *North and South* that argues vigorously against what she perceives to be the very conservative reading of previous commentaries. For Harman, the traditional view is summed up by Barbara Hardy: 'Mrs Gaskell is never a propagandist; or if she is, she is only a propagandist for sympathy'.[36] On the contrary, Harman argues: Gaskell illustrates the dangers of middle-class women entering the public sphere but also shows how such an entry nevertheless can refashion it. The problem with such an approach, however, is that it is in danger of maintaining the valorised binary logic of the public/private and thus ends up recirculating nineteenth-century ideology.

■ [T]he central event for my purposes is Margaret's emergence into the public arena during the strike at Thornton's mill. She goes to the mill on an errand from home – to fetch a water bed for her ailing mother – and finds herself when she gets there in the midst of a crisis.

Margaret is asked to help secure the house against strikers – to 'shut down the windows' and stay inside – as the bolted gates are repeatedly attacked. This time, it seems, the intruders will not be kept out, and the language of sexual violation in the scene is almost egregiously clear: 'they could all hear the one great straining breath; the creak of wood slowly yielding; the wrench of iron; the mighty fall of the ponderous gates' (p.231). But instead of defending herself even further against what amounts to a serious threat of intrusion, Margaret first challenges Thornton to face the angry strikers and then, fearful of the consequences of her challenge, moves to face them herself. In a scene that revises and then reverses Margaret's panicky self-enclosure in the Helstone drawing room (when she thinks she hears poachers), she 'threw the window wide open', then 'tore her bonnet off; and bent forwards to hear', and finally 'rushed out of the room, down-stairs, – she had lifted the great iron bar of the door with an imperious force – had thrown the door open wide – and was there, in face of that angry sea of men, her eyes smiting them with flaming arrows of reproach' (p.233).

John Pikoulis has justly described this scene as 'one of the most thrilling moments in Victorian literature, representing, as it does, the first time that a woman has convincingly established herself on the public stage in her own right'.[37] The scene is, indeed, both thrilling and unprecedented, describing in a way quite unlike that of any previous novel, a woman who steps dramatically and fearlessly into the political turmoil of a chaotic strike, unprotected and unmediated by the presence of others. It is also crucial to read Gaskell's scene in relation to that of her friend and predecessor Charlotte Brontë, especially because Gaskell told Lady Kay-Shuttleworth that she 'disliked a good deal in the plot of Shirley' – a significant remark in light of the fact that the strike scene in *North and South* could easily be read as a revision of Brontë's riot at the mill.[38] Brontë's Shirley finds herself in circumstances not entirely unlike Margaret's – presented with a situation in which she thinks she can prevent a violent attack.

In Margaret's appearance before the angry crowd scene in *North and South* Gaskell rewrites Shirley's restraint and highlights the physical conspicuousness, and surprising bodily openness, of Margaret's action. The strikers themselves are stopped in their tracks, 'arrested' by her appearance (p.233). At first, she is unable to speak and can only stand and '[hold] out her arms towards them'. But perhaps most significantly, Margaret stations herself 'between [the strikers] and their enemy', covering Thornton, at least partially, with her own body. Thornton stands 'a little on one side . . . away behind her', not wanting her protection and seeking to recover his own proper place, 'jealous of anything that should come between him and danger' (p.234). The movement is a slight one, but it betokens the rivalry here between Thornton and Margaret: Who shall occupy the public stage? Who shall take command? Who shall speak? Who shall act? Who shall really 'appear'?

Margaret, whose voice had earlier lacked 'tone', speaks first. Her voice rings out, though her assurances to the crowd are empty ones ('you shall have relief from your complaints, whatever they are') and in that sense only incites the strikers. But when the crowd erupts and Margaret sees a group of young men about to take aim at 'he whom she had urged and goaded to come to this perilous place', she acts again: 'she only thought how she could save him. She threw her arms around him; she made her body into a shield from the fierce people beyond. Still, with his arms folded, he shook her off. "Go away," said he, in his deep voice. "This is no place for you." "It is!" said she' (p.234).

Gaskell returns here to Margaret's conspicuous presence, to her willingness to use her body and to her sense of its powerful instrumentality. When Margaret makes 'her body into a shield' to protect Thornton, her action suggests that she is willing to risk exposure; she believes she can manage and control her intercourse with others – even in the public realm – and is willing to risk unwanted intrusion even while she feels she can deflect it. That she should associate this power with her body seems especially intriguing since it confirms the physical and even sexual significance of female public appearance to which Margaret's earlier responses to life in the out-of-doors (at Helstone) and life in the city streets (of Milton) have already pointed.

As it turns out, however, Margaret overestimates the power of the maiden to deflect assault, for as Gaskell remarks, 'if she thought her sex would be a protection, – if, with shrinking eyes she had turned away from the terrible anger of these men, in any hope that ere she looked again they would have paused and reflected, and slunk away, and vanished, – she was wrong' (p.234). The assertion that Gaskell wants to make is that 'if she thought her sex would be a protection . . . she was wrong'. But she makes it both more difficult to detect, and at the same time even stronger, by inserting the parenthetical 'if': if Margaret imagines that she can turn away 'with shrinking eyes' – in other words, turn away in maiden shame – in the hope of recovering the protection that maidenly innocence provides, she will learn that it is too late to do so. Gaskell notes that the strikers' 'reckless passion had carried them too far', but Margaret's has too (p.234). She has crossed a sequence of boundaries – opened the windows, torn off the (protecting) bonnet, flung wide the doors, stepped outside, and placed herself between Thornton and the crowd. This insertion of herself into public space and into the great struggle between masters and men challenges the notion that she will be granted the chivalric protection upon which she depends.

The insistently violating sexual language of the strike scene emerges with greater power in the following passage as Margaret suffers her first actual injury: 'a sharp pebble flew by her, grazing her forehead and cheek, and drawing a blinding sheet of light before her eyes. . . . [The strikers] were watching, open-eyed, and open-mouthed, the thread of dark-red blood which wakened them up from their trance of passion. Those nearest the gate stole out ashamed' (p.235). The language of this passage shows that the real risk of public exposure is sexual violation, and even though Margaret is only 'symbolically' deflowered,[39] the complications that attend her public appearance all serve to intensify its sexual meanings. As Margaret remembers her action at home, in its aftermath, she thinks both of the shame associated with involving herself in a public disturbance – 'I, who hate scenes . . . I went down and must needs throw myself into the mêlée, like a romantic fool!' (p.247) – and the shame associated with courting a man in public as others, it turns out, think she has done.

Margaret thus suffers, as Bodenheimer points out, 'exactly the consequences that Shirley foresees for Caroline',[40] and I would argue, foresees for herself – namely, the misconstruction of character from which both Shirley and Caroline are protected by Shirley's constraint. Margaret enters public space without cover (Shirley and Caroline do not: Brontë declares, in language that Gaskell uses almost verbatim, that 'they both knew they would do no good by rushing down into the mêlée') and the meaning of her act is, for those who witness it, genuinely difficult to interpret. This difficulty is acute because in one sense Margaret reverses the conventional understanding of gender relations (in which men take public stands on behalf of women, not women on behalf of men) and in another she seems to reinstate it (women convert even political events into romantic ones, public events into private ones). Thornton himself is struck by the first reading: once the strike scene is over he openly asserts 'I don't know where I should have been but for her. . . . Not many girls would have taken the blows on herself which were meant for me' (pp. 242–43) – a statement that again recalls, in comparison, Brontë's assertion that Shirley and Caroline 'desired neither to deal nor to receive blows'.[41]

But the second reading is powerful too: everyone (including Thornton himself) sees Margaret's act as a sexual one. The servants have watched the mêlée from 'the front garret' where they 'could see it all, out of harm's way' (again, like Shirley and Caroline). They describe the scene to Thornton's sister, Fanny, who has fainted and missed the entire event; and what they report is a romantic encounter: 'Miss Hale with her arms about Master's neck' (p. 239). The servants regard Margaret's action not merely as sexual but as sexual self-display in action ('hugging him before the people', p. 239). Margaret's own language illustrates how difficult it is to keep sexual innuendo out of an account of the strike scene: she remembers 'throw[ing] myself into the mêlée, like a romantic fool' (p. 247).

This, however, is a sign not that women contain, or are used to contain, politically explosive scenes by reducing them to romantic encounters but, rather, that female participation in public life and female appearance itself are both politically and sexually explosive. Margaret interprets the strike scene by attempting to refute its sexual meaning and by claiming its collective, and thoroughly conventional, character. Hers was not 'a personal act between you and me', she tells Thornton when he later proposes marriage to her, but, rather, an act consistent with her membership in the female sex as a whole and, in some sense, an impersonal class action (p. 253). 'We all feel the sanctity of sex as a high privilege when we see danger,' she declares, and 'any woman, worthy of the name of woman, would come forward to shield, with her reverenced helplessness, a man in danger of the violence of numbers' (pp. 252, 253). Margaret invokes here – though in a revised form – the 'woman's mission' argument about woman's helplessness when she suggests that female passivity is so revered by men that it literally suppresses their desire to injure and calls up, instead, their wish to conserve and protect. She should have been able, Margaret implies, to shield Thornton from the rioters precisely because of her inability to shield herself. Her extreme vulnerability should have arrested the violent activity that threatened them both as the strikers joined with her to confirm the vision of womanhood to which everyone collectively subscribed.

What Margaret fails to appreciate, of course, is the way in which her appearance on a public stage revokes the very protection that she wished to elicit. For as T.H. Lister commented in [an] 1841 review article [. . .]:

> The deference, the tenderness, the courtesy of man towards the other sex, are founded principally on the feeling that they need his protection, and can never question his power. But let women be made ostensibly powerful; let a sense of competition be introduced; let man be made to feel that he must stand on the defensive – and the spirit of chivalry . . . will speedily cease; and it will be useless to expect a continuance of that feeling, to which women can now appeal with confidence, and which lends the most essential charms to the ordinary intercourse of civilised society. Women, as a class, cannot enjoy, at the same time, the immunities of weakness and the advantages of power.[42]

Lister makes his claim in relation to arguments about suffrage, but it is a claim that repeats itself frequently in debates about women's access to public life throughout the nineteenth century. What Margaret does not fully realise is that she has made herself 'ostensibly' and conspicuously powerful, and in so doing she has relinquished the female 'immunity' she might otherwise have enjoyed. In one sense, her debate with Thornton about men and gentlemen, and more prominently the implicit debate about men and women, re-emerges here too. Chivalric relations do not govern the intercourse of men and women in public space – at least not if those women insert themselves into the public domain. Margaret's old insistence on the language of class, and on class separation, disintegrates in this scene. If Lister is right, the class to which Margaret really belongs is the class of women, and she has relinquished that class's right to protection from the other class – from the class of men.

Margaret's defence of herself is interesting for its insistent conservatism in the face of what is clearly an unconventional act on her part. No one, it seems, reveres her helplessness (Thornton certainly doesn't). Everyone is astounded either by the courage, or by the presumptuousness, of her act. Thornton is alternately proud of her bravery and jealous of the way *she* appropriates *his* role as protector. And Margaret's own insistence on her purity is given the lie both by her symbolic defloration and by the 'deep sense of shame' she feels whenever she contemplates her own actions (p. 249).

This sense of shame is linked to what Margaret calls 'be[ing] the object of universal regard' (p.249) – a phrase that evokes the identification between publicity and sexuality to which the opponents of legal reform, the expansion of female employment opportunities, and female suffrage regularly referred. To be universally regarded is to be seen by anyone – to have no control over those who do the looking, over the mere fact that they look, or over the kind of looking they might do. Margaret's painful self-consciousness is a self-consciousness both about indiscriminate or, to use a more loaded term, promiscuous, regard and also about the very fact of regard pure and simple. As Victorians were only too aware, when a middle-class woman took to the public stage she brought her body, ordinarily confined to the drawing room, before the eyes of others. This meant that her appearance virtually always had both class and sexual implications – unless special steps were taken to 'cover' and block her from regard (this is why Shirley always 'screens' herself in Brontë's novel). In Margaret's case no such steps are taken. Fanny faints and is carried upstairs; the servants watch from the garret; but Margaret stands before the striking workers and covers Thornton – not the other way around. The related ideas of class erosion and sexual tainting that get bonded to her by the plot and language of *North and South* are affiliated with Margaret's crossing of boundaries and her entrance into the public realm – and they are, in a variety of forms, persistent features of female public appearance both here and elsewhere in Victorian writing.

In the courtroom scene of her earlier novel *Mary Barton* (1848), Gaskell invoked the association between female publicity and female sexuality and yet went to significant lengths to de-emphasise the impropriety that might be thought to attach to it. Mary's great – and effective – act of courage actually precedes the courtroom scene. It is embodied in the wild errand of mercy on which she goes in advance of her appearance there: she races through the streets of Liverpool, hires a boat at the dock where 'the cries of the sailors, the variety of languages used by the passers-by, and the entire novelty of the sight' make her feel 'helpless and forlorn' – not excited, as they might make Margaret feel.[43] Mary's intention is to stop the ship that is bearing away the man who might provide an alibi for her lover, Jem Wilson, and in a scene that anticipates Margaret's own first gesture before the striking workers, she 'stood up, steadying herself by the mast, and stretched out her arms, imploring the flying vessel to stay its course by that mute action, while the tears streamed down her cheeks. The men caught up their oars, and hoisted them in the air, and shouted to arrest attention' (p.357). Like Margaret's cry at the beginning of the strike scene, Mary's too lacks tone: 'her throat was dry; all the musical sound had gone out of her voice; but in a loud harsh whisper she told the men her errand of life and death, and they hailed the ship' (p.358). Though the captain refuses to release the sailor who can prove the alibi, Mary's effort will eventually bear fruit: the young man will emerge later at the trial and his testimony will exculpate Jem.

Mary's own public appearance at the trial, however, will have little bearing on the outcome: the evidence she has to give is not deci-sive. Still, like Margaret, Mary looks out on a 'sea of faces, misty and swimming before her eyes' and sees the 'hundreds [who] were look-ing at her' (pp.388, 389), just as Margaret remembers afterwards 'a sea of men', a 'cloud of faces', and the 'unwinking glare of many eyes' (pp.233, 248, 249). But what is strikingly different about the two scenes is that although the trial is actually the scene of Mary's sexual self-representation – she confesses her love for Jem in public when a lawyer asks her 'to tell, before that multitude assembled there, what a woman usually whispers with blushes and tears, and many hesita-tions, to one ear alone' (p.390) – her appearance in court does not bring with it any sense of sexual impropriety at all. Indeed, Gaskell seems determined in this earlier novel *not* to associate Mary's court-room appearance with the sort of taint that publicity carries in *North and South* and she accomplishes this in a variety of ways: by separating Mary's public appearance from her earlier heroic act (Margaret's public appearance *is* her heroic act), by having her confess to a love that others would be loath to acknowledge (she loves a man on trial for murder, a man 'abhorred of men', p.390), and by having her 'los[e] all command over herself' after her testimony ends (p.392).

In other words, Mary's public appearance lacks the agency that Gaskell attributes to Margaret's. That agency is reserved for the earlier, heroic scenes in Liverpool. By the time Mary gets to the courtroom she is able to speak with clarity and composure, but she can only do so while averting her eyes and, when she is done speaking, covering her face with her hands. Those who watch her are struck by the 'higher kind of beauty' that her face suggests (p.389), not by the 'conspicuous notice' that Sally Leadbitter, at the dress shop where Mary had been working, associates in advance with Mary's court appearance. Mary will prove 'quite an attraction to customers', Sally says, 'many a one would come and have their gowns made by Miss Simmonds just to catch a glimpse at you, after the trial's over. Really, Mary, you'll turn out quite a heroine' (p.353).

Mary does turn out a heroine, but not in the way Sally thinks. Gaskell imagines publicity and heroism separately in *Mary Barton*, and she explores public sexual self-representation hemmed round with self-determining protections. In *North and South* Gaskell confronts the risks of a bold, and boundary-crossing heroism and, building on the earlier book's innovations, explores much more openly the sexual taint to which female publicity would increasingly find itself attached.[44] [. . .]

What I would call the generosity of Gaskell's vision of sexual impropriety extends itself beyond her rendering of Margaret and Thornton's relationship and into her treatment of Margaret's role in the social world of London where she plans to 'set apart for freedom in working' a portion of her own life (p. 508). Instead of abandoning, as she might have done, Margaret's interest in public causes, Gaskell refashions her vision of female publicity, suggesting – in an admittedly reticent portrait – that Margaret will become a nineteenth-century lady visitor, wearing, as Edith humorously remarks, 'brown and dust-coloured' dresses to avoid showing 'the dirt you'll pick up in all those places' (p. 509). The critic Dorice Williams Elliott states that Margaret differs from the traditional Lady Bountiful, supported by the landed gentry or the church, and even from the lady visitor who is an 'emissary for a philanthropic association', because Gaskell intimates that she will operate independently and on her own authority.[45] But of course Margaret has been operating independently for much of the novel in her home visits to the Higginses and their neighbours. Gaskell suggests at the end that Margaret will professionalise her independent visiting in London (where she would be unlikely to go visiting on her own), committing herself to it in a way that implies she will join a visiting society.

It would be easy to see such work as part of a project of containment in which Margaret is transformed from a potent strike scene participant into a fledgling lady visitor, a woman who extends the domestic sphere outward into the homes of the poor. In this reading the emergence of a woman onto the public stage somehow becomes the feminisation, and thus the conversion and reduction, of a literally explosive relation to the public realm. But as Anne Summers points out in her analysis of women's philanthropic work, 'treating social problems on an individualistic basis rather than subjecting them to a structural analysis' did not make women's work 'reactionary'. Although Summers acknowledges the conservative features of visiting (especially as it bears upon the poor themselves), she clearly sees it as providing middle-class women with access to 'power outside their homes'.[46]

The implication that such work brought one into the 'glare of publicity' and that it might even be attached to some undefined 'opprobrium' intimates that Margaret has not entirely altered her instinct to strike out on her own potentially dangerous path. She will follow her own authority and 'her own ideas of duty' by committing herself more fully to the tasks, and the risks, of nineteenth-century female visiting. Gaskell treats lightly and humorously the scene in which Margaret discusses her plans with Edith, and Edith warns her against becoming 'strong-minded', but the indication that Margaret's work will be perilous is nonetheless unmistakable (p. 508).

Gaskell's representation of Margaret's complex circumstances reveals her serious interest in refashioning the meaning of female publicity and reconceiving the relations between private and public life. Unlike the domestic ideologists upon whose thinking she initially draws, Gaskell does not finally portray her heroine as a woman who feminises the public realm by extending domestic life outward (Margaret crosses the boundary between public and private and relinquishes the immunities associated with private life) nor as a woman who purifies public life of its taint by conserving her own private principles as a sustaining resource (the lie, I have argued, makes this stance impossible). Gaskell abandons both of these visions and focuses first on what happens when a woman enters an unreconstructed and unpurified public realm: she is penetrated by it and initiated into it, where penetration consists in physical violation and initiation consists both in enduring public exposure and in suffering the shame of an implied promiscuity. Gaskell also imagines her way beyond her heroine's public initiation and into a new version of public endeavour – even though public space is promiscuous space in Gaskell's novel and entry into it both risky and potentially compromising.

To say this might appear to suggest that Gaskell rejected one set of Victorian conventions (those defining female domesticity with moral power) only to adopt another (those defining public life as sexually compromising) – and in one sense this is indeed the case. But what makes *North and South* interesting and surprising is that Gaskell neither saw the danger of public life as a reason to exclude women from it nor sought to imagine entry into that realm as an opportunity to domesticate it. The sexualisation of public life can only be seen as an effort to imagine its domestication if femininity is really felt to be benign – if a woman's entrance onto the public stage might be seen as an opportunity to neutralise a dangerous world. But Gaskell suggests here both that female sexuality is potent – affiliated with exposure, criminality, indiscretion, and immoral secrecy – and, at the same time, that this is emphatically not stigmatising. She never reduces our sense that public life is dangerously thrilling: Margaret's excitement about the universe of power or accomplishment in Milton and her determined authority about 'freedom in working' emphasise this point. Nor does Gaskell seek entirely to eliminate the sexual shame that gets attached first to Margaret's public appearance and later to her supposed relation with a secret lover. Instead, she converts public into private shame, and private shame into the acknowledgement of mature sexuality, thus affirming rather than condemning the inevitable connectedness of public and private life and imagining a world in which their explosive union might actually be accommodated – as it is in the marriage of Thornton and Margaret, which begins as a business proposition (on Margaret's part) and ends as an intensely erotic proposal of marriage (on Thornton's).

Many critics have seen Gaskell's ending as a conservative project of accommodation.[47] In my view it is the opposite. *North and South* does equate public with private life by equating female publicity with female sexuality, and it transforms private sexual shame into an opportunity for sexual self-recognition, a new form of female public appearance, and, of course, public marriage. But its equations never appear in the service of exclusion, neutralisation, containment, or even romantic reduction. The novel confirms what critics of female emancipation tended to fear – that access to public life means access to potentially dangerous kinds of sexual intimacy for women – and it does so while affirming, and hence finally legitimising, both female public action and female sexuality. This double affirmation does not narrow, but rather expands, the range of possibilities. It does not convert and thus reduce the public into the private, but grants the private its disturbingly public dimension.[48] □

The question of female authority with which Harman engages is also tackled in an earlier study but in quite a different way. Hilary M. Schor is interested in questions of literary authority, language and the marketplace and, in a chapter on *Mary Barton*, draws lucidly from recent feminist theory to suggest that the issue circulates round the figure of Mary's dead mother.[49] Schor illustrates how the private sphere can be empowered in Gaskell's fiction through the maternal.

■ The dead mother is the key to much of [the] recasting of authority [in *Mary Barton*] – and of fiction. The parent previously in this novel has been the angry father; if God is the father, the Bible told John Barton, we must bear what he sends us, and the critique of the cold, indifferent father extends beyond the home into the marketplace. What brings grace for Mary is a mother who will take her back to a time when she was not hungry rather than tell her to bear her hunger more cheerfully now, who might offer a way out of patriarchal authority. Mother love offers a similar model of care to Esther, who says that Mary is like her own child; to Mrs Wilson, who tells the orphaned Mary that she shall be her own 'ewe-lamb'; to the dying Alice Wilson, who talks once more to her dead but forgiving mother. Maternal wisdom suggests a way of watching over that protects, nurtures, binds, connects – that restores what has been lost.

That is to say, this 'watching over' is a narrative impulse, which in turn will revision authority. Maternal authority, unlike supervision, is an authority that can *name* its charges. Its opposite is embodied in Mr Carson, who, when Wilson goes to his home to ask for a medical order for the dying Davenport, does not 'know the name' of this man. Wilson reminds him he 'worked in your factory better nor three year'. 'Very likely', says Carson, 'I don't pretend to know the names of those I employ: that I leave to the overlooker' (p. 109). The overlooker – like Carson – does, indeed, manage to overlook: to overlook breaks in machinery like the one that cripples Jane Wilson, or those injuries that even the doctors at the hospital where Barton once stayed know come late in the day when the workers are tired. 'Overlooking', barely listening, judging harshly are all forms of missed connections and failed love in the novel – real 'overlooking', in the sense that Gaskell means to reinstate here, is the watching out of sympathetic love, the provenance of mothers – or here, of mothers turned novelists. Reinstating the authority of the mother also places Gaskell as (maternal) author at the centre of her text, and makes the mother the perfect novelistic authority. If mother love is to redeem the world, who better to write novels than Gaskell herself? Just as Mary assumes her dominant role in the second half of the novel in part by taking on the authority of the *dead* Mary Barton, so the providence behind the fiction becomes female, a different kind of authorship.

At this point, my argument might be seen as overlapping with recent feminist theory, which argues that it is through the mother – and specifically, through the mother's body – that we get the kind of textual disruption I am arguing Gaskell invokes here. For such critics, maternal language, as Mary Jacobus explains it, has the power to disrupt phallogocentric authority: the 'discourse of maternity', the 'archaic language of the pre-oedipal . . . rhythms, melodies, and bodily movements' 'precede[s] and prepare[s] the way for the language of signification'. Though the paternal, 'symbolic dimension of language works to repress the semiotic . . . the maternal nonetheless persists in oral and instinctual aspects of language which punctuate, evade or disrupt the symbolic order – in prosody, intonation, puns, verbal slips, even silences'. Such a criticism, rooted in a psychoanalytical view of language, argues, in Julia Kristeva's words, that language separates itself from the body through the mother's body; 'the woman-subject' is a 'thorough-fare, a threshold where "nature" confronts "culture"'.

One could read the scenes of maternal visitation in *Mary Barton* in such a way, as Mary's mother's ghost invokes the *sounds* of memory, speaking the soft dialect Mary recognises. The scene's disruption of genre, its gothic use of the mother's haunting return, might be seen as disrupting the symbolic order, as does the repetition of the maternal figure in the text. The mother blurs into her darker self, the prostitute Mary almost became, or, most movingly, as in the hallucination Aunt Esther recounts, her own daughter, her mother, and her sister (Mary's mother) walk around and around her bed as she lies in prison. In this Burne-Jones-like duplication of some eternal (familiar) woman, endlessly repeating herself in Esther's nightmares, endlessly authoring and erasing herself, we see what Kristeva recounts: the mother who 'by giving birth . . . enters into contact with her mother; she becomes, she is, her own mother; they are the same continuity differentiating itself' – that is, the mother/daughter who is *both* Mary Bartons, and neither.

But I want to historicise this psychoanalytic move, to ask again what particular power the 'semiotic' might have in this novel's political economy – to argue, in fact, that the nightmare/vision of maternal presence has a more powerful (and specifically political) authority. Elizabeth Gaskell imagined a maternal authority that would make of England a home; that would cure the condition of England; that would feed the hungry workers; that would redeem the lost children. More than a maternal, slippery language (the 'fond mimicry of affection') Gaskell describes something like a maternal plot: an alternate structure of power, an alternate family, an alternate England. In the new world, families 'will go up as well as down', so that Mary and Jem can bring Mrs Wilson with them to Canada, instead of a child; in the new world, as Mrs Wilson somewhat comically but hopefully announces, 'perhaps in them Indian countries they'll know a well-behaved lad when they see him'; in the new world, Mary will be restored as 'a ewe lamb' to a new mother. In this new world, there is more than maternal 'continuity differentiating itself'; there is a potentially new order.

We can ask, of course, how far the 'authority' of these dead mothers extends. To make only the most obvious point, the end of the novel finds Aunt Esther dead ('she held the locket containing her child's hair still in her hand, and once or twice she kissed it with a long soft kiss'), finds Mary Barton transformed into Mary Wilson, and the voice of her dead mother presumably silenced. Judith Newton has noted that female authority too often takes the form of 'influence' instead of 'ability'; as she quotes Sarah Ellis's *The Wives of England*, to have influence, 'all that has been expected to be enjoyed from the indulgence of selfishness must then of necessity be left out of our calculations, with all that ministers to the pride of superiority, all that gratifies the love of power, all that *converts the woman into the heroine* (emphasis added)'. Only in Mary's efforts to save Jem from hanging do we find female action directly embraced by the text; later, when Mary wants to perform the same redemptive work for Aunt Esther, 'vehemently' rising 'as if she was going on the search there and here', Jem, 'fondly restrain[s] her', ending the progress of 'the woman into the heroine'. But the other conversion, of woman into mother, remains, and maternal activity, as it can be learned and imitated, is at the novel's heart. The scene where Job Legh carries his dead daughter's child from London, wearing a woman's nightcap to try to calm the baby's screams,[50] suggests that it is as mothers that we will love, teach, travel best.

But even if one allows it to be a real power, with a wider sphere than that of 'influence', matriarchal authority creates a second problem: what does wielding this power do to those around you? If the problem with the patriarchal power of the masters is that it turns workers into animals to be guided and governed, matriarchal power in the novel seems to make the workers infants. The recipients of maternal wisdom move back, almost beyond language, to what Tennyson described as a state of 'no language but a cry'. (In *Mary Barton*, once you get the mother back in the world, you can't talk to her.) In Gaskell's mind, all her characters are like 'terrified children', only 'secure of safety when near the protecting care' of the mother, and they attain moral goodness only when they become 'protecting'.

On the text's conscious level, that protection is Christ's, the 'friend of the orphan', but on its deepest level, it is the care of the mother. The messianic overtones of Mary's 'you are come at last!' are echoed in the 'they know not what they do' of Mr Carson's final revelation, and its implicit message (be like Christ, be like a mother) is brought out in a series of scenes with children. When John Barton leaves home to assassinate Carson, he stops long enough to help a small child; in the scene before Mary's mother's 'return', Mary has been stopped in her panicked run by a little Italian boy who utters 'in his pretty broken English', the words 'Hungry! so hungry!' Mary races past him, only to think better of her impatience, and returns to where 'the little hopeless stranger had sunk down . . . in loneliness and starvation, and was raining down tears as he spoke in some foreign tongue, with low cries for the distant "Mamma mia!"' (p. 284). The most important scene of conversion in the novel, Mr Carson's, is also prepared for by an encounter with a child. After he has left the home of John Barton, still unwilling to forgive the worker who claims not to have known what he was doing, Carson sees a rough young boy run headlong into a beautiful, well-dressed girl and knock her down. The girl's governess pounces on the boy, only to have the angelic young girl forgive him, exclaiming that he didn't know what he was doing; this message haunts Carson till he goes home, takes down the family Bible and reads the Gospels. Then he comes to 'the end: the awful End. And there were the haunting words of forgiveness' (p. 440). Only after witnessing the young child's forgiveness toward her enemy on account of his essential ignorance can Carson absorb the message of this explicitly Christian novel, picking up the text he and John Barton share and have both 'puzzled over'. But for this to happen, for Carson to be moved to compassion for Barton, Barton must become like that child and be forgiven for not knowing what he is doing. For Carson to be Christ-as-mother, Barton's autonomy (his most articulate demands, the wickedness of the masters) must be denied.

The problem with mothering, then, is that it requires children: the more hungry they are like the Italian boy, uttering brokenly, 'Hungry! so hungry' the better. People are returned to that world where desire and demand become one; they have a language to ask for only the simplest needs to be fulfilled. The workers themselves become, in the words of one of Barton's visitors before his trip to London, people who have 'been clemmed long enough, and [who] donnot see whatten good they'n been doing, if they can't give what we're all crying fo sin' the day we were born' (p. 128). However moving this plea is, and it is in some ways the perfect summary of the blighted lives of the workers, it is also reductive, compared to the strongest arguments for dignity Barton makes in the course of the novel. There is a difference, which Gaskell never addresses, between Barton's reasoned arguments for work, for reform, for individual autonomy, and the crying of starving children, to which this statement reduces the Charter – there was more at stake, somehow, before.

However much we might prefer the sympathising mother to the angry father, and whatever the creation of maternal narratives allowed Gaskell to do, the mother's return does not seem to solve all the problems the novel set out to answer. The difficulty Gaskell faces as she nears the end of her novel is to avoid setting up yet another structure of authority that will silence people like John and Mary Barton as effectively as did the structure she set out to criticise. As John Barton's voice gets swallowed up by the discourse around him, be it Job Legh's or Carson's, so the potential for transforming the language of authority seems to disappear as well. Gaskell appears to have trouble imagining a world without authority, in England at least, and this may be why she moves the novel to Canada for its final chapter. It may also be why she tells us so little of life in Canada, that mythic place where class relationships will no longer exist. If happy marriages could not take place in the world of Manchester but had to occur in the new world, perhaps free, unlegislated space can exist only there as well. And perhaps that space exists only outside the novel; to impose any narration may be to freeze it into something supervised and 'overlooked'. It may, further, reduce the narrative to one of expertise, of 'political economy', rather than 'truth'. Gaskell's novel does not promise a solution; it promises, rather, a changed heart.

If the move to Canada is not a solution, Gaskell's vision of maternal narrative presence, along with her questioning of narrative authority in general, does present solutions of a different kind. If the world cannot be transformed absolutely, our ways of seeing and describing it can – and as the novel's critique of received languages suggests, to write the story differently may be to write a different story. *Mary Barton* contains within it the story of Gaskell's learning to speak, a rewriting of stories of female heroism and female authorship played out in a world of spectacle and silencing in which Gaskell finds for herself a language 'expressing her wants' that is more than just 'a cry' and for her heroine, a chance to speak openly, choose her life, and overcome some of the plots that have been written for her.[51] □

Another commentary on the two roles of public woman in *Mary Barton*, the streetwalker (neglected in particular by contemporary reviews, which are blind to Esther's disruptive presence) and the social worker, unravels their associations with the female novelist and offers an alternative approach to Gaskell's treatment of the separate spheres. Deirdre D'Albertis's sensitive and engaging study of Gaskell's fiction argues, like Harman, that the novel aims to break down the distinction between masculine and feminine norms of fiction. In addition, she points to the problematic association between the woman writer and the fallen woman, for both were engaged in the public sphere of commerce.[52]

■ Gaskell introduces the idea of the prostitute and social worker as 'secret sharers' by downplaying the observational power of her protagonist. *Mary Barton* is a novel with a disappointing heroine: incurious, unself-aware, prevented from any meaningful involvement in political thought or action in a 'Condition-of-England' novel. Gaskell intended originally to focus the narrative on the tragedy of Mary's father, John Barton, a radical Chartist and assassin. Yet as Catherine Gallagher points out, in the battle of generic conventions underway in this text, domestic fiction (and by extension, the domestic heroine) emerges triumphant.[53] And this is a traditional domesticity: the dramatic interest of the novel springs from various assaults on Mary's purity and her own and others' heroic efforts to expunge from her consciousness any taint of guilty sexual or political knowledge. The price of this protection, which enables Mary to function ethically and socially as an insulated middle-class subject, is the assumption of knowledge and experience, or 'sin', by another woman, her mysterious Aunt Esther, who serves as the girl's secret guardian throughout the story.

Mary Barton opens with the disappearance of Esther from the relatively stable domestic world of the Barton household. John Barton, prophesying her eventual ruin, has just reprimanded his strong-willed sister-in-law for 'stopping out when honest women are in their beds', asserting 'you'll be a street-walker, Esther'.[54] The plot of the novel unfolds to fulfil this prediction, yet it is both Esther and John Barton who alienate themselves from the domestic sphere represented by Mary and her mother. Barton, radicalised through economic hardship and working-class politics, drifts into an underworld of secret societies, union agitation, and class warfare, forsaking home and family in pursuit of social justice. He acts not as an 'honest man' but as a conspirator and assassin. Esther, on the other hand, estranged from a traditional sexual role through her economic independence and work in the factories, inadvertently relinquishes the protection of family and home when she becomes the mistress of a soldier. She loses her status as a 'true woman' along with her 'honour,' denigrating into meretricious display and sexual self-abandonment. The criminal and the prostitute, to quote Peter Brooks, here jointly emblematise the 'deviant body' of Victorian culture, 'the maximal, most daring social deviance' imaginable in nineteenth-century England.[55] The homology between John and Esther's fates is made utterly clear by the conclusion of *Mary Barton*: Both die, physically broken and dehumanised, and their final resting place in a common grave 'without name, or initial, or date' (p.463) to mark their passing.

Barton and Esther, the most flamboyant characters in *Mary Barton*, flaunt their disaffection with the order of things – he rejects a system of political representation that recognises workers only in the form of caricature, while she rebels against a standard of feminine conduct that rewards only self-abnegation. Consequently, the two are driven underground: leading subterranean existences, they become silent and thoroughly ineffectual watchers of society they can neither destroy nor support. The bitter knowledge each possesses proves utterly devastating to the possessor. Mary Barton's ignorance is valorised by the novel, but it can only be protected by the heroine's removal from the England that produced her father and her aunt. Even so, the dangerous wisdom these outcasts import into the represented frame of the novel cannot be so easily dispelled. Esther's role, in particular, is to provide a contrasting definition against which Gaskell strives to describe the female philanthropist's activities as a watcher and intermediary.

The prostitute is unequivocally marked as a sinner for Gaskell – more than unwomanly, less than human – and described as one of the 'obscene things of night' (p.275). The streetwalker seemingly breeds only infection and contamination: 'hers is the leper-sin, and all stand aloof dreading to be counted unclean' (p.185). By nature shut out of the domestic space of the family dwelling (in the final stages of consumption, Esther lingers outside the windows of the Barton home, gazing in wistfully upon Mary and her fiancé, Jem Wilson), the prostitute's only alternative to the inhospitable streets are the carceral 'homes' of the workhouse or prison. Perpetually subject to charges of 'disorderly vagrancy', the hapless streetwalker temporarily shelters in entries and on doorsteps, liminal zones of residential buildings, until driven by hunger or cold to return to the streets. She explains to the uncomprehending Jem: 'do you think one sunk so low as I am has a home? Decent, good people have homes. We have none. No; if you want me, come at night, and look at the corners of the streets about here. The colder, the bleaker, the more stormy the night, the more certain you will be to find me' (p. 193).

Despite her misery and her bitterness, Esther refuses Jem's pleas to return to the domestic haven she has left behind: 'I tell you, I cannot. I could not lead a virtuous life if I would' (p. 192). Gaskell was well acquainted with the low success rate of reclamation campaigns for prostitutes; only a small percentage of the women she visited in prison were actually 'reformed' through placement in group homes or emigration. Social patronage of 'fallen women', like designs for model low-income housing or hostels for young female factory workers, was entirely dependent upon the willing co-operation of those being helped. Writing to Samuel A. Steinthal with regard to one such housing scheme, Gaskell expressed reservations:

> It requires that the factory girls should themselves be conscious of wants of a high kind . . . *before* they consent to enter the place where these advantages are offered, but where [other] certain liberties and licenses are denied them, [of] liberties & licenses . . . which they [recognise the (*sic*)] set above the higher privileges offered to them in a 'home'. . . . They leave home (in general) because some home regulation is distasteful to them . . . the other causes for such a step would unfit them for being inmates of a 'Home'.[56]

Gaskell tacitly acknowledges the dilemma facing such women between the economic hardship and physical dangers of street life on the one hand and the oppressiveness of disciplinary regimes, whether in the family or an institutional 'home', on the other. Esther's fear of the lock-up (she suffers hallucinations and withdrawal symptoms for a month in the New Bailey jail) mirrors the terror of a family like the impoverished Davenports, who are threatened with internment in a Poor Law Union workhouse. Neither 'home' is designed to attract new inmates.

In other words, independence, no matter how high the cost, was preferable to the illusory comforts of this sort of 'home'. Victorian prostitutes often preferred the discomfort and risks of streetwalking to the uncertain prospect of entering a protected house or brothel. Streetwalkers retained greater freedom in contracting for rooms with lodging-house keepers, according to historian Judith Walkowitz, than they could in an organised establishment such as those inhabited by 'dress-lodgers'.[57] Being outside these oppressive 'houses' afforded the streetwalker some fraction of self-determination in pursuing her livelihood. With passage of the Contagious Diseases Acts of 1864 and 1866, establishment of venereal disease 'lock-hospitals', and escalating debate over 'the criminalisation of street-soliciting', the streetwalker's distrust of institutions and her reliance on collective action with her fellow sex-trade workers was confirmed, as was her sense of identity as an outcast from both her own class and society in general.[58]

Esther's plight, like that of many Victorian streetwalkers, resonated – however distantly – with middle-class women who abandoned the safe (if cloying) confines of private domesticity writ small for the uncertainty of public domesticity writ large. Gaskell clearly was of two minds when it came to weighing the benefits and the disadvantages of quitting one for the other. 'To be shut out of home is the worst fate in this novel', declares Hilary Schor; it 'may be variously cold, dark, or cheerless, but it is home'.[59] Yet to be an outcast or 'disorderly vagrant' is to enjoy a paradoxical freedom of movement in the urban landscape. In a dark parody of Walter Benjamin's *flâneur*, Gaskell's streetwalker is a detached observer of city life, interested in protecting only one other dweller there – her niece – from the degradations she herself endures. Esther's 'fallen' status allows her to go anywhere, to observe anything, as if she were invisible or immune to the restrictions ordinarily placed upon her sex. Acting as a private investigator, Esther provides the clues and information that establish Barton's guilt and guard Mary's innocence. The narrator remarks that 'in her wild night wanderings, she had noted the haunts and habits of many a one who little thought of a watcher in the poor forsaken woman' (p. 185). Although Esther is denied entrance (except through subterfuge) into any but the lowest dwelling, she is acutely aware of the doings of her former friends and neighbours.

Gaskell's cautionary tale, while designed ostensibly to warn, thus informed her female readers of the intricate social mapping of Manchester's city streets. The streetwalker, much like the middle-class district visitor Gaskell later wrote about and herself became, enjoyed unparalleled access to the social geography of the city, seeing and hearing every aspect of human life in her nightly perambulations, no matter how forbidden or dangerous. The prostitute was able to accomplish most of the things middle-class social workers did, in terms of observing and noting the habits of the poor, yet she moved through this terrain with a claim to special knowledge unrivalled by visitors from outside the slums.

Gaskell's streetwalker struggles to do more than passively observe in her role as invisible 'watcher'; she actively attempts to intervene in the respectable world that has rejected her as 'fallen'. Moreover, Esther acts to influence events in the novel, first by soliciting the assistance of Barton in saving Mary's honour, and later, bent on the same mission, in apprehending Jem Wilson on a lonely street corner. Esther is shown performing a traditional 'feminine' task – practising moral suasion over men in the manner prescribed by domestic ideologues – in a striking inversion of her anti-domestic role in society. Although Esther uses her painfully won power of mobility to serve the very sphere of society that has disowned her, her special form of 'solicitation' is possible only in the streets: she perversely reinvents feminine influence to encompass seduction, culpability, and carnal experience, all ostensibly beyond the domestic sphere.

Unfortunately, Esther's unique perspective, while unfettered by domestic conventions, is nearly impossible to communicate or to enforce. John Barton's response to her street-corner pleas is to fling her 'trembling, sinking, fainting from him' and to stride away without heeding her words (pp. 144–45). If Gaskell uses the streetwalker's Cassandra-like quandary to explore the failures of feminine advocacy, her narrator resists the urge to move through urban space as Esther does. Despite her perpetual disclaimers with regard to her own authority, Gaskell's narratorial perspective is more extensive and varied than that of the streetwalker/observer. Able to draw back at a distance from her subject, Gaskell's narrator alternates between intensive examination of individual actions – detailed scrutiny of particular people and places – and a more comprehensive gaze seemingly capable of taking in the mass of working-class humanity and explaining it to Victorian readers in universal terms. Drawn to identify with the pathos of Esther's impotent testimonials, Gaskell ultimately resists the temptation to merge the prostitute's point of view with that of the clearly vulnerable narrator, preserving the latter's power of superordinate vision at the expense of such an identification.

From her initial dramatic presentation of the fire at Carson's mill, complete with heroic rescues, before an eager audience of breathless, sympathetic workers, to her description of the benighted Chartist march through the thickly populated avenues of London, Gaskell's narrator – through her all-encompassing perspective – possesses the power to rise above city streets and represent them as the only public forum accessible to the working classes in the novel. As such, Gaskell exploits the theatrical potential of her crowd scenes, orchestrating them to assert her own theories about the 'mob' so feared by the middle classes: 'the people rise up to life; they irritate us, they terrify us, and we become their enemies. Then in the sorrowful moment of our triumphant power, their eyes gaze on us with mute reproach. Why have we made them what they are; a powerful monster, yet without the inner means for peace and happiness?' (p. 199). Gaskell flatters her middle-class readers by granting them 'triumphant power', while expecting them to feel and to answer the workers' 'mute reproach'. 'The actions of the uneducated seem to me typified', the narrator explicitly declares, 'in those of Frankenstein, that monster of many human qualities, ungifted with a soul' (p. 199). Confounding the creator with his creature, Gaskell speaks directly here (literally as 'me') to the 'masters' on behalf of their erring 'men'. Shuttling back and forth between the particular and the general – from John Barton, 'a Chartist, a Communist', to the maddened mob, 'all that is commonly called wild and visionary' (p. 199) – Gaskell's narrator is torn between two modes of observation or perception.

As stage manager of all these crowd scenes, Gaskell confirms Asa Briggs's observation that Manchester was the mid-Victorian urban 'theatre of contrasts' par excellence. *Mary Barton* is carefully structured around a series of contrasts or theatrical moments: quasi-allegorical encounters punctuate the text at crucial plot structures. Street life furnishes Gaskell's characters (and readers) with lessons in charity, tolerance, and even political economy. Set-piece passages such as the journey of John Barton and Wilson through the most squalid courts and alleyways of Manchester to the cellar slum-dwelling of the destitute Davenport family, have encouraged critics to assert Gaskell's own disgust with the urban environment she recreated in her novels. Enid Duthie's critique of the 'claustrophobic world' of the workers assumes that such an alien place could only feel 'naturally uncongenial' to Gaskell; the contrast 'between the Davenports' miserable cellar and lighted, well-filled shops' nearby, rather than an unrelenting catalogue of filth and despair, suggests Angus Easson, makes the urban setting of Manchester ideally suited to Gaskell's didactic purposes as a novelist.[60]

If the image of Frankenstein's monster establishes one means of representing the mass of people in the public realm, Gaskell also employs the countertechnique of isolating individual characters in surreal street encounters that emphasise the author's moral design in the novel. En route to his clandestine task as political executioner, Barton stumbles upon a lost boy, whom he guides home to a grateful Irish family. The encounter stimulates memories of Barton's own dead son and excites in him sensations of pity, yet it fails to prevent him from carrying out his murderous resolve against the masters.

Likewise, when Mary encounters a starving Italian child in 'the busy, desolate crowded street' (p. 269), she rouses herself only momentarily from her personal cares to share what little food she has with the urchin. The act of charity briefly diverts her 'from the thought of her own grief', but Mary's good deed seems futile, leaving her despair essentially untouched.

These momentary encounters suggest that personal charity is unmotivated save by impulse and unrelated to any real social change. Yet Gaskell uses them to prepare the reader for a third street scene. Carson, the vengeful millowner intent on punishing his son's murderer and the class that produced such a man, witnesses an act of unintentional violence in the roadway. A 'rough, rude errand boy' accidentally tramples a middle-class girl, whose outraged nurse collars and berates the boy, threatening to summon the police. Carson observes the struggle, amazed to see the injured 'fairy-child' urge her nurse to release the boy: 'he did not mean to do it. *He did not know what he was doing*' (p. 434). The incident proves deeply affecting for Carson, who remembers these words in conjunction with John Barton's crime and eventually overcomes his bitterness to forgive his son's murderer.

Gaskell uses these allegorical moments to construct a moral framework for the narrative that is marked specifically as transcendent. That is, by offering her readers otherworldly interpretative strategies through the medium of allegory, Gaskell situates her narrator on a plane higher than the localised and experiential one occupied by the streetwalker. In the third encounter, the reader is trained to interpret the urban landscape as a form of morality play directed by a persuasive, gently didactic narrator. Asa Briggs has characterised the industrial fiction writers of the 1840s and 1850s as 'social explorers'. Gaskell takes on the responsibility of an urban 'explorer' when she translates her findings into a discourse legible to middle-class readers. Yet she also aspired to a truly universal readership. Intelligent people of every class consulted Gaskell's novel as a guide or hand-book, a veritable social map of the new urban culture in Manchester; '*Mary Barton* was read by the cotton operatives also – they clubbed together to buy it –' Asa Briggs notes, 'because it helped them to realise "the heights as well as the depths" of their nature'. Nothing less than an emissary to the rest of England, Gaskell represented 'an acute and sympathetic outsider' who strove to interpret what was new and dangerous and thrilling about 'Cottonopolis' to her readers.

Gaskell's allegory of the streets was structured to teach middle-class readers, particularly Londoners, how to 'read' northern industrial life. *Mary Barton* also aspired to translate the experience of urban poverty into a humanistic language that would reflect working-class life through the lens of middle-class morality back to the workers it purported to represent. In addition, it was meant to speak to potential female intermediaries of class conflict who might learn from the novel's example how to avoid the pitfalls of over-involvement, impotent observation, and personal loss of reputation suffered by the streetwalker as a 'body double' for the female philanthropist.

The chief problem the narrator of *Mary Barton* has with persuasion is that it is obviously linked to sexual experience, not social exploration, through the most 'acute and sympathetic outsider' in the novel, the prostitute Esther, known colloquially as 'the Butterfly'. (For all her flitting from street corner to street corner, Esther as 'Butterfly' is never simply a 'bearer of the word', to recall Margaret Homans's influential work on domestic realism.) There is too much continuity between Esther's powers and the prerogative assumed by the narrator of *Mary Barton*. In offering to guide readers through the labyrinth of working-class Manchester, for example, Gaskell's narrator speaks as urgently to her audience as Esther does to the male characters in *Mary Barton*. Critics have reacted with much the same mixture of confusion and dismay to Gaskell's imploring narrator as Jem and Barton do to Esther's hysterical appeals.[61] Stephen Gill, for instance, complains about 'bewildering shifts of voice where Mrs Gaskell interpolates a comment or addresses her audience direct'.[62] Gaskell, like Esther, seeks in her address to persuade a disinterested auditor, and both work to guide the auditor's sympathies into new channels. Thus the writer inevitably courts being discounted as 'false' or fallen woman, literally incapable – as Esther is said to be – of conveying truth to others. Indeed, Gaskell comes close to taking on the role of outcast in allying herself with this most common form of female public appearance, at moments seeming to erase distinctions between a woman who walks the streets – Esther's 'wild night wanderings' – and one who traverses them under the cover of urban social work. Both the night visitor, Mrs Wightman, and the prostitute can be accused of 'stopping out', in John Barton's words, 'when honest women are in their beds'. Rather than accept the rhetorical conflation of 'criminal, prostitute, mother', however, as Hilary Schor asks us to do in understanding the woman novelist's problematic authority in mid-Victorian England, it is crucial to recognise the separation the novel itself enforces between women who walk the streets for money and women who walk the streets for the sake of charitable causes.[63]

Esther's presence, no matter how powerful, is rendered insignificant by her failure to interact with others in the proper manner, place, or time (she is incapable, for instance, of entering a court of law, working instead for justice in the dark byways of the city). So too, the language Esther speaks and the literary discourse she mobilises in the novel is strictly limited. 'Gaskell isolates melodrama and romance as the specific genres of prostitution and fallenness', observes Amanda Anderson: 'Esther is a ghost from another genre'.[64] Regarding the prostitute as a peculiarly 'literary' figure, Anderson proposes that Esther's primary role is 'to allegorise literary reformism'. Gaskell feared that the seductions of reading could come to substitute for the proper, active exercise of sympathy through charity. She thus approaches prostitution as a melodramatic construct, a form of romance representing only one of several competing genres in *Mary Barton*. As a genre, melodrama reinforces and rewards quietism in its audience. But Gaskell employs sympathy to rouse her readers to action. The narrator therefore positions herself not with the prostitute Esther, the suffering subject of melodrama, but with the ambulatory observer capable of standing outside, deciphering and transmitting 'the wild romances' of working-class lives as a call to reform the world that produces such tales (p. 70). Gaskell wrote in 1859 to her sister-in-law, Nancy Robson, 'I don't call the use of words *action*: unless there is some definite, distinct, practical *course of action* logically proposed by those words'.[65] Her experiments in genre underscore a fine gradation between words that lead to action and words that do not; clearly she preferred those that ended in deeds, even if she undercut her own stated purpose as a writer by creating conflicted, hybrid plots composed in equal parts of reportage-like realism and melodrama.

Using two separate but closely linked forms of solicitation, Gaskell aligns Esther's powers of observation with melodrama while she identifies her narrator's with social investigation. We might plausibly ask why Gaskell chose to combine two such incompatible modes of representation or address. Does not the dilution of industrial fiction with melodramatic excess, which is never given a chance to succeed in the novel, weaken her call to action, her charge to potential philanthropists? Esther may fleetingly take on the trappings of respectability, but she will never be able to disguise, disavow, or explicate her 'crimes'. *Mary Barton* forcefully reinstates a system of difference among women by endorsing the narrator's beseeching anonymity and compassionate objectivity as the true stance of social realism while purging the narrative of a melodramatic strain of feminine power and persuasion represented by the streetwalker. Esther dies a wretched death at the end of the novel, in plain sight, as it were, of domestic bliss. [. . .] [T]his system of difference among women was often organised through an aggressive campaign against masculine intervention in philanthropy. Esther's form of observation is brought down by her polluting contact with the world of men. So too, melodrama appears to be a representational mode Gaskell may have associated with victimised women pleading their causes before powerful men. As much as she disapproved of this form of suasion, however, Gaskell was not about to drop it from her representational repertoire. Instead, she incorporated melodramatic appeals into the larger structure of *Mary Barton*. Gaskell both needed Esther and needed to dispense with her. It was this local use of 'melodramatic tactics',[66] the introduction and eventual disposal of the 'Butterfly's' story, I would contend, that enabled women such as Mrs Wightman to walk through city streets at night without fear, confident in their new identity as female social workers. Mapping urban space through the twinned perspectives of an all-too-experienced Esther and a self-doubting neophyte of a narrator, as well as the formal fusion of melodrama and social realism, Gaskell began her literary career with a voice and a perspective that was bound to be equivocal.[67] □

The last and longest extract in this chapter is Linda K. Hughes and Michael Lund's analysis of the relationship between serial publication and erotic pleasure. Their analysis is impressive for the way in which it combines the new historicist interest in reclaiming contexts – in this case, the circumstances of *North and South*'s serial publication – with feminist theory of woman's sexuality. The essay returns to what is becoming a favourite subject for critics in the 1990s, Gaskell's fraught relationship with Dickens during the publication of *North and South* in *Household Words*. The extracts that discuss this issue all suggest the different and divergent ways the power relationship between the two authors can be read. Hughes and Lund offer an alternative reading that, ambitiously, attempts to change the way we think about all serial publication and urges us to consider the literary struggle between Gaskell and Dickens in terms of the reader of Gaskell's fiction.

Not K.

■ While best known as a medium for male authors, the serial novel's intrinsic form more closely approximates female than male models of pleasure. Rather than inviting sustained arousal of attention until the narrative climax is reached, spending the driving energy of narrative and sundering the readers from the textual experience, the instalment novel offers itself as a site of pleasure that is taken up and discharged only to be taken up again (some days or weeks later), and again, and again. Moreover, the engagement and discharge of pleasure in each instalment is always oriented toward the future, toward new beginnings and sustained connections with the text, since an instalment ends but the narrative continues, 'to be continued' until the novel's serial run concludes. Finally, this rhythm of textual pleasure is not entirely controlled by serial readers; no matter how much they might want to sustain interest and pleasure in the text, they must wait until the next instalment is scheduled to appear.

Considerations of serial publication have traditionally discounted the extended time frame and periodic structure it imposed on the narrative. Modern studies of reading place great emphasis on narrative endings, resolutions that retrospectively validate patterns throughout a text. Thus, critical assessments of serial texts have generally downplayed the experience of first readers who spent months without an ending to authorise response. Yet instalment literature and extended reading times dominated nineteenth-century literary experience, not just in England, but in America, France, Russia, and elsewhere. Instalment readers enjoyed the parts of Dickens's *Pickwick Papers* (March 1836 to November 1837) and Gaskell's *North and South* (2 September 1854 to 27 January 1855) for the many months they received instalments without endings. The crucially authoritative texts today, however, are the volume editions in which the hesitations, speculations, reversals, and surprises of the serial text are lost in a form retrospectively defined from the point of closure.

The preference for volume editions and whole texts is, however, related to a traditional, masculinist critical paradigm. Susan Winnett argues that male sexual experience has provided the pattern for contemporary critical models of pleasure in reading. Many narrative plots do rise in tension, peak, and return to equilibrium. Winnett notes, however, that such a definition of plot structure encourages the interpretation of 'a particular action in the light of what it *will have meant* at a future moment that it is simultaneously determining and resisting'.[68] Furthermore, other, generally unexplored aspects of plot involve excitement that does not end in quiescence, arousals that look forward as beginnings and are not dependent on later endings or resolutions. Winnett explains that experiences of tumescence or detumescence associated with female sexuality – pregnancy and breast feeding – are ultimately oriented not toward re-establishing the state of quiescence that preceded arousal (as in male sexuality) but toward inaugurating and sustaining new beginnings and connections. Moreover, the rhythm of female tumescence/detumescence is partly controlled by forces and an individual (the nursing child) outside the mother. Winnett concludes that new models of plot and pleasure need to be constructed: 'I want to explore the different narrative logic – and the very different possibilities of pleasure – that emerge when issues such as incipience, repetition, and closure are reconceived in terms of an experience (not *the* experience) of a female body'.[69]

The serial has traditionally been viewed, then, as an inferior artistic form that fractures or impedes unified plots driving toward endings that confer meaning on entire novels. More recently it has been shown to be an expression of capitalist practices that appropriate storytelling and intimate audience relations to mask rationalised production of text and the creation of additional demand for the product.[70]

We suggest that the serial form also can be reconceptualised in relation to feminine issues, especially the material and cultural conditions of Victorian women readers, and feminist theoretical paradigms. Though the financial control of serial publication rested with Victorian men,[71] the prevalence of women as readers and writers of fiction played a significant role in the serial's popularity. In this sense the serial can be said to 'have it all', since it does not subvert dominant economic structures or aesthetic paradigms but nonetheless can offer particular pleasure to women readers.[72] This can be so for serials written by male and female writers alike, but it will be instructive to look at the principal unit of the serial – the part – to see how major writers' conceptions of part structure are manifested along gender lines.

Though women were a major presence among novelists in the first third of the century, and though some prominent women (for example Harriet Martineau) emphatically rejected serialisation as a suitable medium for fiction, women's entry into the literary market as mass readers and popular writers and the emergence of serial fiction as a dominant publication mode in the nineteenth century can be seen as related phenomena.[73] So great was the association of novels with female authorship that, as Gaye Tuchman and Nina Fortin discovered in examining the Macmillan publishing archives, 'in the 1860s and 1870s men submitting fiction were more likely to assume a female name than women were to use either a male or neuter name'.[74] And male serial authors regularly inscribed the expectation of female readership even when subject matter might seem to dictate male readership.[75] Women readers and writers, then, dominated the fiction market when serial publication flourished, and cultural conditions as well as models of female pleasure on the lines Winnett suggests could have fostered women's pleasure in the serial form.

Victorian and twentieth-century commentators have often noted the sense of intimacy and connection serial publication created between audience and text, or audience and author. This result of serial publication, besides helping to perpetuate Victorian domestic ideology, could have worked to extend female readers' associations of pleasure with renewed and sustained relationships, as they met and came to know characters in part after part over as much as a two-year period.[76] And at least one serial female novelist has recorded that her own close relation to the audience affected her production of text. Mary Elizabeth Braddon revamped the ending of her adaptation of Flaubert's *Madame Bovary* because in the process of writing she found herself 'so apt to be influenced by little scraps of newspaper criticism, & by what people say to me'.[77]

The intimacy encouraged between text and audience by serial publication could have suited women readers on additional grounds.

Recently Mary Field Belensky and others have argued that women
best respond to what the authors term 'connected knowing', learning
in which women develop a relationship to what they study and integrate material with their lived experience to construct personally
empowering knowledge. Belensky *et al* do not suggest that men are
excluded or fail to profit from this kind of learning process but only
that women resist being forced into other learning models, for
example those requiring them to consider material as separate and
autonomous, subject to impersonal procedures.[78] Serial publication
fostered a similarly 'connected' relation of readers to fiction, since, as
we argue elsewhere, 'readers and reviewers engaged in provisional
assumptions and interpretations about the literary world, which then
shaped the evolving understanding of works as they continued to
unfold part by part. And a work's extended duration meant that serials
could become entwined with readers' own sense of lived experience
and passing time'.[79] Because authoritative pronouncements were not
available on a work of fiction in progress, moreover, serial fiction
offered women – even within the confines of dominant male social
structures – a space in which to explore and discover their own
reactions to a literary work.

The material format of the serial was also adapted to the material
conditions of middle-class female readers. Though the issuing of fiction in parts has sometimes been related to increasing pressures on
time and leisure in the male-dominated commercial world of Victorian
society, female lives were also defined by their vulnerability to interruption. In *Cassandra*, Florence Nightingale has given perhaps the
most famous statement of this condition:

> Women are never supposed to have any occupation of sufficient
> importance *not* to be interrupted, except 'suckling their fools'; and
> women themselves have accepted this, have written books to sup-
> port it, and have trained themselves so as to consider whatever
> they do as *not* of such value to the world or to others, but that they
> can throw it up at the first 'claim of social life'. They have accus-
> tomed themselves to consider intellectual occupation as a merely
> selfish amusement, which it is their 'duty' to give up for every
> trifler more selfish than themselves.[80]

If this condition held for the single, upper-middle-class Nightingale,
married women and mothers of small children, even with the help of
servants, could hardly have immersed themselves all day long in a
novel. Conduct books nonetheless encouraged women to maintain
reading programs. Isabella Beeton urged that the 'mistress of the
house' save time late in the morning for, among other things, 'the

pleasures of literature'; regarding domestic evenings, Beeton stated, 'it has often been remarked . . . that nothing is more delightful to the feminine members of a family, than the reading aloud of some good standard work or amusing publication'.[81] Short stories, of course, could have responded to the demand for reading in restricted units of time, but short stories feature the gathering and dispersal of narrative energy in a single burst rather than the slowly accreting and intimate form of the serial novel – itself a form defined by its interruptions in the text.

The periodicity of the serial narrative could also have functioned to make such literary work congenial to women while not excluding or marginalising male readers. The scheduled release of literary parts should bring to mind the monthly scheduling of a female bodily activity also not subject to willed intentions, menses. As a nineteenth-century American physician at Harvard remarked, 'periodicity characterises the female organisation, and develops feminine force. Persistence characterises the male organisation, and develops masculine force'.[82] The serial novel, which incorporated periodicity as well as persistence, may have been an ideal mass-market strategy not only because it was attuned to capitalism and gender ideology but also because it presented structures attuned to actual female experience in an era when women were major consumers of literature. Of course, novels appeared in weekly, biweekly, and bimonthly instalments as well as in monthly parts, but the cyclic periodicity that typifies serial fiction differs significantly from the model of the whole volume and should remind us that periodicity suppressed in critical discourse has an analogue in the biological periodicity that was an important part of every Victorian woman's life – an experience outside the confines of accepted social or literary discourse in the Victorian age.[83]

Serial fiction did not serve, and most likely could not have served, as a medium for what today is called *écriture féminine*, but the form did, in certain instances, allow women authors to inscribe the female body in the silent spaces between numbers that answered to the silencing of female experience in the larger culture. In *Daniel Deronda* George Eliot (who practised some form of birth control while living in extralegal union with George Lewes) raised the possibility of unwanted pregnancy for Gwendolen after Grandcourt's death in the novel's book 7, published August 1876. Serial readers had to wait a full month, until book 8 was published in September 1876, to learn this crucial element of Gwendolen's fate. For women readers this month-long interval could have gestured toward bodily functions signalling pregnancy or menses so familiar as not to require verbal articulation.

Though not as striking as in *Daniel Deronda*, Elizabeth Gaskell also made use of the interval between parts to indicate female bodily change and the introduction of physiological cycles. Between the first and second parts of *Wives and Daughters* (published from August 1864 to January 1866 in the monthly *Cornhill Magazine*), Molly Gibson underwent puberty. A young girl of twelve in the first part (August 1864), Molly was a postpubescent young woman of seventeen who attracted sexual attention in the second instalment (September 1864). Gaskell used the space between parts to indicate a change that may be said always to occur offstage, but one that is dramatic and certain nonetheless. By calling attention to this physical change in a young girl's body at the same time she omitted to narrate it, Gaskell exemplifies Elaine Showalter's point that a female subculture emerged from a whole array of physical experience, 'increasingly secretive and ritualised', that was shared but could not be openly articulated.[84] The inherent periodicity and silent spaces between parts that characterised serial fiction could have enabled women writers and readers to indicate and recognise female bodily experiences that were not permitted direct articulation.

Although the serial may not be a form of *écriture féminine*, many of the distinctive features of serial fiction are analogous or even homologous with models of feminine narrative developed by a number of theorists and critics.[85] As Hélène Cixous remarks in 'Sorties', if a woman 'is a whole, it is a whole made up of parts that are wholes, not simple, partial objects but varied entirety, moving and boundless change, a cosmos where eros never stops travelling'; similarly, a woman's 'writing also can only go on and on, without ever inscribing or distinguishing contours . . . she goes on and on infinitely'.[86] Estelle Jelinek has advanced a comparable argument about the structuring of feminine, as opposed to masculine, autobiographies. Feminine autobiographies, she proposes, tend to be irregular and fragmentary, 'organised into self-sustained units rather than connecting chapters', thus mirroring the 'pattern of diffusion and diversity' in women's social (and socially constructed) lives.[87] A serial novel is itself a whole made up of parts that at once function as self-contained units and as building blocks of a larger aesthetic structure. Though the serial eventually ends and takes its place within the literary establishment as an entire, completed work awaiting interpretation and judgement, the long middle of a serial form approximates in significant terms the patterns identified by Cixous and Jelinek. Indeed, as Margaret Beetham remarks of the periodical genre as a whole:

> 'Closed' or 'masculine' forms are seen as those which assert the dominant structures of meaning, by closing off alternative options and offering the reader or viewer only one way of making sense of the text and so, by analogy, of the world and the self. By contrast

the 'open' form, the form which refuses the closed ending and allows for the possibility of alternative meanings, is associated with the potentially disruptive, the creative, the 'feminine'.[88]

She terms the periodical 'a potentially creative form for its readers', though noting as well that the regular issue and format in the periodical implicitly position readers in social groups and in given vantage points.[89]

Many patriarchal terms used to describe the female rather than male body have been used to describe the serial novel as well. As Rachel Du Plessis and others remark, masculine terms are often those used to describe 'good writing' – 'lean, dry, terse, powerful, strong, spare, linear, focused, explosive' – versus the feminine terms often associated with 'bad writing': 'soft, moist, blurred, padded, irregular, going around in circles'.[90] The serial has often been censured for padding, digression, and irregularity, all evoked in Henry James's famous term for Victorian novels, 'baggy monsters'. It is precisely the bag, however, that Ursula Le Guin advances as a preferred, feminist model of narrative in her 'Carrier Bag Theory of Fiction'. She repudiates the notion that 'the proper shape of the narrative is . . . the arrow or spear, starting here and going straight there and THOK! hitting its mark (which drops dead)'. Instead, she proposes that 'the natural, proper, fitting shape of the novel might be that of a sack, a bag'. In this model of narrative, conflict is only one of many possible elements in shaping plot, not *the* determinant, since the purpose of 'narrative conceived as carrier/belly/box . . . is neither resolution nor stasis but continuing process'. She argues that her own plots are 'full of beginnings without ends, of initiations, of losses, of transformations and translations'.[91] Le Guin's terms can also be usefully applied to serial fiction, to stories that depend on beginnings that end only provisionally, at the end of a part, before the narrative is further transformed in additional parts.[92]

Yet even if, from material, cultural, and theoretical vantage points, serial fiction has particular relevance to female readers, the serial form did not subvert or exclude dominant male experience or ideology; an individual instalment, viewed as an independent entity, was both an apt commercial product and a single instance of aroused and discharged interest and textual pleasure. And, of course, the name most closely associated with the serial form was that of a male: Charles Dickens. Tuchman suggests that the history of nineteenth-century fiction can be viewed as a story of the displacement (by men) of women as authors and the elevating of the aesthetic prestige of the novel. Although she focuses on the customary volume editions rather than serial novels, Tuchman's account of the prevalence and then decline of women novelists in the publishing industry roughly coincides with the heyday and decline of serial fiction. Citing 1840–79 (when serialisation also flourished) as the period in which women dominated the submission and acceptance of novels, Tuchman argues that 1880–99 marked the redefinition of the novel, when the number of submissions and acceptances was distributed evenly between men and women, whereas men dominated submissions and acceptances between 1900 and 1917 – the latter period, we argue, also a time when modernist aesthetics caused the serial to decline as a preferred form for 'high' literary art.[93] Tuchman's detailed research on Macmillan's publishing archives may suggest as well, then, that the serial form was a particularly congenial medium for women writers and readers. Indeed, she notes that when the aesthetic paradigm shifted to the shorter, 'high art' novel in the 1890s, women were either unwilling or unable to abandon the long form of the novel that flourished in mid-century.[94]

Two traditional accounts of serial composition and response – one success story and one apparent failure, the former masculine and the latter feminine – serve to illustrate further how certain concepts of plot have shaped critical understanding of serial form and neglected important elements of literary experience. The rocketing sales of Charles Dickens's *Pickwick Papers* after the fifth monthly number in July 1836 (from 400 to 40,000) represent the achievement of genius as his narrative captured the first genuine mass audience for literature. The pattern of this development, from slow start to later explosion, has dominated our understanding of this particular text and of literary history in the nineteenth century. However, the sustained appeal of *Pickwick* through the remaining fourteen months of its publication needs additional exploration; and here the sources for prolonged reading pleasure suggest different dynamics, one perhaps more accessible in the fiction of a Dickens contemporary.

Elizabeth Gaskell serialised *North and South* in Dickens's weekly *Household Words* (2 September 1854 to 27 January 1855). But she and Dickens disagreed about what constituted proper and effective structure for individual instalments.[95] This battle about editorial policy involved different narrative aims and rival assumptions about readers' pleasure. While Dickens wanted each part to be self-contained – with a clear climax and resolution – Gaskell wanted a more leisurely pace for the development of plot and the entanglement of her audience.

North and South was not the first serial fiction Gaskell published under Dickens's editorship. 'Lizzie Leigh', a story serialised in three parts in *Household Words*, opened the inaugural number of the magazine on 30 March 1850. Each part of 'Lizzie Leigh' was certainly self-contained. The story's subtitle is 'In Four Chapters', and the first and second parts 'contained' one chapter each. The first part, moreover, ended on a distinct note of suspense. Anne Leigh, whose husband James dies at the beginning of the part, rents out the farm and moves the family of two sons to Manchester to look for their 'fallen' sister Lizzie; Will, the eldest, has fallen in love with Susan Palmer and feels inhibited in his courtship by his mother's quest to reclaim Lizzie. The part ends with him poised to encounter his mother. But if the part ends on a note of suspense, it looks forward, not to an event or action, but to a conversation, a relationship, between a mother and her son. It is easy to see why this part construction might satisfy both the editor Dickens and the author Gaskell. The ending of the second part is not skewed toward suspense, since the ending of this part coincides with the end of a revelatory conversation between Mrs. Leigh and Susan Palmer, during which Mrs. Leigh learns that Susan's 'niece' is the daughter of Lizzie. Yet because Mrs. Leigh has yet to encounter her daughter, the part also looks forward to a final part, and a final meeting, suggested by the story's title. In this short serial, then, Gaskell maintained a balance between 'connectedness' and suspense, self-containment and anticipation, as forms of narrative pleasure; and Dickens was pleased enough to solicit more work from her for his periodical.

The successful serialisation of *Cranford* in *Household Words* owed much to its special character as a series of related tales and to the fact that, as Winifred Gérin writes, Gaskell was able to write for once 'under no professional or personal pressures'.[96] This work has long been a favourite among Gaskell's readers, and Dickens's major concern was to secure additional parts for *Household Words*. Were it not for the novel's rich, quiet humour and engaging characters, an editor's delight with it might be surprising, for this work is an unusually clear instance of 'arousal' and 'desire' in plot emerging in patterns contrary to traditional concepts. The first four instalments presented assorted vignettes of life in Cranford but neglected a sustained 'rising action'; rather than a forward-driving plot, the four parts appearing from 13 December 1851 to 3 April 1852 invited renewed and deepening acquaintance with a community. There followed a nine-month hiatus in *Cranford*'s publication;[97] when it resumed in the 8 and 15 January 1853 issues of *Household Words*, the fifth part quickened with an advancing plot and concluded on a note of suspense as the still-unnamed narrator wondered if the Aga Jenkyns could be Matty Jenkyns's lost brother Peter. Thereafter *Cranford* became in large part Matty's story, with a clearly advancing plot, until the work concluded in the 21 May 1853 issue. Yet even here, as readers later discovered, *Cranford* had not reached a definitive climax that cut off the text from author and audience, for a separate sketch entitled 'The Cage at

Cranford' appeared in the November 1863 *All the Year Round*. In 1853 and 1854, meantime, *Cranford* pleased Gaskell, Dickens, and the readers of *Household Words*. Some parts of *Cranford* manifested the suspense and rising action traditionally associated with Dickens's own parts structure; but in other respects the novel's larger plot, serial issue, and parts structure resembled the model of narrative pleasure offered by Winnett and others. The publication of Gaskell's next serial work, however, revealed conflicting ideas about literature and its pleasures.

When Dickens first reviewed the manuscript of *North and South*, he praised its 'character and power' and noted especially 'a strong suspended interest in it (the end of which, I don't in the least foresee)'. However, Dickens's advice about the work's serialisation was presented in absolute terms: 'let me endeavour to shew you as distinctly as I can, the divisions in which it must fall'.[98] In an outline, he presented what he thought should be the first six instalments; each entry began with the phrase 'I would end No. [ ] with . . .', showing his concern that each part have an effective conclusion. In another letter Dickens also insisted, 'I believe you are aware that it will at least be necessary to begin every weekly portion as a new chapter'.[99] Although Dickens summarised the content of three of the proposed first six instalments, he identified the last event to be narrated in every case. Thus, the rhythm of reading, as it was shaped by the sense of each part's beginning in a precise place and coming to a felt conclusion, may have been more important to Dickens as editor than what element of the narrative's subject should be presented by the author every week. Dickens also stated unequivocally that 'if it were divided in any other way – reference being always had to the weekly space available for the purpose in *Household Words* – it would be mortally injured'.[100] Dickens, of course, was the magazine's editor; but he seemed to assume that Gaskell was unable to conceive on her own of an appropriate division into parts.[101]

Dickens's plan for the novel rearranged some of Gaskell's material; and his efforts almost always were directed at creating self-sufficient units with powerful conclusions.[102] He even offered to take over the matter of parts structure completely, including 'sometimes' writing 'a word or two of conclusion' for the author. Even as he admits, 'I hope these remarks will not confuse you', Dickens's letter ends with additional stress on the absolute necessity of turning the parts structure over to him as editor: 'I am bound to put before you my perfect conviction that if I did not [follow this pattern], the story would be wasted – would miss its effect as it went on – *and would not recover it when published complete*' (Dickens's emphasis).[103] For Dickens, the entire life of this novel through all its editions would be a product of the rhythm of its first appearance, a rhythm he was intent on controlling.

The entire plot of *North and South* reveals important distinctions from traditionally conceived (masculinist) plots. The opening number hardly contained within itself the germ of its resolution. The first two chapters, in fact, were so carefully crafted that they constitute a brilliant, complete short story. It is also difficult to argue that the novel's end point determined or conferred sole meaning on this beginning when there was no hint of the removal to Milton or of John Thornton. And after even the first five parts of the novel had appeared, so astute a reader as Charlotte Brontë thought the novel was to focus on religious doubt.[104] This discontinuity between beginning and end has been one basis for censuring the novel, but if we recur to Cixous's or Le Guin's notions of transformations and ongoing process, or Winnett's model, in which narrative arousal can occur at unforeseen (and even arbitrary) moments, this larger narrative shape is less disturbing.

The shape of an individual part could also, in Gaskell's hands, diverge from Dickens's emphasis on 'strong suspended interest' or from the traditional, linear emphasis on event. Interest in the affective lives of characters, more than in events' outcomes, often characterises individual parts of *North and South*. The twelfth part, for instance, takes the shape of 'woman's work' as identified by Margaret Hale in that instalment: 'if I saved one blow, one cruel, angry action that might otherwise have been committed, I did a woman's work'.[105] The part opens when tension during the strike has built to a point of impending explosion, and the thrust of the narrative seems to be toward explosive violence. But the tension building toward a cataclysmic event is deflected into the connectedness of a courtship plot instead. When workers threaten Thornton, Margaret throws her arms about him and is the one wounded (not seriously, as it turns out) rather than John. This protective action then initiates the forward movement of the courtship plot, and the part ends looking ahead, not to another explosive event but to the developing relationship of Margaret and John. In this instalment, too, then, Gaskell 'saves a blow', prevents an 'angry action', and focuses on 'woman's work' of nurturing and affection instead.[106]

The divergence between Dickens's and Gaskell's notions of serial publication, however, is most evident in the major textual variant between the serial version, over which Dickens exercised some authority, and the volume edition, which Gaskell could superintend with less external interference. The volume edition differed from the serial *North and South* primarily in its conclusion, where the final four chapters were expanded by Gaskell to make eight. Most of this addition involved a return visit paid by the heroine Margaret Hale from England's industrial North to her old home in the country's rural

South. The life of her father's old friend, Mr. Bell, is nicely extended (he had died suddenly in the serial text) so that he can accompany her on the trip. But what was kept out of the narrative by Dickens and *Household Words* was not so much event as commentary and reflection.[107]

The entire novel of *North and South* had progressed through a series of stages in understanding as different or opposing perspectives clashed: North against South, Church of England against Methodism, men against women, worker against employer, servant against mistress. Each instalment, then, constituted a debate from different positions: capital versus labour, wealth versus poverty, age versus youth, old versus new, agriculture versus industry. And the completion of every number generally represented a new moderation of views, as characters (and readers) slowly but steadily moved closer to shared values.[108]

The expanded conclusion was needed less to complete a sequence of action than to provide one more stage in the dialectical evolution toward a new, transforming perspective.[109] In the expanded last chapters Margaret sees the limits of her past life against the promises of a new. And the most memorable passages from the new text involved more time devoted to acknowledging and coming to terms with contraries. Margaret, for instance, recognises that even in 'timeless' old England, represented by her native village of Helstone, 'there was change everywhere; slight, yet pervading all' (p.481). She admits to continual change within herself as well: 'and I too change perpetually – now this, now that – now disappointed and peevish because all is not exactly as I had pictured it, and now suddenly discovering that the reality is far more beautiful than I had imagined it' (p.489). One of the most frequently cited passages from Gaskell's revision is Margaret's long meditation after Mr. Bell's death, the passage that concluded chapter 48 in the volume edition. The heroine uses this occasion to moderate her estimate of life's opportunities: 'on some such night as this she remembered promising to herself to live as brave and noble a life as any heroine she had ever read or heard of in romance . . . And now she had learnt that not only to will, but also to pray, was a necessary condition in the truly heroic' (p.502). Such balancing of opposed principles, such extended description of a character's relation to her environment and circumstances, were important enough to Gaskell's novel that they figured prominently in her revisions of the serial text.

In her own account of composition and serialisation, Elizabeth Gaskell felt the need to extend both the time of her own work on the novel and the length of the story's natural form.[110] In January 1855 she complained to her friend Anna Jameson of not having 'happy leisure hours' for her own work, and she insisted that, if 'the story had been poured just warm out of the mind, it would have taken a much larger mould'. She wrote to Anna Jameson late in the process of composition that the

> story is huddled and hurried up . . . But what could I do? Every page was grudged me, just at last, when I did certainly infringe all the bounds & limits they set me as to quantity. Just at the very last I was compelled to desperate compression. But now I am not sure if, when the barrier gives way between two such characters as Mr. Thornton and Margaret it would not go all smash in a moment.[111]

However, Gaskell also seemed to accept Dickens's judgement about the necessities of magazine publication and to admit to her own inability to work within this mode. She wrote, for instance: 'I have tried to shorten & compress [the 20 January 1855 instalment] . . . but, there were [sic] a whole catalogue of events to be got over . . . but, *if you will keep the MS for me, & shorten it as you think best for HW*, I shall be very glad. Shortened I see it must be'.[112] Later letters and comments show that Gaskell resented, even if she could not escape, the magazine's shaping of her novel.[113] The ways in which her own structuring of *North and South* attempted to avoid sharp divisions of plot into chapters and instalments suggest that Gaskell felt the pleasure of reading a text derived from more than engaging well-constructed parts. She faced similar pressures to compress material in her masterpiece, *Wives and Daughters*, serialised in the monthly *Cornhill*. However, the instalment shape of all Gaskell's serial fiction derives from fundamental patterns of narrative that complement and expand traditional, masculinist formulations.

A final element of *North and South* deserves attention in an exploration of sexual and textual pleasure in the serial form, one that has often been censured in critical estimates: the novel's eroticism. Beginning with part 12, when Margaret casts her arms about John Thornton, a pattern of erotic tension begins to develop and is sustained until the novel's final pages, when it is released in the couple's second embrace that mirrors the first: 'he gently disengaged her hands from her face, and laid her arms as they had once before been placed to protect him from the rioters' (pp.529–30). From the moment John is first touched by Margaret he becomes intensely aware of her physical presence and returns again and again to the memory of their embrace:

> Mr. Thornton remained in the dining-room, trying to think of the business he had to do at the police-office, and in reality thinking of Margaret. Everything seemed dim and vague beyond – behind – besides the touch of her arms around his neck – the soft clinging which made the dark colour come and go in his cheek as he thought of it. (p.244; see also p.274)

Yet because Margaret spurns with stinging words his marriage proposal offered the next day, Thornton thereafter combines apparent indifference to Margaret's presence with intense erotic awareness: '[Margaret] fancied that, from her being on a low seat at first, and now standing behind her father, he had overlooked her in his haste. As if he did not feel the consciousness of her presence all over, though his eyes had never rested on her!' (p.276). Margaret eventually realises she has fallen in love with Thornton, but a number of obstacles prevent their union until the final page: Thornton's mistaking Margaret's brother Frederick for her lover, Margaret's lie to the police to protect Frederick, the hurt Margaret and John inflict on each other by their forthright (if not ingenuous) comments, and more. This strand of the novel is a familiar one: it is the erotic plot that characterises romance fiction.

The eroticism in romance fiction, as in Gaskell's work, consists of the feminine desire of being desired, and the impetus toward, yet prohibition of, desire for a male erotic figure. This structure prolongs and intensifies erotic arousal, making desire, more than its release, the focal point. It is of course a model of desire predicated on cultural norms for middle-class women. If they are encouraged to attract an erotic partner and to form intimate emotional bonds made possible in part by the postponement of sexual activity, they are also prohibited from directly expressing their own desire for a heterosexual partner. Such a structure suggests male control of female sexuality to ensure paternity but also a feminine quest for emotional security and protection from abandonment.

This Victorian pattern has persisted into twentieth-century romance fiction, as Janice Radway makes clear in a study based on interviews with readers of the genre. According to these readers, Radway explains, the middle of a romance narrative 'must create some form of conflict to keep the romantic pair apart until the proper moment[;] many authors settle for misunderstanding or distrust as the cause of the intermediary delay of the couple's happy union'. The heroine should be 'strong' or 'fiery', and possessed of 'intelligence, a sense of humour, and independence'. The romance hero should be 'strong and masculine, but equally capable of unusual tenderness, gentleness, and concern for [the heroine's] pleasure'.[114] The plot of the romance must above all be developmental and filled with anticipation, traits linked by Radway to the form's eroticism:

> [Readers] want to identify with the heroine . . . The point of the experience is the sense of exquisite tension, anticipation, and excitement created within the reader as she imagines the possible resolution and consequences for a woman of an encounter with a

member of the opposite sex. . . . In all their comments about the nature of the romance, the Smithton women placed heavy emphasis on the importance of development in the romance's portrayal of love. [Thus,] [i]t matters little whether that care and attention [from the hero] are detailed in general terms or presented as overtly sexual as long as they are extensively described. However, this focus on his attention to her is itself erotic, for even the most euphemistic descriptions of the heroine's reception of his regard convey the sensual, corporal pleasure she feels in anticipating, encouraging, and finally accepting those attentions of a hero who is always depicted as magnetic, powerful, and physically pleasing.

Though scholars offer varied reasons for romance readers' attraction to this genre, most agree that the eroticism it offers is defined by 'waiting, anticipation, anxiety'.[115]

The features of waiting, anticipating, and postponing fulfilment are also salient features of serial fiction. The serial might be said to further prolong the duration of desire; and, since this prolongation is identified as a central feature of romance fiction, the prolonged narrative of the serial form may lead to erotic intensification in a feminine economy of desire. In the case of *North and South*, serial issue, moreover, could have allowed erotic tension to fade in the intervals between parts only to revive and extend its duration with each succeeding part.[116] Winnett's narrative model is again relevant here, especially her reminder that female arousal can occur at any time during the sexual act and can resurface again and again and again. Margaret remarks in part 19, when she realises she loves Thornton, 'it [her love for him] has come upon me little by little, and I don't know where it began' (p.401). The frequently expressed impatience with Gaskell's deflection of an industrial novel plot into a romance plot is a shrewd critique from the vantage point of political strategies and concerns, but it may also be useful to assess this narrative structure in terms of feminine sexuality and patterns of pleasure.

Serial publication by male and female authors in the Victorian age could 'have it all' in its ability to integrate female and male structures of experience. Readers could have the pleasure of each instalment read as a satisfying unit, with the bound whole volume always the final product of the publication process. Or readers could, without threatening the status quo, enjoy a serial text's pleasure by having all the parts over the months of publication, thus making of reading a prospective and ever-renewed experience until the end was reached long after the text began. This was so even when women read fiction by the age's best-known male authors, such as Dickens. But their pleasure in serial fiction could have been heightened in instalments by writers like Elizabeth Gaskell, whose handling of individual parts suggests approaches to plot that lie outside traditional, masculinist norms of textual pleasure, and whose distinctive strategies in a given part remind us why serial publication as a whole may have been a pleasure to its female readers.[117] □

NOTES

INTRODUCTION

1 J.A.V. Chapple and Arthur Pollard, eds., *The Letters of Mrs Gaskell* (Manchester: Manchester University Press, 1966), p.116. Citations from this edition will be denoted *Letters*.

2 Angus Easson, ed., *Elizabeth Gaskell: The Critical Heritage* (London: Routledge, 1991), p.203. Subsequent references will be cited as *Critical Heritage*.

3 *Critical Heritage*, p.202.

4 Five of these are collected in Jenny Uglow, ed., *Curious, If True: Strange Tales by Mrs Gaskell* (London: Virago, 1995). In her Introduction, Uglow notes: 'the basis of her art is realistic, displaying an acute observation of domestic detail and a marvellous ear for dialogue – from Manchester tenements to Paris salons – but in all her work, from time to time, realism gives way to fantasy. A darker side emerges, a writer fascinated by the alien, the Other' (p.vii).

5 Macdonald Daly, introduction to *Mary Barton* (Harmondsworth: Penguin, 1996), p.xxvii.

6 Raymond Williams, *The English Novel from Dickens to Hardy* (London: The Hogarth Press, 1984 [1970]), pp.9–11. See chapter three of this Guide for a fuller discussion of Williams, including his approach to Gaskell's fiction. For an emphasis upon the response of women writers to the social conditions of the 1840s, see particularly Joseph Kestner, *Protest and Reform: The British Social Narrative by Women 1827–1867* (Madison, Wisconsin: The University of Wisconsin Press, 1985), Chapter 3, and Rosemarie Bodenheimer, *The Politics of Story in Victorian Fiction* (Ithaca: Cornell University Press, 1988).

7 Kate Flint suggests a direct comparison between the Chartists and Gaskell: 'Manchester became a centre for the Chartist activity, when the workers, frustrated by their political powerlessness, sought redress through attempting to redefine the terms of parliamentary representation. Gaskell's own early fiction, in particular, can be linked to this desire for public representation, since it sets out to give a voice to the otherwise silent, whether the mill-worker or the unmarried working-class mother'. See *Elizabeth Gaskell* (Plymouth: Northcote House, 1995), p.4.

8 Thomas Carlyle, *Chartism*, second edition (London: Chapman and Hall, 1842 [1839]), p.1.

9 Thomas Carlyle, *Past and Present* (London: Chapman and Hall, 1889 [1843]), pp.1–2.

10 Frederick Engels, *The Condition of the Working Class in England from Personal Observation and Authentic Sources*, with an introduction by Eric Hobsbawm (Frogmore, Herts: Panther, 1969), pp.78–9. The first authorised translation into English was published in 1887 in New York.

11 For an analysis that suggestively picks up Gaskell's use of the word 'elbowed', see Deborah Epstein Nord, 'Elbowed in the Streets: Exposure and Authority in Gaskell's Urban Fictions', in *Walking the Victorian Streets: Women, Representation, and the City* (Ithaca: Cornell University Press, 1995).

12 In Chapter 2 of *The Literature of Change: Studies in the Nineteenth-Century Provincial Novel* (Sussex: Harvester Press, 1977), Lucas compares the representations of Manchester offered by Engels with *Mary Barton*. See my discussion of Lucas in chapter three of this Guide.

13 Engels, *Condition of the Working Class*, pp.84–5.

14 Ibid., pp.86–7.

15 *Ruth* and *The Life of Charlotte Brontë* also caused her pain. Gaskell, on the publication of *Ruth*, states: 'how I shrink with more pain than I can tell you from what people are saying, though I wd do every jot of it over again to-morrow. "Deep regret" is what my friends here . . . feel & express. In short the only comparison I can find for myself is to St

Sebastian tied to a tree to be shot at with arrows' (letter to Anne Robson, January 1853; *Critical Heritage*, p.202). On the problems she encountered with the publication of her biography, see Deirdre D'Albertis, '"Bookmaking Out the Remains of the Dead": Elizabeth Gaskell's *The Life of Charlotte Brontë*', *Victorian Studies* 39.1 (Autumn 1995), pp.1–31. For further discussion of Gaskell's biography, see Gabriele Helms, 'The Coincidence of Biography and Autobiography: Elizabeth Gaskell's *Life of Charlotte Brontë*', *Biography: An Interdisciplinary Quarterly* 18.4 (Fall 1995), pp.339–59; and Juliet R.V. Barker, 'Saintliness, Treason and Plot: The Writing of Mrs Gaskell's *Life of Charlotte Brontë*', *Brontë Society Transactions* 21.4 (1994), pp.101–15.

16 Gaskell to Eliza Fox, 26 April 1850; *Letters*, p.113.

17 Winifred Gérin, *Elizabeth Gaskell* (Oxford: Oxford University Press, 1980 [1976]), p.261.

18 Hilary M. Schor, 'Elizabeth Gaskell: A Critical History and a Critical Revision,' *Dickens Studies Annual* 19, pp.345–69 (p.349).

19 Virginia Woolf, 'Mrs Gaskell', in Michèle Barrett, ed., *Virginia Woolf on Women and Writing* (London: The Women's Press, 1979), p.145. The essay was first published in 1910.

20 Schor, 'Elizabeth Gaskell', p.349.

21 Ibid., p.350.

22 Ibid., p.345.

23 Patsy Stoneman begins her study with a useful analysis of Gaskell criticism; see *Elizabeth Gaskell* (Brighton: Harvester, 1987). Arthur Pollard also begins his monograph with a review of the history of Gaskell criticism in *Mrs Gaskell: Novelist and Biographer* (Manchester: Manchester University Press, 1965).

24 Deanna L. Davis, 'Feminist Critics and Literary Mothers: Daughters Reading Elizabeth Gaskell', *Signs* 1992, pp.507–32 (p.507).

CHAPTER ONE

1 Elizabeth Gaskell to Catherine Winkworth, 23 December 1848; *Letters*, p.66.

2 Writing to her publisher Edward Chapman on 10 July 1848, Gaskell is puzzled by his suggestion that a Preface should be written: 'the only thing I should like to make clear is that it is no catch-penny run up since the events on the Continent have directed public attention to the consideration of the state of affairs between the Employers, & their work-place' (*Letters*, p.58).

3 See Gérin, p.90. Julia Swindells notes: 'Gaskell's nervousness about writing, about publication and about the critical process, is characteristic of an existence on the periphery of the production process'. See *Victorian Writing and Working Women: The Other Side of Silence* (Cambridge: Polity Press, 1985), p.109.

4 ?Late 1848; *Letters*, p.67.

5 December 1848; ibid., p.64.

6 Perhaps the best known of Gaskell's flights from the publication of her novels is her stay in Italy while the controversy over her biography of Charlotte Brontë raged in Britain, unknown to the author. For a discussion of Gaskell's influences, and change of emphases, in the process of writing *North and South*, see Catherine Barnes Stevenson, '"What Must Not be Said": *North and South* and the Problem of Women's Work', *Victorian Literature and Culture* 19 (1991), pp.67–84; and Jerome Meckier, *Hidden Rivalries in Victorian Fiction: Dickens, Realism, and Revaluation* (Lexington, Kentucky: The University Press of Kentucky, 1987).

7 January 1855; *Letters*, p.329.

8 While Gaskell and some early critical response to her fiction (especially posthumous revaluations) stress the book's very personal genesis from Gaskell's grief, this does not necessarily mean the novel is so personal as to be autobiographical. It is important to recall the many literary influences that shaped the narrative, and which later critics

note, such as those of Disraeli, Carlyle and Harriet Martineau.

9 23 December 1848; *Critical Heritage*, p.84.

10 Ibid., p.85

11 Hilary M. Schor points out that this is what Sandra Gilbert and Susan Gubar term a 'cover story': a vehicle for paradoxically attaining authority through feigning ignorance. See *Scheherezade in the Marketplace: Elizabeth Gaskell and the Victorian Novel* (Oxford: Oxford University Press, 1992), pp.21–2.

12 Probably the death at nine months of her son William in August 1845. [William was born on 23 October 1844 and died on 10 August 1845. Some critics give his age at his death as nine months, others as ten months.]

13 No such text has survived.

14 Christ draws a moral from the widow contributing two mites to the treasury in Mark 12:41–44.

15 Gaskell's father had, in fact, written expressly on the subject, and she was also familiar with her Unitarian friend Harriet Martineau's famous *Illustrations of Political Economy* (9 vols., London: Charles Fox, 1834), whose 'A Manchester Strike' is clearly a major influence on *Mary Barton*. Her disavowal of Political Economy is perhaps intended to forestall criticism of her novel's lack of practical prescriptions for tackling the 'unhappy state of things' it delineates. For a highly readable account of the year, see Raymond Postgate, *The Story of a Year: 1848* (London: Cassell, 1955).

16 The European revolutions of 1848 in France, Austria and Italy. Britain and Ireland, however, were hardly free of disturbances.

17 Elizabeth Gaskell, *Mary Barton: A Tale of Manchester Life*, ed. by Macdonald Daly (Harmondsworth: Penguin, 1996), pp.3–4.

18 For an introduction to realism, see Damian Grant, *Realism* (London: Methuen, 1970).

19 For more on Victorian gender ideology of female creativity, see Nancy Armstrong, *Desire and Domestic Fiction: A*

Political History of the Novel (Oxford: Oxford University Press, 1987); Mary Poovey, *Uneven Developments: The Ideological Work of Gender in Mid-Victorian England* (Chicago: University of Chicago Press, 1988); and Elizabeth Langland, *Nobody's Angels: Middle-Class Women and Domestic Ideology in Victorian Culture* (Ithaca, New York: Cornell University Press, 1995). Elaine Showalter, in *A Literature of Their Own: British Women Novelists from Brontë to Lessing* (Princeton, New Jersey: Princeton University Press, 1977) argues that women's novels from 1820 to 1880 largely imitated and internalised the dominant patriarchal norms. She terms this period the 'Feminine' phase of British women's writing. While a hugely oversimplistic analysis, and a rather blinkered dismissal of their potential for subversion, Showalter's study is important because of its emphasis upon the difficulties – personal, literary, economic, cultural, political – that women faced in this period when they chose to write fiction. See in particular Chapter 2.

20 For more on feminine narrative, see for example Barbara Leah Harman, *The Feminine Political Novel in Victorian England* (Charlottesville: The University Press of Virginia, 1998), an extract from which is given in chapter five of this Guide, and Showalter.

21 Unsigned review, the *Examiner*, 4 November 1848, pp.706–9; *Critical Heritage*, p.68.

22 8 November 1848; ibid., p.72.

23 Maria Edgeworth to Mary Holland, 17 December 1848; ibid., p.89.

24 Ibid., p.65.

25 4 November 1848; ibid., p.69.

26 9 March 1849; ibid., p.150.

27 Ibid., p.132.

28 ?Late 1848; *Letters*, p.67.

29 29 May 1849; *Critical Heritage*, p.85.

30 1 February 1849; ibid., p.113.

31 Ibid., pp.104–6.

32 28 February 1849; ibid., p.121. See *Critical Heritage*, pp.128–30 for a reply to the hostile review by D. Winstanley, and the editor's response.

33 April 1849; ibid., p.176. Greg was a family friend of the Gaskells. See Gaskell's response to his comments in a letter to his wife, in *Letters*, pp.73–4.

34 21 October 1848; *Critical Heritage*, pp.62–3.

35 15 November 1848; ibid., p.77.

36 The best and most accessible edition of Elizabeth Barrett Browning's *Aurora Leigh* is edited by Margaret Reynolds (New York: Norton, 1996).

37 13 December 1850; *Critical Heritage*, pp.187–8.

38 Gaskell was influenced in this, as in other aspects of her writing, by Carlyle. See *Critical Heritage*, p.71.

39 *Letters*, p.70.

40 ?Early 1849; ibid., p.74.

41 1 January 1849; ibid., p.68.

42 *Prospective Review*, 1 February 1849; *Critical Heritage*, pp.139, 142.

43 See, for example, the comments of William Ellis and Mary Turner Ellis, who argue that a solution is for the next generation to implement (ibid., p.156).

44 27 December 1848; ibid., pp.89, 90.

45 In a letter to Mary Holland, Edgeworth suggests that she would have concluded the plot by allowing Jem to stay and overcome people's suspicions with his good character (ibid., p.90).

46 Early 1849; ibid., p.89. Lucas points out that this is Gaskell at her most accurate and realistic: Manchester had an exceptionally high mortality rate and the average age of death among the working class was seventeen (*The Literature of Change*, p.42). Compare Gaskell's comment to Dickens about *North and South*: 'I think a better title than N.&S. would have been "Death and Variations". There are 5 deaths, each beautifully suited to the character of the individual' (?17 December 1854; *Letters*, p.324).

47 *Critical Heritage*, pp.90–1.

48 Hilary M. Schor, 'Elizabeth Gaskell', p.350.

49 Pollard, p.108.

50 Swindells, p.111.

51 13 April 1853; cited in Gérin, p.142.

52 3 May 1853, ibid., p.142.

53 See Elizabeth Gaskell to John Forster, 23 February 1854; *Letters*, p.281.

54 24 [25?] December 1854; ibid., p.325.

55 Ibid., pp.330–1.

56 ?17 December 1854; ibid., p.323.

57 January 1855; ibid., pp.328–9.

58 *North and South*, p.3.

59 Cited in Gérin, p.153.

60 Ibid., p.126.

61 14 April 1855; *Critical Heritage*, p.335.

62 Ibid., p.336.

63 7 April 1855; ibid., pp.331–2.

64 30 September 1854; ibid., p.330.

65 Ibid., pp.346–7.

66 October 1855; ibid., p.353.

67 For two excellent discussions of how the oppositions work in *North and South*, see Schor, *Sheherezade in the Marketplace*, Chapter 4, and Deirdre D'Albertis, *Dissembling Fictions: Elizabeth Gaskell and the Victorian Social Text* (London: Macmillan, 1997), passim.

68 14 April 1855; *Critical Heritage*, p.333.

69 14 April 1855; ibid., p.337.

CHAPTER TWO

1 Elizabeth Gaskell to an unknown addressee, 4 June ?1865 (*Letters*, p.761). This letter illustrates Gaskell's hostility to biographers. Gérin suggests this may be because of the controversy surrounding Gaskell's own biography of Charlotte Brontë (p.vii).

2 For an exploration of culture's fascination with the Brontës, see Patsy Stoneman's *Brontë Transformations: The Cultural Dissemination of 'Jane Eyre' and 'Wuthering Heights'* (London: Harvester Wheatsheaf, 1996). Tricia Lootens offers an account of the nineteenth-century fascination with the persona of the poetess in *Lost Saints: Silence, Gender, and Victorian Literary Canonization* (Charlottesville: The University Press of Virginia, 1996). When the author inhabits criticism in this way, the first casualty is the historical personage. For an account of this process in relation to Christina Rossetti, see Alison Chapman, 'History, Hysteria, Histrionics:

The Biographical Representation of Christina Rossetti', *Victorian Literature and Culture* 24 (forthcoming).

3 *Critical Heritage*, p. 489.

4 Ibid., p. 490.

5 Ibid., p. 495.

6 Ibid., p. 505.

7 For another reviewer uncomfortable with the notion of a woman writer, see the barbed comment of George Barnett Smith in the *Cornhill Magazine*, February 1874: '[Gaskell's] life was one of those which furnish the best evidence that woman is frequently fitted to accomplish greater work than that which is usually assigned to her sex' (*Critical Heritage*, p. 540).

8 *Critical Heritage*, pp. 514–15.

9 Ibid., p. 516.

10 [Charlotte Elizabeth Tonna, known as Charlotte Elizabeth, was an Evangelical writer.]

11 [As we see in chapter one of this Guide, this is not at all the case.]

12 [For an analysis of how this parable echoes throughout *Mary Barton*, see Michael Wheeler, *The Art of Allusion in Victorian Fiction* (London: Macmillan, 1979).]

13 Louis Cazamian, *The Social Novel in England 1830–1850: Dickens, Disraeli, Mrs Gaskell, Kingsley*, trans. Martin Fido (London: Routledge and Kegan Paul, 1973 [1903]), pp. 211–12.

14 Professor Minto's conjecture that *Mary Barton* was suggested by Disraeli's social novels does not seem plausible. Mrs Gaskell's novel was started in the same year as *Coningsby* (1844), and shows no sign of having been influenced by it. The two writers share a common spirit, but it is only that of the interventionist reaction, which was in the air at the time. *Mary Barton* and *Sybil* are alike products of the emotional needs that turned the novel to the social predicament (cf. *Fortnightly Review*, New Series, vol. xxiv [1878]). Nor does Mrs Gaskell ever seem to have owed anything to Dickens; on the contrary, Dickens was indebted to her; many of the characters

and incidents in *Hard Times* (1854) were suggested by *Ruth*.

15 Cazamian, p. 214.

16 Yvonne ffrench, *Mrs Gaskell* (London: Home and Van Thal, 1949), p. 27.

17 Ibid., pp. 22–5.

18 Ibid., p. 27.

19 [This is, of course, because both Charlotte Brontë and George Eliot were established writers before their marriages.]

20 David Cecil, *Victorian Novelists: Essays in Revaluation* (London: Fontana, 1964 [1934]), pp. 154–6.

21 Ibid., p. 157.

22 Ibid., p. 163.

23 Cecil's pronouncements about Gaskell's quiet uneventful life are common in early responses to her death. Edward Dicey, for example, states: 'if you can pardon the paradox, I should say that the most remarkable feature about Mrs. Gaskell's life was that there was so singularly little to be said about it' (*The Nation* 7 December 1865; *Critical Heritage*, p. 519).

24 Gérin, pp. 266–7.

25 Cecil, p. 183.

CHAPTER THREE

1 Preface, *Mary Barton*, p. 3.

2 Carlyle, *Past and Present*, p. 196.

3 F. R. Leavis, *The Great Tradition: George Eliot, Henry James, Joseph Conrad* (London: Oxford University Press, 1948).

4 Cited in *Critical Heritage*, p. 71.

5 From *Past and Present*; cited in *Critical Heritage*, p. 71. For an introduction to Marxist literary criticism, see Terry Eagleton, *Marxism and Literary Criticism* (London: Methuen, 1976).

6 Arnold Kettle, 'The Early Victorian and Social-Problem Novel', in Boris Ford, ed., *The New Pelican Guide to English Literature, vol. 6: From Dickens to Hardy* (Harmondsworth: Penguin 1982 [1958]), pp. 164–81, particularly p. 175.

7 Ibid., p. 173.

8 Ibid., p. 173.

9 Ibid., p. 174.

10 Williams, *The English Novel*, p. 9.

11 Ibid., p. 11.

12 Raymond Williams, *Culture and Society 1780–1950* (New York: Columbia University Press, [1958] 1983).

13 Compare the analysis of David Cecil, cited in the previous chapter, which juxtaposes Gaskell with the critic's norm, in this case male novelists such as Dickens.

14 *North and South*, ch. li, p. 459 (1889 edition).

15 Williams, *Culture and Society*, pp. 87–92.

16 There has been critical controversy surrounding the aptness of these terms. See Kettle, and also John Lucas, 'Mrs Gaskell and Brotherhood', in *Tradition and Tolerance in Nineteenth-Century Fiction: Critical Essays on Some English and American Novels*, ed. David Howard, John Lucas and John Goode (London: Routledge and Kegan Paul, 1966), pp. 142–3.

17 Kathleen Tillotson, *Novels of the Eighteen-Forties* (Oxford: Clarendon Press, 1954), p. 9.

18 Ibid., p. 208.

19 Ibid., p. 202.

20 Ibid., p. 222.

21 Preface to first edition, 1848.

22 Review of *Wives and Daughters* in *The Nation* (22 February 1866), collected in *Notes and Reviews* (Cambridge, Massachusetts, 1921), pp. 154–5.

23 'Libbie Marsh's Three Eras', 'The Sexton's Hero', and 'Christmas Storms and Sunshine', published in that order in vols. i–iii, under the pseudonym 'Cotton Mather Mills'. The Howitts had been her friends for some years, and it was William Howitt who, after seeing the first volume of her novel in manuscript, urged her to continue.

24 *Blackwood's Magazine* (January 1837), pp. 48–50; the heading is 'Sketches among the Poor, No. 1', but no further instalment followed. The authorship was first pointed out by John Mortimer, 'A Lancashire Novelist', *Manchester Quarterly* xxi (1902), p. 205.

25 Draft of letter to Mrs Greg, published in A. W. Ward's introduction to *Mary Barton* (Knutsford edition, vol. i, 1906, pp. lxii–lxiv).

26 Preface to *Mary Barton*, first edition. This does not seem to have survived, though it is possible that it has some relation to *Sylvia's Lovers*.

27 Letter to Mrs Greg.

28 William, the only son, died at the age of ten months in August 1845; and the Preface to *Mary Barton* (dated October 1848) speaks of 'three years ago'. Some writers, following A. W. Ward, have given the year wrongly as 1844; the point is set right by G. D. Sanders, *Elizabeth Gaskell* (Cornell Studies in English, 1929). [See chapter one, note 12, of this Guide.]

29 Her sixth child and fifth daughter was born in September 1846.

30 Not only because of the European revolutions, but also because of the closing of many Lancashire mills owing to the failure of the American cotton crop, and the Chartist meeting in April. The novel was published on 14 October.

31 *Westminster Review* (1849), p. 48.

32 April 1849, pp. 429–32. Other interesting reviews are in the *Athenaeum* (21 October 1848), the *Prospective Review* v (1849), pp. 36–57; and the *North British Review* (August 1851).

33 Greg, author of *The Creed of Christendom* (1851), was himself a mill-owner until 1850. He reviewed *Mary Barton* in the *Edinburgh Review* (April 1849), and reprinted his article in *Mistaken Aims and Attainable Ideals of the Artisan Class* (1876).

34 See *Westminster Review* (April 1849).

35 *Letters addressed to Mrs. Gaskell by Celebrated Contemporaries . . .*, ed. R. D. Waller (Manchester, 1935).

36 William Minto, *Fortnightly Review* (1 September 1878), pp. 353–69.

37 Letter of 30 October 1852; *The Brontës, their Lives, Friendships, and Correspondence*, 4 vols. (Shakespeare Head Brontë, Oxford, 1932), vol. iv, p. 14.

38 *Sybil*, Book II, ch. x.

39 Ch. vi. It is in fact so little detachable that it would not 'tell' in selective quotation or summary.

40 Letter to Mrs Greg, op. cit., p. lxiii.

41 Another is defined only retrospec-

tively; his early attempt to 'live Gospel-wise' and how he 'gave it up in despair, trying to make folks' actions square wi' th' Bible; and I thought I'd no longer labour at following th' Bible myself'. This is related only on his death-bed (ch. xxxv) and the delay is surely part of a deliberate avoidance of emphasis on his turning away from religion.

42 Ch. xv.

43 Presumably Chapman and Hall insisted on this. They also demanded, when the novel was in the press, several extra pages to fill out the second volume (letter to Mrs Greg, op. cit., p.lxiv). These are said, I do not know on what authority, to have been added in chs. xxxiii, xxxiv, and especially in ch. xxxvii (Thomas Seccombe, Introduction to Everyman edition).

44 Ch. xi.

45 [Sylvia Robson is the heroine of Sylvia's Lovers by Elizabeth Gaskell (1863).]

46 'Our readers need not be alarmed at the prospect of penetrating the recesses of Manchester. The king's daughter, washing the linen of the Phæacian palace, is scarcely more unsuggestive of anything like vulgarity, than are these descriptions' (North British Review, August 1951 [sic], p.426).

47 Ch. ii; 'A Manchester tea-party' is the title in the collected edition.

48 Ch. i.

49 Ch. ix.

50 Ch. x.

51 Ch. xxxvii.

52 Ch. xviii.

53 Ch. xxxvii.

54 Henry James, speaking not of this quality but of the completeness of the world in Wives and Daughters (review, 1866; Notes and Reviews, 1921, p.154).

55 Letters of Mrs Gaskell to Charles Eliot Norton (1932), p.20 (letter of 1858).

56 Lucas, 'Mrs Gaskell and Brotherhood' p.141.

57 All quotations come from the first edition, London, 1848.

58 Tillotson, p.202.

59 Vol. 84 (part 3 for 1848).

60 Vol. LI, July 1849.

61 [Parataxis is the placing of clauses, etc. one after the other, without words to indicate coordination or subordination (Oxford English Dictionary).]

62 John Lucas, 'Mrs Gaskell and Brotherhood', pp.161–74. Compare the feminist interest in Gaskell and sisterhood: see in particular Amy K. Levin, The Suppressed Sister: A Relationship in Novels by Nineteenth- and Twentieth-Century British Women (Lewisburg: Bucknell University Press; London: Associated University Press, 1992) and Pauline Nestor, Female Friendships and Communities: Charlotte Brontë, George Eliot, Elizabeth Gaskell (Oxford: Clarendon Press, 1985).

63 Compare Arthur Pollard who refuses to compare Gaskell with Engels's Condition of the Working Classes in England in his analysis of the truth of her representation of Manchester, 'because of the propagandist intention of that work' (p.40).

64 John Lucas, The Literature of Change: Studies in the Nineteenth-Century Provincial Novel (Sussex: Harvester Press, 1977), pp.1–2. A recent critic who takes the realist argument to task is Catherine Barnes Stevenson, who points out that the representation of the Preston strike is crucially inaccurate on one count: it ignores the 55.8 per cent of women factory workers (p.68).

65 Pollard, p.35

66 Ibid., p.61.

67 Ibid., p.47.

68 Carol Lansbury, Elizabeth Gaskell: The Novel of Social Crisis (London: Paul Elek, 1975), p.7.

69 Claud Welch, Protestant Thought in the Nineteenth Century, 2 vols. (New Haven, 1972), vol. 1, p.184.

70 Quoted in Francis E. Mineka, The Dissidence of Dissent (Chapel Hill, 1944), p.19.

71 Quoted in R.K. Webb, Harriet Martineau (New York, 1960), p.65.

72 Thomas Belsham, Memoirs of the late Reverend Theophilus Lindsey M.A. (London, 1873), p.279.

73 [The exception here is, of course, Gaskell herself.]
74 Letter to Mrs Long, April 1850, quoted in Waldo Hilary Dunn, *James Antony Froude* (Oxford, 1961), p.167.
75 Quoted in F.D. Cartwright, ed., *Life and Correspondence of Major Cartwright*, 2 vols. (London, 1826), vol. 1, p.300.
76 Lansbury, pp.11–15.
77 W.A. Craik, *Elizabeth Gaskell and the English Provincial Novel* (London: Methuen, 1975), p.1.
78 Craik, pp.4–5.
79 Showalter, p.84.

CHAPTER FOUR

1 Lord Houghton on the death of Elizabeth Gaskell, the *Pall Mall Gazette*, 14 November 1865; *Critical Heritage*, p.505.
2 For an exploration of the tensions between feminism and new historicism, see Ros Ballaster, 'New Hystericism: Aphra Behn's *Oroonoko*: The Body, the Text and the Feminist Critic', in Isobel Armstrong, ed., *New Feminist Discourses: Critical Essays on Theories and Texts* (London: Routledge, 1992), pp.283–95. See also Katherine Kearns, *Psychoanalysis, Historiography, and Feminist Theory* (Cambridge: Cambridge University Press, 1997).
3 Stoneman, *Elizabeth Gaskell*, p.45.
4 Adrienne Rich, *On Lies, Secrets, and Silence: Selected Prose: 1966–1978* (London: Virago, 1979), p.186.
5 In Nannerl O. Keohane, Michelle Z. Rosaldo and Barbara C. Gelpi, eds, *Feminist Theory: A Critique of Ideology* (Brighton: Harvester, 1982), p.56.
6 *Mary Barton*, ed. Martin Dodsworth (Harmondsworth: Penguin, 1970), p.460.
7 Stoneman, pp.118–20.
8 Terry Lovell, *Consuming Fiction* (London: Verso, 1987), p.74.
9 Lovell, cited and introduced by Schor, 'Elizabeth Gaskell', p.366.
10 Ien Ang, *Watching Dallas* (London and New York, 1985).
11 Williams, *Culture and Society*.
12 Ibid., p.87.

13 Ibid., p.89.
14 Elizabeth Haldane, *Mrs Gaskell and her Friends* (London, 1930), p.47. [This letter is given as an extract in chapter one of this Guide.]
15 Williams, *Culture and Society*, p.88. [See the extract from this letter in chapter one of this Guide.]
16 Lovell, *Consuming Fiction*, pp.86–8.
17 Rosemarie Bodenheimer, *The Politics of Story in Victorian Fiction* (Ithaca: Cornell University Press, 1988), pp.6–7.
18 For a discussion of Gaskell's personal 'endorsement of female communality', especially her friendships with other women writers, see Nestor, *Female Friendships and Communities*, ch. 2.
19 Bodenheimer, p.23. Victorian social paternalism evolves as a response to industrialisation and a rigorous, and cruel, market economy. Paternalists believed the kinship between employer and worker to be both economic and ethical. This kinship rested on a reciprocal relationship between the two classes: the rich would protect the poor in exchange for their deference and duty (ibid., p.21).
20 Ibid., p.60.
21 Ibid., p.55.
22 For Gaskell's comments on *Shirley*, see her letter to Lady Kay-Shuttleworth, 14 May 1850 (*Letters*, p.116).
23 The work of Luce Irigaray on parody and mimicry would be a useful avenue to pursue in the relationship between Gaskell and Dickens. See Luce Irigaray, *Speculum of the Other Woman*, translated by Gillian C. Gill (Ithaca, New York: Cornell University Press, 1985 [1974]) and Toril Moi's cogent discussion of Irigaray and mimicry in *Sexual/Textual Politics: Feminist Literary Theory* (London: Routledge, 1988). Catherine Barnes Stevenson's article contains an excellent section on Dickens and Gaskell's tussles over *North and South* (see the extract in chapter five of this Guide).
24 Meckier, *Hidden Rivalries*, pp.76–7.
25 Gallagher, *Industrial Reformation*, p.xi.
26 *Harriet Martineau's Autobiography*, ed. Marie Weston (Boston, 1877), vol. 1, p.83.

27 Quoted in James Drummond, *The Life and Letters of James Martineau* (New York, 1902), vol. 2, pp. 262–3.

28 Quoted in R.K. Webb, *Harriet Martineau: A Radical Victorian* (New York, 1960), p. 96.

29 Drummond, vol. 2, p. 262.

30 James Martineau, 'The Three States of Unitarian Theology', in *Essays, Reviews, and Addresses* (London: 1891), vol. 4, p. 574.

31 Ibid., vol. 4, p. 574.

32 W. Arthur Boggs, 'Reflections of Unitarians in Mrs Gaskell's Novels' (Dissertation, University of California, Berkeley, 1950), p. 23.

33 Quoted in William Robbins, *The Newman Brothers: An Essay in Comparative Intellectual Biography* (Cambridge, Massachusetts, 1966), p. 152.

34 From Francis Newman, *Four Lectures on the Contrasts of Ancient and Modern History* (1846), quoted in Robbins, *Newman Brothers*, p. 93.

35 Catholic Union, *Essays Toward a Church of the Future as the Organisation of Philanthropy* (London, 1854), p. 13; first published in 1844.

36 *Four Lectures*, p. 93.

37 From *Biographical Memoranda*, by James Martineau, quoted in Drummond, *Life and Letters of James Martineau*, vol. 2, p. 273.

38 Ibid., vol. 2, p. 273.

39 *Letters of Mrs Gaskell*, p. 70.

40 Ibid., p. 74.

41 Ibid. p. 74.

42 *British Quarterly Review*, 9 (1849), p. 128.

43 *Mary Barton: A Tale of Manchester Life*, ed. Stephen Gill (Baltimore, 1976), p. 121.

44 *Letters of Mrs Gaskell*, p. 74.

45 Tillotson, p. 214.

46 Gaskell's description from a letter to Mary Howitt, *Letters*, p. 33. The sketch was published in *Blackwell's Magazine*, 41 (1837), pp. 48–51, under the title 'Sketches among the Poor, No. 1'.

47 *Letters*, p. 74.

48 Tillotson, *Novels of the Eighteen-Forties*, p. 222.

49 Gallagher, *Industrial Reformation*, pp. 62–87.

50 See, in particular, Nancy Chodorow, *The Reproduction of Mothering: Psychoanalysis and the Sociology of Gender* (Berkeley: University of California Press, 1978) and Carol Gilligan, *In a Different Voice: Psychological Theory and Women's Development* (Cambridge, Massachusetts: Harvard University Press, 1982).

51 See Moi.

52 Those interested in Gaskell and motherhood should consult her fascinating diary, recently published in an excellent edition with helpful introductory material. The diary is written about and for her daughter Marianne. See J.A.V. Chapple and Anita Wilson, eds, *Private Voices: The Diaries of Elizabeth Gaskell and Sophia Holland* (Keele, Staffordshire: Keele University Press, 1996). The diary is particularly compelling as a celebration of maternity, a facet of Gaskell's writing that has attracted competing feminist interpretations as either conservative or subversive. On 4 August 1835, Gaskell writes: 'how all a woman's life, at least so it seems to me now, ought to have a reference to the period when she will be fulfilling one of her greatest and highest duties, those of a mother' (p. 53). For a metacritical analysis of motherhood and Gaskell, see the extract from Deanna L. Davis's article in the Introduction. A useful analysis of maternity and the Victorian novel is Matus, *Unstable Bodies*. It is interesting to note Gaskell's perhaps rather mischievous comment to an unknown correspondent, which suggests that her knotty relationship between writing and maternity is neither straightforwardly conservative nor subversive: 'when I had *little* children I do not think I could have written stories, because I should have become too much absorbed in my *fictitious* people to attend to my *real* ones' (*Letters*, pp. 694–5). Compare another contradictory letter to Eliza Fox in February 1850 (*Letters*, pp. 106–7).

53 A.W. Ward, introduction to *Mary*

Barton (1848; reprint, Knutsford Edition, London: Smith and Elder and Co., 1906), vol. 1, pp. xxvii–xxviii. Although I have not been able to trace Ward's source for this story – all Gaskell's letters from the time of William's death to 1847 were destroyed at her wish – it has been accepted as fact by Gaskell's readers.

54 Gaskell gives the epigraph in the original German of J. L. Uhland; the translation is from the Knutsford edition, p. xlix:

> Take, good ferryman, I pray
> Take a triple fare to-day:
> The twain who with me touched
> the strand
> Were visitants from spirit-land.

55 Printed in the introduction to the Knutsford edition, pp. xxvi–xxvii.
56 Gaskell, *Diary*, p. 19.
57 Margaret Homans, *Bearing the Word: Language and Female Experience in Nineteenth-Century Women's Writing* (Chicago: University of Chicago Press, 1986), pp. 223–6.

CHAPTER FIVE

1 See Paul Rabinow, ed., *The Foucault Reader* (London: Penguin, 1986) and Lois McNay, *Foucault: A Critical Introduction* (Cambridge: Polity Press, 1994).
2 These two modes of criticism are epitomised by the different practices of Stephen Greenblatt (see, for example, his *Renaissance Self-Fashioning: From More to Shakespeare* [Chicago: University of Chicago Press, 1980]) and Jerome McGann (see, for example, his *The Beauty of Inflections: Literary Investigations in Historical Method and Theory* [Oxford: Oxford University Press, 1985]). For an introduction to new historicism, see John Brannigan, *New Historicism and Cultural Materialism* (Basingstoke: Macmillan, 1998) and Claire Colebrook, *New Literary Histories: New Historicism and Contemporary Criticism* (Manchester: Manchester University Press, 1997).
3 Schor, *Scheherezade in the Marketplace*, p. 5.

4 Mary Ann O'Farrell, *Telling Complexions: The Nineteenth-Century English Novel and the Blush* (Durham: Duke University Press, 1997), pp. 6–7.
5 Ibid., p. 7.
6 Compare John Kucich's very different approach to the question of lying, impulsiveness and sexual inversion, in his *The Power of Lies: Transgression in Victorian Fiction* (Ithaca: Cornell University Press, 1994), Chapter 3.
7 [O'Farrell is arguing here that bodily signs, such as the blush, are not an index to truth. Body language does not disclose a stable meaning.]
8 O'Farrell, *Telling Complexions*, pp. 67–8.
9 Pierre Macherey, *A Theory of Literary Production*, trans. Geoffrey Wall (London: Routledge and Kegan Paul, 1978), pp. 85, 87. Cited in Stevenson, p. 67.
10 Gallagher, *Industrial Reformation*, pp. 128–9.
11 Elizabeth Gaskell, *North and South* (Harmondsworth: Penguin, 1981), p. 133.
12 J. F. C. Harrison, *The Second Coming: Popular Millenarianism 1780–1850* (New Brunswick: Rutgers University Press, 1979), p. 228.
13 *Letters*, p. 227.
14 Annette B. Hopkins, 'Dickens and Mrs Gaskell', *Huntingdon Library Quarterly* 9 (1945–46), pp. 357–85; Dorothy Collin, 'The Composition of Elizabeth Gaskell's *North and South*', *Bulletin of John Rylands University Library* 54.1 (1971), pp. 67–93.
15 Walter Dexter, *The Letters of Charles Dickens*, 3 vols. (London: Nonesuch, 1958), vol. 2, p. 457.
16 Hopkins, p. 359.
17 Dexter, vol. 2, p. 542.
18 Dexter, vol. 2, p. 561.
19 Dexter, vol. 2, p. 561.
20 Hopkins, p. 371.
21 Collin, p. 81.
22 Dexter, vol. 2, p. 561.
23 Hopkins, p. 370.
24 Anne Lohrli, *Household Words: A Weekly Journal 1850–1859 Conducted by Charles Dickens* (Toronto: University of Toronto Press, 1973), p. 15.
25 Dexter, vol. 2, p. 581. Dickens's con-

cern that Gaskell would ruin his profits seems to have been ill-founded in the long run. William E. Buckler points out: 'it is obvious from the table of profits . . . that *North and South* while it did not equal the success of *Hard Times* maintained the circulation of the journal'. 'Dickens' Success with *Household Words*', *The Dickensian* 46 (June 1950), pp. 197–203 (p. 201).

26 Malcom Andrews, 'A Note on Serialisation', *Reading the Victorian Novel: Detail into Form*, ed. Ian Gregor (New York: Barnes and Noble, 1980), pp. 243–7 (p. 246).

27 Hopkins, p. 374. See also Gerald G. Grubb, 'Dickens' Editorial Methods', *Studies in Philology* 40 (1943), pp. 79–100 (p. 97) and also Gérin, p. 151.

28 Swindells, *Victorian Writing and Working Women*, p. 111.

29 *Letters*, p. 325.

30 Ibid., p. 595.

31 Catherine Winkworth describes Dickens with the diction one might use for a seducer: 'Mr Dickens writes to her praisingly, but he does not please me, and I hope she won't be "wiled by his false flattering tongue" into thinking him true and trustworthy, like Mr Forster'. See J. A. V. Chapple, ed., *Elizabeth Gaskell: A Portrait in Letters* (Manchester: University of Manchester Press, 1980), p. 130.

32 N. N. Feltes, *Modes of Production of Victorian Novels* (Chicago and London: University of Chicago Press, 1986), p. 6.

33 Dorothy Collin, 'The Composition and Publication of Elizabeth Gaskell's *Cranford*', *Bulletin of John Rylands University Library* 69 (1986), p. 60.

34 *Letters*, p. 274.

35 Stevenson, ' "What Must Not be Said" ', pp. 70–5.

36 Harman, *Feminine Political Novel*, p. 52.

37 John Pikoulis, '*North and South*: Varieties of Love and Power', *Yearbook of English Studies* 6 (1976), pp. 176–93 (p. 189 n. 1).

38 *Letters*, 14 May 1850, p. 115; Gaskell

and Brontë had not yet met.

39 Deirdre David, *Fictions of Resolution in Three Victorian Novels: 'North and South', 'Our Mutual Friend' and 'Daniel Deronda'* (Basingstoke: Macmillan, 1981), p. 43.

40 Bodenheimer, *Politics of Story*, p. 66.

41 Charlotte Brontë, *Shirley* (Harmondsworth: Penguin, 1974), pp. 336, 337.

42 T. H. Lister, 'Rights and Conditions of Women', *Edinburgh Review* 73 (1841), pp. 189–209 (p. 204).

43 Elizabeth Gaskell, *Mary Barton* (Harmondsworth: Penguin, 1985), pp. 351–52; further citations will appear in the text.

44 Harman, *Feminine Political Novel*, pp. 63–9.

45 Dorice Williams Elliot, 'The Female Visitor and the Marriage of Classes in Gaskell's *North and South*', *Nineteenth-Century Literature* 49 (1994), pp. 21–49 (p. 33).

46 Anne Summers, 'A Home from Home: Women's Philanthropic Work in the Nineteenth Century', in *Fit Work for Women*, ed. Sandra Burman (New York: St Martin's Press, 1979), pp. 58, 45.

47 For additional proponents of this view, see, for example, Françoise Basch, *Relative Creatures: Victorian Women in Society and the Novel* (New York: Schocken, 1974), p. 250; Judith Lowder Newton, *Women, Power, and Subversion: Social Strategies in British Fiction, 1777–1860* (Athens: University of Georgia Press, 1981), pp. 164, 168; and Stoneman, *Elizabeth Gaskell*, p. 120.

48 Harman, *Feminine Political Novel*, pp. 73–5.

49 Another critic who emphasises the importance of language in Gaskell's fiction, but with a different approach from Schor's, is Terence Wright in *Elizabeth Gaskell: 'We are not angels': Realism, Gender, Values* (Basingstoke: Macmillan, 1995). Compare Coral Lansbury: '[Gaskell's] sense of reality was never translated into a realm of symbolic metaphor. Smoke remained smoke in Manchester' (p. 95). For more on the fallibility of authority see Stoneman, *Elizabeth Gaskell*, pp. 56–64.

50 [Schor has made an error here. It is, of course, Jennings who wears the night-cap.]

51 Schor, *Scheherezade in the Marketplace*, pp. 32–7.

52 For a discussion of Victorian women poets and fallenness, see Angela Leighton, '"Because men made the laws": The Fallen Woman and the Woman Poet', in Angela Leighton, ed., *Victorian Women Poets: A Critical Reader* (Oxford: Blackwell, 1996), pp. 215–34.

53 Gallagher, *Industrial Reformation*, pp. 77–87.

54 Elizabeth Gaskell, *Mary Barton*, ed. Edgar Wright (Oxford: Oxford University Press, 1987), p. 6.

55 Peter Brooks, *Reading for the Plot: Design and Intention in Narrative* (New York: Vintage Books, 1984), p. 158.

56 *Letters*, p. 806.

57 Judith Walkowitz, *Prostitution and Victorian Society: Women, Class, and the State* (Cambridge: Cambridge University Press, 1980). For more on the plight of the dress-lodger, see Mariana Valverde, 'The Love of Finery: Victorian Fashion and the Fallen Woman in Nineteenth-Century Social Discourse', *Victorian Studies* 32 (Winter 1989), pp. 168–88. [A 'dress lodger' was a prostitute fashionably attired who was watched, and possessed, by an older female pimp or brothel keeper (Valverde, p. 180).]

58 Valverde links the 'dress lodger' explicitly to the history of the Contagious Disease Acts (pp. 169–88).

59 Schor, *Scheherezade in the Marketplace*, pp. 31–2.

60 Enid Duthie, *The Themes of Elizabeth Gaskell* (London: Macmillan, 1980), pp. 66, 67; Angus Easson, *Elizabeth Gaskell* (London: Routledge and Kegan Paul, 1979), p. 50.

61 See, for example, the unsigned review of *Mary Barton*, published in *The British Quarterly Review* (1 February 1849), pp. 117–36.

62 Stephen Gill, introduction to *Mary Barton* (Harmondsworth: Penguin, 1970), p. 23.

63 Schor, *Scheherezade in the Marketplace*, p. 39.

64 Amanda Anderson, *Tainted Souls and Painted Faces: The Rhetoric of Fallenness in Victorian Culture* (Ithaca, New York: Cornell University Press, 1993), pp. 110, 116.

65 *Letters*, p. 530.

66 This term is borrowed from Elaine Hadley's *Melodramatic Tactics: Theatricalised Dissent in the English Marketplace, 1800–1855* (Stanford, California: Stanford University Press, 1995).

67 D'Albertis, *Dissembling Fictions*, pp. 50–8.

68 Susan Winnett, 'Coming Unstrung: Women, Men, Narrative, and Principles of Pleasure', *PMLA* 105 (1990), p. 515.

69 Ibid., p. 509.

70 Norman N. Feltes, in *Modes of Production of Victorian Novels* (Chicago: University of Chicago Press, 1986), has provided the fullest assessment of the serial's effect from a Marxist perspective. See also Mary Poovey's chapter on Dickens and the serial in *Uneven Developments*.

71 Gaye Tuchman with Nina E. Fortin, *Edging Women Out: Victorian Novelists, Publishers, and Social Change* (New Haven: Yale University Press, 1989), p. 209.

72 Elaine Showalter proposes a model for gynocentric criticism that never loses sight of the appearance of women's writing within dominant social structures; see 'Feminist Criticism in the Wilderness', in *Writing and Sexual Difference*, ed. Elizabeth Abel (Chicago: University of Chicago Press, 1982), pp. 31–3.

73 For further evidence that women functioned as major forces in the production and consumption of nineteenth-century fiction, see Showalter, *A Literature of Their Own*, pp. 20–1; G. D. Klingopulos, 'The Literary Scene', in *From Dickens to Hardy*, ed. Boris Ford (1958; Harmondsworth: Penguin, 1972), p. 71; Elizabeth K. Helsinger, Robin Lauterbach Sheets, and William Veeder, *The Woman Question: Society and Literature*

in Britain and America, 1837–1883 (3 vols; Chicago: University of Chicago Press, 1983), vol. 3, p. 8; and Tuchman, p. 7.

74 Tuchman, p. 53. By the 1880s this pattern had changed, and women were more likely to use male pseudonyms (Tuchman, p. 54).

75 Thus, Edward Howard paused in the midst of his largely nautical *Life of a Sub-Editor*, serialised in *Metropolitan Magazine* from 1834–1836, to explain the finer points of naval rigging for his female readers.

76 Elizabeth Gaskell's letter to an aspiring woman novelist with young children is usually cited to illustrate women's enforced subordination of personal achievement to domestic responsibility. Yet Gaskell's remarks also suggest that she perceived her relation to fictional characters in much the same way she did her relation to her family: 'when I had *little* children I do not think I could have written stories, because I should have become too much absorbed in my *fictitious* people to attend to my real ones' (*Letters*, pp. 694–5).

77 David Skilton, introduction to *Lady Audley's Secret* by Mary Elizabeth Braddon (Oxford: Oxford University Press, 1987), p. xi.

78 Mary Field Belenky, Blythe McVicker Clinchy, Nancy Rule Goldberger and Jill Mattuck Tarule, *Women's Ways of Knowing: The Development of Self, Voice, and Mind* (New York: Basic Books, 1986).

79 Linda K. Hughes and Michael Lund, *The Victorian Serial* (Charlottesville: University Press of Virginia, 1991), p. 8.

80 Florence Nightingale, *Cassandra* (New York: Feminist Press, 1979), p. 32.

81 Janet Murray, ed., *Strong-Minded Women and Other Lost Voices from 19th Century England* (New York: Pantheon, 1982), pp. 84, 88. For the dilemma of interruption for women writers, see Helsinger, Sheets and Veeder, vol 3, pp. 10, 12; and Dale Spender, *The Writing or the Sex? or Why You Don't Have to Read Women's Writing to Know It's No Good*, Athene Series (New York: Pergamon

Press, 1989), pp. 127–30.

82 Helsinger, Sheets and Veeder, vol. 2, p. 83. The physician was Edward H. Clarke. Dr Clarke's pronouncement is notorious because he went on to argue that women's periodicity, rather than persistence, meant that women were unsuited either for intensive study associated with higher education or for sustained professional work outside the home. Elaine Showalter and English Showalter, in 'Victorian Women and Menstruation', *Suffer and Be Still*, ed. Martha Vicinus (Bloomington: Indiana University Press, 1972), p. 42, as well as Helsinger, Sheets and Veeder (vol. 2, pp. 86–8, 104), record contemporary refutations of this strand of Clarke's argument. Yet the works they cite also assert the periodicity of feminine physiology, though noting that such biological functions did not preclude persistence of intellectual or physical energies.

83 Murray, p. 211; Spender, pp. 113, 117.

84 Showalter, *A Literature of Their Own*, p. 15.

85 We are particularly interested in the analogy between the serial and notions of feminine form as process-oriented and open. However, because the nonverbal spaces between parts are a fundamental part of the form, the serial's enfolding of silence into the text might usefully be examined in relation to the notion of the preverbal (the 'semiotic', according to Julia Kristeva) that has been identified with the feminine in Lacan's and related theorists' work.

86 Hélène Cixous, 'Sorties', in Hélène Cixous and Catherine Clement, *The Newly-Born Woman*, trans. Betsy Wing (Minneapolis: University of Minnesota Press, 1986), pp. 87, 88.

87 Estelle C. Jelinek, 'Introduction: Women's Autobiography and the Male Tradition', in *Women's Autobiography: Essays in Criticism*, ed. Estelle C. Jelinek (Bloomington: Indiana University Press, 1980), p. 17.

88 Margaret Beetham, 'Towards a

Theory of the Periodical as a Publishing Genre', in *Investigating Victorian Journalism*, ed. Laurel Brake, Aled Jones and Lionel Madden (New York: St. Martin's Press, 1990), p.27.

89 Beetham, pp.27–9; see also Poovey, p.104.

90 Mary Eagleton, ed., *Feminist Literary Theory: A Reader* (Oxford: Basil Blackwell, 1986), p.228.

91 Ursula K. Le Guin, 'The Carrier Bag Theory of Fiction', in *Dancing at the Edge of the World* (New York: Grove Press, 1989), pp.169–70.

92 Susan Morgan argues that nineteenth-century British heroines embody the virtues of change and connectedness that may be celebrated in novels but have been 'traditionally undervalued and labelled as feminine'. *Sisters in Time: Imagining Gender in Nineteenth-Century British Fiction* (New York: Oxford University Press, 1989), p.17.

93 Linda K. Hughes and Michael Lund, 'Linear Stories and Circular Visions: The Decline of the Victorian Serial', in *Chaos and Order: Complex Dynamics in Literature and Science*, ed. N. Katherine Hayles (Chicago: University of Chicago Press, 1991), pp.167–94; see also *The Victorian Serial*, pp.229–74.

94 Tuchman, pp.7–8, 188.

95 In *Elizabeth Gaskell*, Coral Lansbury says that serialisation was 'a mode of publication that she detested, scrambling to fit the work into twenty separate numbers, instead of the twenty-two that she insisted Dickens had promised her' (p.36). See also Angus Easson, *Elizabeth Gaskell* (London: Routledge and Kegan Paul, 1979), p.88.

96 Gérin, *Elizabeth Gaskell*, p.124.

97 As Gérin explains, the nine-month hiatus in *Cranford*'s serialisation was most likely occasioned by Gaskell's turning from this story to the composition of *Ruth*, issued as a whole novel in January 1853, after which *Cranford* resumed (p.126).

98 David Paroissien, ed., *Selected Letters of Charles Dickens* (Boston: Twayne, 1985),

p.320.

99 In a letter dated 26 July 1854 that discusses five later instalments, Dickens again explains his idea of parts structure by stressing how each must 'close' (Paroissien, p.322).

100 Ibid., p.320.

101 Dorothy Collin, in 'The Composition of Mrs. Gaskell's *North and South*', notes how Dickens assumed that he, rather than Mrs Gaskell, would take care of the whole question of parts structure. She cites Dickens's 18 February 1854 letter, written before he received any manuscript:

Don't put yourself out at all as to the division of the story into parts. I think you had far better write it in your own way. When we come to get a little of it into type, I have no doubt of being able to make such little suggestions as to breaks of chapters as will carry us over all that easily. (p.70)

102 Collin compares the parts endings proposed by Dickens to the conclusions of instalments actually published, which, presumably, were approved by Mrs Gaskell (pp.89–91). J. Don Vann, in 'Dickens, Charles Lever and Mrs. Gaskell', *Victorian Periodicals Review* 22, 2 (Summer 1989), p.67, explains that Dickens was guided not only by his notion of effective parts structure for fiction but by concern for the overall shape of each issue of *Household Words*.

103 Paroissien, p.320.

104 Martin Dodsworth, introduction, *North and South* by Elizabeth Gaskell, ed. Dorothy Collin (Harmondsworth: Penguin, 1970), p.7.

105 Elizabeth Gaskell, *North and South*, p.247. Subsequent citations will be given in the text.

106 Gaskell's emphasis on social relations and characters' contexts is evident in the title she preferred. Her choice for the novel's title, *Margaret Hale*, roots the story in personal circumstances, whereas Dickens's choice of title, which prevailed, emphasises conflict, abstraction and

ideological issues that rest on but supersede given individuals.

107 In August, Dickens was angered to find proofs returned from Mrs Gaskell *unaltered* by the author (letter dated 20 August 1854). The editor had wanted 'a great condensation and a considerable compression, where Mr. Hale states his doubts to Margaret' (Paroissien, p. 323). Mrs. Gaskell apparently did not want to reduce this kind of narrative, which presents argument and counterargument rather than advancing the story's action.

108 See also Rosemary Bodenheimer, 'North and South: A Permanent State of Change', *Nineteenth Century Fiction* 34 (1979), pp. 281–301.

109 Mrs Gaskell asked several of her friends if she should revise the serial text for volume publication. To Mrs Anna Jameson she wrote, 'I can not insert small pieces here & there – I feel as if I must throw myself back a certain distance in the story, & re-write it from there; retaining the present incidents, but filling up intervals of time &c &c' (*Letters*, p. 329). Mrs Jameson responded that 'there should be more gradation in effect [in the novel's conclusion], and the rapidity of the incidents at the close destroys the proportions of your story as a work of art'. Cited in Collin, 'Composition', p. 88. Bodenheimer argues 'it may be that the difficulty of ending [the novel] had something to do with the stubbornly open presentation of character and social change in the main part of the story' (p. 301).

110 Deirdre David, in *Fictions of Resolution*, says that Gaskell wrote this novel 'feeling perhaps that her woman's knowledge was not the "correct knowledge", and it was a painful experience for her' (p. 9). See also Lansbury, p. 36.

111 Gérin, p. 154; *Letters*, pp. 330, 328–9.

112 *Letters*, p. 323.

113 Although not all of Mrs Gaskell's letters to Dickens about serialisation have survived, Dorothy Collin argues 'it may be shown that disregard was not [Gaskell's] attitude to serial divisions in the case of *North and South*', but 'there is evidence that the disagreement between Dickens and Mrs. Gaskell was bruited abroad at least among the circle of her correspondents' (pp. 73–4).

114 Janice A. Radway, *Reading the Romance: Women, Patriarchy, and Popular Literature* (Chapel Hill: University of North Carolina Press, 1984), pp. 65, 54, 77, 81. Just as Margaret Hale is displaced from her family homes in London and Helstone at the novel's outset, so the ideal romance, according to Radway's study, 'begins with its heroine's removal from a familiar, comfortable realm usually associated with her childhood and family' (p. 134), a move that allows the heroine to adopt unconventionally assertive behaviour and to encounter the hero.

115 Ibid., pp. 64–5, 105; Ann Barr Snitow, 'Mass Market Romance: Pornography for Women is Different', *Radical History Review* 20 (1979), p. 146.

116 Cixous indicates the regressive politics of such desire, which she perceives as a masculinist strategy: 'the good woman [in patriarchy], therefore, is the one who "resists" long enough for him to feel both his power over her and his desire . . . to give him the pleasure of enjoying, without too many obstacles, the return to himself which he, grown greater – reassured in his own eyes, is making' (pp. 79–80). But John Thornton does not return to his single, same self as a result of desire; like Margaret, he changes over the course of the novel, spurred in part by his vulnerability to Margaret's attacks or praise.

117 Linda K. Hughes and Michael Lund, 'Textual/Sexual Pleasure and Serial Publication', pp. 143–64.

BIBLIOGRAPHY

Bibliography of Works Cited

D'Albertis, Deirdre. '"Bookmaking Out the Remains of the Dead": Elizabeth Gaskell's *The Life of Charlotte Brontë*'. *Victorian Studies* 39.1 (Autumn 1995), pp. 1–31.

D'Albertis, Deirdre. *Dissembling Fictions: Elizabeth Gaskell and the Victorian Social Text*. London: Macmillan, 1997.

Anderson, Amanda. *Tainted Souls and Painted Faces: The Rhetoric of Fallenness in Victorian Culture*. Ithaca, New York: Cornell University Press, 1993.

Armstrong, Nancy. *Desire and Domestic Fiction: A Political History of the Novel*. Oxford: Oxford University Press, 1987.

Barker, Juliet R.V. 'Saintliness, Treason and Plot: The Writing of Mrs Gaskell's *Life of Charlotte Brontë*'. *Brontë Society Transactions*, 21.4 (1994), pp. 101–15.

Basch, Françoise. *Relative Creatures: Victorian Women in Society and the Novel*. New York: Schocken, 1974.

Bodenheimer, Rosemarie. *The Politics of Story in Victorian Fiction*. Ithaca, New York: Cornell University Press, 1988.

Boggs, W. Arthur. 'Reflections of Unitarians in Mrs Gaskell's Novels'. Dissertation, University of California, Berkeley, 1950.

Carlyle, Thomas. *Chartism*, second edition. London: Chapman and Hall, 1842 [1839].

Carlyle, Thomas. *Past and Present*. London: Chapman and Hall, 1889 [1843].

Cazamian, Louis. *The Social Novel in England 1830–1850: Dickens, Disraeli, Mrs Gaskell, Kingsley*. Translated by Martin Fido. London: Routledge and Kegan Paul, 1973 [1903].

Cecil, David. *Victorian Novelists: Essays in Revaluation*. London: Fontana, 1964 [1934].

Chapman, Alison. 'History, Hysteria, Histrionics: The Biographical Representation of Christina Rossetti'. *Victorian Literature and Culture*, 24, forthcoming.

Chapple, J.A.V., ed. *Elizabeth Gaskell: A Portrait in Letters*. Manchester: Manchester University Press, 1980.

Chapple, J.A.V., and Pollard, Arthur, eds. *The Letters of Mrs Gaskell*. Manchester: Manchester University Press, 1966.

Chapple, J.A.V., and Wilson, Anita, eds. *Private Voices: The Diaries of Elizabeth Gaskell and Sophia Holland*. Keele, Staffordshire: Keele University Press, 1996.

Collin, Dorothy. 'The Composition and Publication of Elizabeth Gaskell's *Cranford*'. *Bulletin of John Rylands University Library*, 69 (1986), p. 60.

Collin, Dorothy. 'The Composition of Elizabeth Gaskell's *North and South*'. *Bulletin of John Rylands University Library*, 54.1 (1971), pp. 67–93.

Craik, W.A. *Elizabeth Gaskell and the English Provincial Novel*. London: Methuen, 1975.

David, Deirdre. *Fictions of Resolution in Three Victorian Novels: 'North and South', 'Our Mutual Friend' and 'Daniel Deronda'*. Basingstoke: Macmillan, 1981.

Davis, Deanna L. 'Feminist Critics and Literary Mothers: Daughters Reading Elizabeth Gaskell'. *Signs*, 1992, pp. 507–32.

Duthie, Enid. *The Themes of Elizabeth Gaskell*. London: Macmillan, 1980.

Easson, Angus. *Elizabeth Gaskell*. London: Routledge and Kegan Paul, 1979.

Easson, Angus, ed. *Elizabeth Gaskell: The Critical Heritage*. London: Routledge, 1991.

Elliot, Dorice Williams. 'The Female Visitor and the Marriage of Classes in Gaskell's *North and South*'. *Nineteenth-Century Literature*, 49 (1994), pp. 21–49.

Engels, Frederick. *The Condition of the Working Class in England from Personal Observation and Authentic Sources*. Frogmore, Hertfordshire: Panther, 1969 [1845].

ffrench, Yvonne. *Mrs Gaskell*. London: Home and Van Thal, 1949.

Flint, Kate. *Elizabeth Gaskell*. Plymouth: Northcote House, 1995.

Gallagher, Catherine. *The Industrial Reformation of English Fiction 1832–1867*. Chicago: University of Chicago Press, 1985.

Gaskell, Elizabeth. *Cranford*. Ware, Hertfordshire: Wordsworth Classics, 1993 [1851–53].

Gaskell, Elizabeth. *The Life of Charlotte Brontë*, ed. with an introduction by Alan Shelston. Harmondsworth: Penguin, 1975 [1857].

Gaskell, Elizabeth. *Mary Barton*, ed. with an introduction by Macdonald Davy. Harmondsworth: Penguin, 1996 [1848].

Gaskell, Elizabeth. *North and South*, ed. with an introduction by Angus Easson. Oxford: Oxford University Press, 1973 [1857–55].

Gaskell, Elizabeth. *Ruth*, ed. with an introduction by Angus Easson. Harmondsworth: Penguin, 1997 [1853].

Gaskell, Elizabeth. *Wives and Daughters*, ed. with an introduction by Pam Morris. Harmondsworth: Penguin 1996 [1866].

Gérin, Winifred. *Elizabeth Gaskell*. Oxford: Oxford University Press, 1980.

Harman, Barbara Leah. *The Feminine Political Novel in Victorian England*. Charlottesville: The University Press of Virginia, 1998.

Helms, Gabriele. 'The Coincidence of Biography and Autobiography: Elizabeth Gaskell's *The Life of Charlotte Brontë*'. *Biography: An Interdisciplinary Quarterly*, 18.4 (Fall 1995), pp. 339–59.

Homans, Margaret. *Bearing the Word: Language and Female Experience in Nineteenth-Century Women's Writing*. Chicago: University of Chicago Press, 1986.

Hopkins, Annette B. 'Dickens and Mrs Gaskell'. *Huntingdon Library Quarterly*, 9 (1945–46), pp. 357-85.

Hughes, Linda K., and Michael Lund. 'Textual/Sexual Pleasure and Serial Publication', in John O. Jordan and Robert L. Patten, eds, *Literature in the Marketplace: Nineteenth-Century British Publishing and Reading Practices*. Cambridge: Cambridge University Press, 1995, pp. 143–64.

Kestner, Joseph. *Protest and Reform: The British Social Narrative by Women 1827–1867*. Madison, Wisconsin: The University of Wisconsin Press, 1985.

Kettle, Arnold. 'The Early Victorian Social-Problem Novel', in Boris Ford, ed., *The New Pelican Guide to English Literature: From Dickens to Hardy*, vol. 6. Harmondsworth: Penguin, 1982 [1958], pp. 164–81.

Kucich, John. *The Power of Lies: Transgression in Victorian Fiction*. Ithaca, New York: Cornell University Press, 1994.

Lansbury, Carol. *Elizabeth Gaskell: The Novel of Social Crisis*. London: Paul Elek, 1975.

Levin, Amy K. *The Suppressed Sister: A Relationship in Novels by Nineteenth- and Twentieth-Century British Women*. Lewisburg: Bucknell University Press; London: Associated University Press, 1992.

Lovell, Terry. *Consuming Fiction*. London: Verso, 1987.

Lucas, John. *The Literature of Change: Studies in the Nineteenth-Century Provincial Novel*. Sussex: Harvester Press, 1977.

Lucas, John. 'Mrs Gaskell and Brotherhood', in *Tradition and Tolerance in Nineteenth-Century Fiction: Critical Essays on Some English and American Novels*, ed. David Howard, John Lucas and John Goode. London: Routledge and Kegan Paul, 1966.

Matus, Jill L. *Unstable Bodies: Victorian Representations of Sexuality and Maternity*. Manchester: Manchester University Press, 1995.

Meckier, Jerome. *Hidden Rivalries in Victorian Fiction: Dickens, Realism, and Revaluation*. Lexington, Kentucky: The University Press of Kentucky, 1987.

Nestor, Pauline. *Female Friendships and Communities: Charlotte Brontë, George Eliot, Elizabeth Gaskell*. Oxford: Clarendon Press, 1985.

Newton, Judith Lowder. *Women, Power, and Subversion: Social Strategies in British Fiction, 1777–1860*. Athens: University of Georgia Press, 1981.

Nord, Deborah Epstein. *Walking the Victorian Streets: Women, Representation, and the City*. Ithaca, New York: Cornell University Press, 1995.

O'Farrell, Mary Ann. *Telling Complexions: The Nineteenth-Century English Novel and the Blush*. Durham: Duke University Press, 1997.

Pikoulis, John. '*North and South*: Varieties of Love and Power'. *Yearbook of English Studies*, 6 (1976), pp. 176–93.

Pollard, Arthur. *Mrs Gaskell: Novelist and Biographer*. Manchester: Manchester University Press, 1965.

Schor, Hilary M. 'Elizabeth Gaskell: A Critical History and a Critical Revision'. *Dickens Studies Annual*,19, pp. 345–69.

Schor, Hilary M. *Scheherezade in the Marketplace: Elizabeth Gaskell and the Victorian Novel*. Oxford: Oxford University Press, 1992.

Showalter, Elaine. *A Literature of Their Own: British Women Novelists from Brontë to Lessing*. Princeton, New Jersey: Princeton University Press, 1977.

Stevenson, Catherine Barnes. '"What Must Not be Said": *North and South* and the Problem of Women's Work'. *Victorian Literature and Culture*, 19 (1991), pp. 67–84.

Stoneman, Patsy. *Elizabeth Gaskell*. Brighton: Harvester, 1987.

Swindells, Julia. *Victorian Writing and Working Women: The Other Side of Silence*. Cambridge: Polity Press, 1985.

Tillotson, Kathleen. *Novels of the Eighteen-Forties*. Oxford: Clarendon Press, 1954.

Uglow, Jenny, ed. *Curious, If True: Strange Tales by Mrs Gaskell*. London: Virago, 1995.

Wheeler, Michael. *The Art of Allusion in Victorian Fiction*. London: Macmillan, 1979.

Williams, Raymond. *Culture and Society 1780–1950*. New York: Columbia University Press, 1983 [1958].

Williams, Raymond. *The English Novel from Dickens to Hardy*. London: The Hogarth Press, 1984 [1970].

Woolf, Virginia. 'Mrs Gaskell' [1910], in Michèle Barrett, ed., *Virginia Woolf on Women and Writing*. London: The Women's Press, 1979.

Wright, Terence. *Elizabeth Gaskell: 'We are not angels': Realism, Gender, Values*. Basingstoke: Macmillan, 1995.

Additional Select Bibliography

Beer, Patricia. *Reader, I Married Him: A Study of the Women Characters of Jane Austen, Charlotte Brontë, Elizabeth Gaskell and George Eliot*. London: Macmillan, 1974.

Carnell, Geoffrey. 'Dickens, Mrs Gaskell, and the Preston Strike'. *Victorian Studies*, 8 (1964), pp. 31–48.

Chapple, J. A. V. '*North and South*: A Reassessment'. *Essays in Criticism*, 17 (1967), pp. 461–72.

Gill, Stephen. 'Price's Patent Candles: New Light on *North and South*'. *Review of English Studies*, 27 (1976), pp. 313–21.

Hawley, John C. '*Mary Barton*: The Inside View from Without'. *Nineteenth-Century Studies*, 3 (1989), pp. 23–30.

McVeagh, J. 'Notes on Mrs Gaskell's Narrative Technique'. *Essays in Criticism* 18 (1968), pp. 461–70.

Samuelian, Kirstin Flieger. 'Lost Mothers: The Challenge to Paternalism in *Mary Barton*'. *Nineteenth-Century Studies*, 6 (1992), pp. 19–33.

Selig, Robert L. *Elizabeth Gaskell: A Reference Guide*. Boston: Hall, 1977.

Smith, Sheila M. *The Other Nation: The Poor in English Novels of the 1840s and 1850s*. Oxford: Clarendon Press, 1980.

Stitt, Megan Perigoe. *Metaphors of Change in the Language of Nineteenth-Century Fiction: Scott, Gaskell, and Kingsley*. Oxford: Clarendon Press, 1998.

Stone, Marjorie. 'Bakhtinian Polyphony in *Mary Barton*: Class, Gender, and the Textual Voice'. *Dickens Study Annual*, 20 (1991), pp. 175–200.

Sutherland, John. 'What kind of a murderer is John Barton?', in *Is Heathcliff a Murderer? Puzzles in Nineteenth-Century Fiction*. Oxford: Oxford University Press, 1996, pp. 78–83.

Weyant, Nancy S. *Elizabeth Gaskell: An Annotated Bibliography of English Language Sources 1976–1991*. Metuchen, New Jersey: Scarecrow, 1994.

Wheeler, Michael D. 'The Writer as Reader in *Mary Barton*'. *Durham University Journal*, 36 (1975), pp. 92–102.

Wright, Edgar. *Mrs Gaskell: The Basis for Reassessment*. London: Oxford University Press, 1965.

ACKNOWLEDGEMENTS

The editor and publishers wish to thank the following for their permission to reprint copyright material: Macmillan (for material from *Dissembling Fictions: Elizabeth Gaskell and the Victorian Social Text*); University of Chicago Press (for material from *The Industrial Reformation of English Fiction 1832–1867*, and *Bearing the Word: Language and Female Experience in Nineteenth-Century Women's Writing*); University Press of Virginia (for material from *The Feminine Political Novel in Victorian England*); Cambridge University Press (for material from *Literature in the Marketplace: Nineteenth-Century British Publishing and Reading Practices*); Paul Elek (for material from *Elizabeth Gaskell: The Novel of Social Crisis*); Verso (for material from *Consuming Fiction*); RKP (for material from 'Mrs89 Gaskell and Brotherhood', in *Tradition and Tolerance in Nineteenth-Century Fiction: Critical Essays on Some English and American Novels*); Oxford University Press (for material from *Scheherezade in the Marketplace: Elizabeth Gaskell and the Victorian Novel*); *Victorian Literature and Culture* (for material from '"What Must Not be Said": North and South and the Problem of Women's Work'); Clarendon Press (for material from *Novels of the Eighteen-Forties*); Columbia University Press (for material from *Culture and Society 1780–1950*).

There are instances where we have been unable to trace or contact copyright holders before our printing deadline. If notified, the publisher will be pleased to acknowledge the use of copyright material.

Alison Chapman is a Lecturer in English at the University of Dundee. She has recently published articles in *Victorian Poetry* and *Victorian Literature and Culture* and her study of Christina Rossetti is forthcoming from Macmillan.

INDEX

Note: EG in the index stands for Elizabeth Gaskell. Titles of literary works are listed under their authors' names, except for *Mary Barton* and *North and South* by Elizabeth Gaskell.